Hiking the Oregon Coast

Help Us Keep This Guide Up to Date

Every effort has been made by the author and editors to make this guide as accurate and useful as possible. However, many things can change after a guide is published—trails are rerouted, regulations change, techniques evolve, facilities come under new management, etc.

We would love to hear from you concerning your experiences with this guide and how you feel it could be improved and kept up to date. While we may not be able to respond to all comments and suggestions, we'll take them to heart, and we'll also make certain to share them with the author. Please send your comments and suggestions to the following address:

The Globe Pequot Press
Reader Response/Editorial Department
P.O. Box 480
Guilford, CT 06437

Or you may e-mail us at:

editorial@GlobePequot.com

Thanks for your input, and happy travels!

A **FALCON** GUIDE®

Hiking the Oregon Coast

Day Hikes along the Oregon Coast and Coastal Mountains

Lizann Dunegan

FALCON®

GUILFORD, CONNECTICUT
HELENA, MONTANA

AN IMPRINT OF THE GLOBE PEQUOT PRESS

A FALCON GUIDE®

All photographs by the author unless otherwise indicated.
Maps created by XNR Productions Inc © The Globe Pequot Press.
The author used MapTech software to produce some source maps.

Library of Congress Cataloging-in-Publication Data is available.

ISBN 0-7627-2574-5

Manufactured in the United States of America
First Edition/First Printing

Contents

Acknowledgments ix
Introduction 1
Beach Safety 1
Weather 2
Camping on the Coast 3
Flora and Fauna 3
Wilderness Restrictions and Regulations 8
How to Use This Book 10
How to Use These Maps 11
Map Legend 12

THE HIKES

North Coast 13
1. Fort Canby State Park 14
2. Cathedral Tree to Astoria Column 18
3. Fort Stevens State Park 21
4. Ecola State Park to Indian Beach 25
5. Cannon Beach 28
6. Saddle Mountain 32
7. Oswald West State Park—Short Sand Beach 36
8. Neahkahnie Mountain 39
9. Cape Meares State Park 43
10. Cape Lookout 48
11. Munson Creek Falls 52
12. Cape Kiwanda State Natural Area 56
13. Pheasant Creek Falls and Niagara Falls 59
14. Kiwanda Beach to Porter Point 63
15. Harts Cove 66
16. Cascade Head 70
17. Drift Creek Falls 74
18. Devil's Punchbowl State Natural Area 78

North Coast Honorable Mentions
A. Banks—Vernonia State Park Trail 82
B. Gales Creek 82
C. Hagg Lake 82
D. King Mountain 83
E. Arcadia Beach State Recreation Site 83
F. Nehalem Bay State Park 84
G. Oceanside Beach State Recreation Site 84
H. Roads End State Recreation Site 84
I. Gleneden Beach State Recreation Site 85

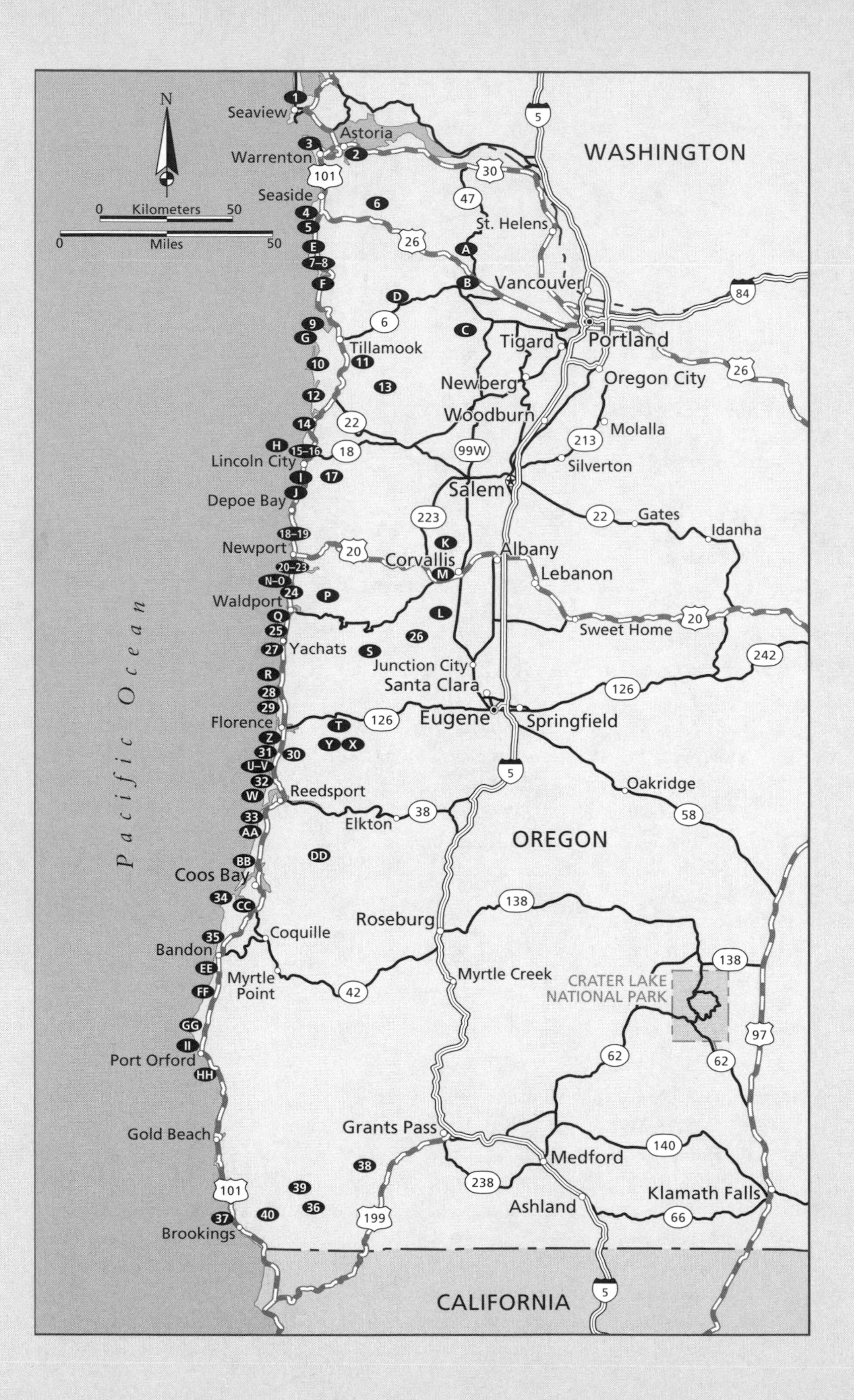

N
0 Kilometers 50
0 Miles 50
Pacific Ocean
WASHINGTON
OREGON
CALIFORNIA
Seaview
Astoria
Warrenton
Seaside
St. Helens
Vancouver
Portland
Tigard
Tillamook
Oregon City
Newberg
Woodburn
Molalla
Lincoln City
Silverton
Salem
Depoe Bay
Gates
Idanha
Newport
Corvallis
Albany
Lebanon
Waldport
Sweet Home
Yachats
Junction City
Santa Clara
Eugene
Springfield
Florence
Oakridge
Reedsport
Elkton
Coos Bay
Roseburg
Coquille
Bandon
Myrtle Creek
Myrtle Point
CRATER LAKE NATIONAL PARK
Port Orford
Gold Beach
Grants Pass
Medford
Ashland
Klamath Falls
Brookings

J. Fogarty Creek State Recreation Area ... 85
K. Valley of the Giants ... 85
L. Finley National Wildlife Refuge ... 86
M. Dan's Trail ... 86

Central Coast ... 87
19. Yaquina Head Outstanding Natural Area ... 89
20. Yaquina Bay State Park and Lighthouse ... 93
21. Hatfield Marine Science Center Estuary Trail ... 97
22. Mike Miller Educational Trail ... 100
23. South Beach State Park ... 104
In Addition: The Oregon Coast Trail ... 108
24. Seal Rock State Recreation Area ... 110
25. Yachats 804 Trail ... 113
26. Alsea Falls and Green Peak Falls ... 117
27. Cape Perpetua Trails ... 121
28. Heceta Head Lighthouse ... 125
29. Sutton Creek Recreation Area ... 129
30. Siltcoos Lake ... 134
31. Siltcoos River Estuary Trails ... 137
32. Tahkenitch Creek ... 141
33. Lake Marie ... 144

Central Coast Honorable Mentions
N. Lost Creek State Recreation Site ... 148
O. Ona Beach State Park ... 148
P. Horse Creek—Harris Ranch ... 148
Q. Beachside State Park ... 149
R. Carl G. Washburne Memorial State Park ... 149
S. Pawn Old Growth Trail ... 150
T. Sweet Creek Falls ... 150
U. Taylor Dunes Trail ... 150
V. Dunes Overlook ... 151
W. Tahkenitch Dunes—Three Mile Lake ... 151
X. Kentucky Falls ... 151
Y. North Fork Smith River ... 152
Z. Jessie M. Honeyman State Park ... 152
AA. Umpqua Dunes ... 153
BB. Blue Bill Lake ... 153

South Coast ... 155
34. Sunset Bay, Shore Acres, and Cape Arago State Parks ... 156
35. Coquille River Lighthouse ... 160
36. Babyfoot Lake ... 164
37. Cape Ferrelo to Whalehead Beach ... 168

38. Illinois River Trail 172
39. Vulcan Lake 177
40. Alfred A. Loeb State Park Nature Trails 181
South Coast Honorable Mentions
CC. South Slough Estuarine Preserve 186
DD. Golden and Silver Falls State Natural Area 186
EE. Bandon State Natural Area 186
FF. New River 187
GG. Cape Blanco State Park 187
HH. Humbug Mountain State Park 188
II. Port Orford Heads State Park 188

The Art of Hiking 189
Getting into Shape 190
Preparedness 191
First Aid 193
Navigation 195
Trip Planning 196
Equipment 197
Hiking with Children 201
Hiking with Your Dog 203
Appendix: Hikes by Interest 207
About the Author 209

Acknowledgments

Thanks to my trail-hiking partners who helped me research the trails in this book—this also includes Ken Skeen and my canine trail partners, Levi and Sage, who always make my hiking trips more fun. Also thanks to Scott Adams, David Singleton, and all of the other folks at Falcon for their help and advice.

Introduction

If this is your first time hiking the Oregon Coast or you are a seasoned coast-hiking veteran, this book will help you get the most out of your hiking adventure. This book contains seventy-five hikes covering the 362-mile Oregon coastline, from Astoria, located on the banks of the Columbia River, to Brookings, near the California state line. In addition this book covers hikes that are in the Coast Mountain Range and the Kalmiopsis Wilderness, both of which are part of the Siskiyou National Forest in southern Oregon.

Luckily for all of us, Oregon passed two Beach Bills, in 1967 and 1972, that allow public access to beaches and headlands along the entire Oregon Coast. When you visit the coast, you can expect a multitude of hiking experiences. You can walk on a long, isolated sandy beach; explore rocky tide pools filled with colorful sea creatures; walk through a rare grove of old-growth trees; walk to the summit of a coastal peak; or walk along a river estuary rich with wildlife.

Windy U.S. Highway 101 hugs the coastline from Astoria to Brookings, offering plenty of opportunities to stop and enjoy spectacular ocean vistas from its many roadside viewpoints as well as opportunities to explore trails that are located on or close to the highway. Many of the hikes in this book are located in the more than eighty state parks and recreation areas present on the Oregon Coast as well as the vast 630,000-acre Siuslaw National Forest, which is host to wilderness areas and protected research areas harboring plants and animals found nowhere else. There are also hikes that explore amazing dune environments in the Oregon Dunes National Recreation Area, a reserve that protects more than 50 square miles of magnificent sand dunes between Florence and Coos Bay.

Beach Safety

When you are visiting Oregon's scenic beaches, keep the following in mind.

- Avoid hiking to isolated rocks, tide pools, on beaches, or around headlands during the incoming tide. You can download tide-table information by visiting www.oregonstateparks.org/images/pdf/tidetable.pdf. You can also view tide tables on-line at www.hmsc.orst.edu/weather/tides/tides.html.
- Be aware of water-saturated logs, which can weigh several tons and may roll on top of you and crush you.
- Don't wade out too far into the surf. Strong currents and waves can swiftly carry you offshore. And the ocean temperatures are very cold and can quickly sap your strength.

◀ *Admiring an old-growth Sitka spruce on the Coastal Trail in Fort Canby State Park*

Break time!

- Watch out for sneaker waves, which can knock you off exposed rocks, headlands, and jetties.
- Don't climb on steep cliffs or rocks. Always assume that all cliff edges are unstable and stay away from them.

Weather

When you visit the Oregon Coast, expect and prepare for wet weather. The Oregon Coast has the highest rainfall in the entire state, with an average rainfall of 80 to 100 inches and some areas in the Coast Mountain Range receiving up to 200 inches. November through March is the wettest time of year. You can expect average temperatures on the coast in the low to mid-60s in the summer months with occasional warm sunny days that reach into the mid-70s. In the winter months you can expect average temperatures to be in the 40s and 50s. The town of Brookings, near the California border, has the warmest and driest weather on the coast, which generally occurs from July through mid-October. However, there are some dry periods during the winter months where temperatures can reach the mid-60s.

Rain, wind, drizzle, and fog are common weather patterns on the coast. If you prepare for these conditions by bringing waterproof shoes, wool socks, a good rain jacket, gloves, a hat, and an extra set of dry clothes, you'll enjoy your outing much more. You'll also find that these weather conditions are all part of the allure of this part of the state. Mist and fog create a mystical backdrop to a hike through an old-growth forest, and high winds and winter storms create unforgettable opportunities to watch huge waves crash into offshore rocks. To find out more about current weather conditions at the coast, visit www.newportnet.com/weather.htm.

Camping on the Coast

If you want to camp while visiting the Oregon Coast, you have many options. There are hundreds of state, county, private, and forest-service campgrounds dotted along the entire coast. Campsites vary from primitive to very posh. Basic sites usually have a picnic table, access to running water, and a fire ring with a grill. Larger campgrounds also often have rest rooms with showers. If you don't want to rough it, many state-park campgrounds have yurts you can rent for the night. Yurts are circular tentlike structures that are 16 feet in diameter with a wooden floor and come equipped with a lockable door, electric heater, skylight, and three beds that sleep five people. These yurts make you feel like you're still roughing it, but they have a few amenities that make your camping experience more comfortable. Yurts are very popular places to stay on the Oregon Coast, so always be sure to call ahead to reserve one of these unique camping lodges. While you are welcome to stay in a yurt, your furry friends are not permitted to stay inside with you. Many campgrounds take reservations, and it is recommended that you make them during the peak camping season, May 1 through September 30. To make a reservation for a state-park campground, call (800) 452–5687. You can also reserve campsites on-line at www.oregonstateparks.org/reserve.php. You can reserve state-park campsites from two days to nine months in advance. Note that not all state-park campgrounds accept reservations. To find out more about forest-service campgrounds, contact the Siuslaw National Forest Service Headquarters at (541) 750–7000 or visit them on-line at www.fs.fed.us/r6/siuslaw. For information about camping opportunities in the Oregon Dunes National Recreation Area, call (541) 271–3611.

Flora and Fauna

The Coast Mountain Range is covered with forests made up of primarily western hemlock, Sitka spruce, red cedar, and Douglas fir. Southern coastal forests contain small pockets of orange-barked madrone trees, Port Orford cedar, coast redwood trees, and myrtle trees. Due to logging, large areas of coastal forest are a patchwork of different ages and types of trees. In areas that have been heavily cut, you'll find thick groves of big-leaf maple and red alder trees. Coastal forests have a rich variety

Scenic dunes in the Oregon Dunes National Recreation Area

of understory plants, including salal, Oregon grape, the white triangular flowers of western trillium, the pink-flowered western columbine, the purple bell-shaped flowers of the coast penstemon, pink-flowered Pacific rhododendron, and the cloverlike leaves and delicate white flowers of wood sorrel. Dominant fern species include sword fern, deer fern, and maidenhair fern that thrive in the cool wet environment. Wildflowers that grow in sunny, open areas include vibrant orange tiger lilies, crimson Indian paintbrush, white meadow chickweed, phlox, and larkspur.

Many coastal headlands are covered with a variety of grasses and unique wildflowers, such as red fescue, wild rye, goldenrod, coastal paintbrush, wild iris, blue violet, lupine, and yarrow. Cascade Head, designated as a National Scenic Preserve, is haven to a rare meadowland ecosystem that protects the federally threatened Oregon silverspot butterfly. Cascade Head is one of six remaining areas where this butterfly is found. Its current range is the coast along northern California, Washington, and Oregon. The best time to see the butterfly is from August through September, when it is in the adult stage. Adults lay eggs on the tall grasses in August and September, and the caterpillar emerges in early spring. The caterpillar forms a cocoon in early summer and reaches the adult butterfly stage in midsummer. The butterfly is about 1 inch wide and has orange and brown markings on the top of the wings and silver spots under the wings.

Black-tailed deer inhabit the coastal forests and feed on bark, buds, leaves, and other plants and grasses. These graceful mammals are named for their distinctive dark brown tail with black trim, which has a white underside. Smaller than their mule-deer cousins, black-tailed deer most frequently are seen grazing in open clearings in the evening and early morning hours.

Black bears can also be found roaming the mountains and valleys on the Oregon Coast. Ranging in color from rich dark brown to light cinnamon in color, these bears range from 35 to 40 inches tall when on all fours and have a length of 4.5 to 6 feet. Depending on area and level of nutrition, black bears range in weight from 125 to 600 pounds, with males being about a third larger than females. Black bears have taste buds for virtually anything that is edible. About 75 percent of their diet is made up of roots, berries, flowers, grasses, sedges, herbs, and tubers. They also feed on decaying animal carcasses, fish, small marine animals, insects, and small mammals.

One of the most magnificent mammals you may see is the Roosevelt elk. Mature bull elk can weigh up to 1,000 pounds and are usually reddish-brown in color. Roosevelt elk are primarily grazers, and they tend to congregate in open meadows where grasses are plentiful. A dominant bull elk is usually in charge of a herd of about twenty cows. Every spring the bulls grow antlers, which are used to ward off rival males during the fall breeding season. Once the breeding season is done, the antlers are shed. Most likely you'll see these magnificent animals on the Cascade Head hike.

The Oregon Coast has dozens of rivers that flow from the Coast Mountains, weave through lush coastal valleys, and eventually flow into the transitional zone of estuaries. The coastline is rich with estuaries that are formed when tides cause seawater to flood the mouths of coastal rivers, mixing freshwater and seawater. The level of the water in estuaries rises and falls with the tide. Estuaries are productive places due to the fairly calm rise and fall of the water, which creates a safe haven for estuarine plants and animals to live. Estuaries have a flat, muddy bottom due to the accumulation of decaying plants, animal matter, and fine sediment that is brought down from the mountains in the coastal rivers. Shellfish such as butter clams, razor clams, and oysters thrive in this rich muddy environment and, in turn, shorebirds find an ample supply of crustaceans, fish, snails, and worms. Estuaries are an excellent place to view different varieties of birds, such as blue herons, belted kingfishers, loons, grebes, and a variety of geese and ducks. Plants that thrive in the nutrient rich soil include arrow grass, giant vetch, salt rush, cattails, bull rushes, and bull thistle.

The coast of Oregon is also host to long stretches of sand dunes. The dunes form desertlike landscapes that intermingle with the coastal forest and freshwater lakes, creating different types of coastal ecosystems. The Oregon Dunes stretch from Heceta Head south to Cape Arago and are protected as part of the Oregon Dunes National Recreation Area, established in 1972. This recreation area protects more than 50 square miles of dunes between Florence and Coos Bay. These ever-changing dunes sit on top of a marine sandstone layer called the Coos Bay Dune Sheet. Wind, tides, and wave action have pushed sand as far inland as 2.5 miles over thousands of years to create some of the world's largest sand dunes. The wind sculpts and shapes the dunes by blowing at a constant rate of about 14 miles per hour from the northwest. Winter storm winds that blow in from the southwest can exceed 100 miles per hour and also have a great influence on dune formation. Ocean currents flowing north in the winter months and south in the summer months also act as a partner in sculpting the dunes by keeping sand deposited by coastal rivers at the shoreline. Large waves then push the sand onto shore, and strong winds blow the sand inland.

The rocky shore has been shaped by its never-ending struggle with the sea. Winter storms and high tides form pounding waves that crash into rocky islands, arches, sea stacks, and cliffs. Atop the headlands and bluffs, you'll find the twisted and bent trunks of shore pines, often referred to as krummholz, that are sculpted by the relentless winds that whip in from the sea. Among these sturdy trees, hardy salal and ceanothus bushes make their stand in the wet, windy environment. Open meadows of grasses and bright wildflowers also grace the slopes along the rocky coast and brave succulents gain a foothold on the steep cliff faces and rocky outcroppings.

Where the ocean meets the rocky shore, sea caves, tide pools, and cobblestone beaches are home to a variety of seashore animals and birds. The most common bird we all associate with the seashore is the vivacious gull. Five different species of gulls live along this coastline, with the glaucous-winged gull being the largest and most common. You can identify this gull species by its white head and chest, gray wings, and yellow bill with a distinctive red spot. Sharing the rocky cliffs with the gulls are the penguinlike common murres, which can be identified by their dark brown feathers and white undersides, and pigeon guillemots, which are distinguished by their black bodies, white wing patches, and bright red beaks and feet. Tufted puffins also nest on rocky cliffs and offshore islands. The males have bright orange beaks, white eye patches, yellow feather tufts, and dark plumage. They feed on small minnowlike fish that they catch by diving underwater and swimming with their wings. Other birds that nest on the rocky ledges and offshore islands are pelagic and brandt's cormorants. These long-necked birds have dark, iridescent plumage and often can be seen resting on rocks with their wings outstretched. This curious behavior is because their feathers become saturated with water after they have been diving for fish. In order to regain flight, these birds have to dry out their waterlogged feathers in the sun. Bald eagles also soar on the air

Sea lions resting on the rocky shore near Heceta Head Lighthouse ▶

currents above the rocky shoreline searching for ill or injured fish. The bald eagle has beautiful dark brown plumage and its distinctive white head, neck, and tail feathers.

Large groups of Steller's sea lions rest and breed on offshore islands. They feed on fish and squid, and males can weigh 2,200 pounds and reach lengths of 11 feet. You can hear the barklike sounds of large herds of Steller's sea lions a mile away.

Another fairly common sight is the spout of a migrating gray whale during the semiannual migration. Gray whales can be seen migrating south to their breeding lagoons in Baja, California, during December and January, and migrating north to feed in the rich Arctic seas during March and April. Mature gray whales are about 35 to 45 feet long, weigh 22 to 35 tons, and can live 60 years. These gentle giants feed on shrimplike amphipods by scraping mud from the ocean bottom and filtering unwanted material through their baleen (a filtering apparatus) while retaining the tasty amphipods, which they then swallow.

If you are exploring the rocky shoreline in the tidal zone, you'll have a unique opportunity to view a wealth of plant and animal life. The black stain you see on some rock faces in the tidal zone is hardy black lichen that consists of algae and fungi that have developed a symbiotic partnership. Rough-shelled acorn barnacles also cluster closely on exposed rocks. When the tide is out, these small creatures seem lifeless, but when the tide comes back in and the shells become submerged, these tiny creatures thrust out a netlike appendage that catches microscopic plankton. Acorn barnacles share their rocky home with limpets and snails that are also especially adapted to live with the changing tide. In the tidal zone you'll also find greenish-yellow rockweed and bright green sea lettuce, whose wrinkled fronds resemble a head of Romaine lettuce. In tide pools black oval-shelled mussels cluster tightly together on the craggy rocks, sharing their underwater habitat with vibrant orange starfish, prickly purple sea urchins, and emerald green sea anemones. Other plants that live here include the light yellowish-brown sea cauliflower, green sea cabbage, and olive-brown crisp leather seaweed. Bustling about in these craggy pools are hermit crabs, purple shore crabs, and Oregon rock crabs.

The Oregon Islands National Wildlife Refuge protects all of these species and many more. More than 1,400 islands, rocks, and reefs are part of this system along the entire Oregon Coast. To learn more about coastal species and to see them up close, visit the Oregon Coast Aquarium (2820 SE Ferry Slip Road, Newport; 541–867–3474; www.aquarium.org), which has interactive displays, hands-on exhibits, and natural outdoor displays that house a variety of coastal species.

Wilderness Restrictions and Regulations

The Oregon State Parks, Bureau of Land Management (BLM), and the USDA Forest Service manage the public lands on the Oregon Coast. Some national-forest and BLM trails require a Northwest Forest Pass, which is $5.00 per day, or you can buy an annual Northwest Forest Pass for $30.00. You can determine the participating national forests and locations for purchasing a Northwest Forest Pass by calling (800) 270–7504 or visiting on-line at www.naturenw.org.

Many state parks on the Oregon Coast require a $3.00 day-use pass, or you can purchase an annual $30.00 Oregon State Park pass. You can also purchase the Oregon Pacific Coast Passport. This passport is valid for entrance, day-use, and parking fees at all state and federal fee sites along the Oregon portion of the Pacific Coast Scenic Byway (U.S. Highway 101), from Astoria to Brookings. An annual passport, valid for the calendar year, is available for $35. A five-consecutive-days passport is available for $10. Call (800) 551–6949 to purchase an Oregon State Park pass or Oregon Pacific Coast Passport. All Washington state parks require a $5.00 day-use parking pass.

How to Use This Book

Hiking the Oregon Coast was designed to be highly visual and easily referenced. The Oregon Coast has been split into three regions: the North Coast, the Central Coast, and the South Coast. Each region begins with an introduction, where you're given a sweeping look at the lay of the land. Following the introduction are each of the hikes featured within that region.

To aid in quick decision making, we start each hike chapter with a summary of the hike. The short summary gives you a taste of the hiking adventure to follow. You'll learn about the trail terrain and what surprises the route has to offer. If your interest is piqued, read on and learn more that the chapter has to offer. If not, skip to the next chapter.

The specs of the hike are fairly self-explanatory. Here you'll find the quick, nitty-gritty details of the hike: where the trailhead is located, the nearest town, hike length, approximate hiking time, difficulty rating, best hiking season, if dogs are permitted, type of trail terrain, what other trail users you may encounter, trail hotlines (for updates on trail conditions), and trail schedules and use fees. Our Finding the Trailhead section gives you dependable directions from a nearby city right down to where you'll want to park. The description of the hike is the meat of the chapter. Detailed and honest, this has been carefully researched and gives an impression of the trail. While it's impossible to cover everything, you can rest assured that what's important won't be missed. The Miles and Directions section provides mileage cues to identify all turns and trail name changes, as well as points of interest. And the Hike Information section at the end of each hike is a hodgepodge of information. In it you'll find some ideas on where to stay, what to eat, and what else to see while you're hiking in the area.

The Honorable Mentions section details additional hikes you can explore. Be sure to read through these. A jewel might be lurking among them.

How to Use These Maps

We don't want anyone, by any means, to feel restricted to just the routes and trails that are mapped here. We hope you will have an adventurous spirit and use this guide as a platform to explore the Oregon Coast and discover new routes for yourself. One of the simplest ways to begin this is to just turn the map upside down and hike the trail in reverse. The change in perspective is fantastic, and the hike should feel quite different. With this in mind, it will be like getting two distinctly different hikes on each map.

You may wish to copy the directions for the course onto a small sheet to help you while hiking, or photocopy the map and cue sheet to take with you. Otherwise, just slip the whole book in your pack and take it all with you. Enjoy your time in the outdoors, and remember to pack out what you pack in.

Elevation Profile: This helpful profile gives you a look at the cross-section of the hike's ups and downs. Elevation is labeled on the left, mileage is indicated on the top. Road and trail names are shown along the route, with towns and points of interest labeled in bold. Elevation profiles are not provided for hikes with less than 250 feet of elevation gain.

Route Map: This is your primary guide to each hike. It shows the accessible roads and trails, points of interest, water, towns, landmarks, and geographical features. It also distinguishes trails from roads, and paved roads from unpaved roads. The selected route is highlighted, and directional arrows point the way.

Map Legend

90 Limited access highway
30 U.S. highway
20 State highway
41 Forest road
Paved road
Gravel road
Unimproved road
Trail
Featured route
Powerline
Railroad grade
Tunnel
Boat launch
Bridge
Campground
Cemetary
Horsetrail
Hospital
Information
Lodging
Overlook/viewpoint
Parking
Peak
Picnic area
Point of interest/other trailhead
Rest room
Steps
START Trailhead
Waterfall
Whale watching

North Coast

Long sandy beaches, dramatic headlands, and large bays characterize the North Oregon Coast. In addition you can expect crowds of people on this part of the coast during the summer months, due to its close proximity to Oregon's three largest cities: Portland, Salem, and Eugene. The Columbia River is the dividing line between the states of Oregon and Washington, and Astoria, Oregon's oldest city, is a gateway to this part of the Oregon Coast. A recommended hike in Astoria is the Cathedral Tree to Astoria Column Hike, which takes you on a tour to view a 300-year-old Sitka spruce tree and then to the top of the historic Astoria Column. Lighthouse lovers can view the Cape Disappointment Lighthouse and North Head Lighthouse by visiting Fort Canby State Park, located about 20 miles north of Astoria off U.S. Highway 101 on Washington's Long Beach Peninsula. If you want to view an old shipwreck, be sure to visit Fort Stevens State Park, located about 9 miles southwest of Astoria off US 101.

The small town of Cannon Beach attracts throngs of tourists to its art galleries and shops as well as its beautiful coastal scenery. You can walk several miles on a long flat sandy beach on the Cannon Beach Hike, walk through a magnificent old-growth forest to a secluded beach and cove on the Oswald West State Park—Short Sand Beach Hike, or trek to the summit of Neahkahnie Mountain.

As you continue south on US 101, be sure to stop to tour some of the scenic headlands by driving on the Three Capes Scenic Route, which travels southwest from US 101 in Tillamook. At Cape Meares State Park, you can tour a historic lighthouse and stop at many cliff-side viewpoints where you can observe large colonies of nesting seabirds. On the Cape Lookout Hike, you can trek through an old-growth Sitka spruce forest to a spectacular viewpoint where you may see migrating gray whales from December through June. The Cape Kiwanda State Natural Area, located in Pacific City, has a long sandy beach and huge sand dune that kids love to climb.

Cascade Head and Harts Cove are two other recommended hikes that are located just north of Lincoln City. Both of these hikes offer spectacular viewpoints of the wild rocky coastline as well as opportunities to view abundant wildlife and rare native plants.

1 Fort Canby State Park

This fun route combines three short trails in Fort Canby State Park and takes you through an old-growth Sitka spruce forest, along scenic rocky coastline, and to the Lewis and Clark Interpretive Center and the historic Cape Disappointment Lighthouse. There are many additional hiking opportunities available in the park, including a short, loop trail leading to the North Head Lighthouse.

Start: Fort Canby State Park, located 20 miles north of Astoria, Oregon, and 3.6 miles north of Ilwaco, Washington, off U.S. Highway 101.
Distance: 4.5 miles (with other options).
Approximate hiking time: 1.5 to 2.5 hours.
Difficulty: Easy due to smooth trail surface and minimal elevation gain.
Total climbing: 65 feet. Elevation profiles are not provided for hikes with less than 250 feet of elevation gain.
Trail surface: Forest path and paved path.
Lay of the land: This route travels through coastal forest and along a scenic rocky shoreline and gives you the opportunity to explore the Lewis and Clark Interpretive Center and the Cape Disappointment Lighthouse.
Seasons: Year-round.
Other trail users: None.
Canine compatibility: Leashed dogs permitted.
Land status: State park.
Nearest town: Ilwaco, Washington.
Fees and permits: $5.00 day-use parking fee.
Map: Maptech map: Cape Disappointment, Washington.
Trail contact: Washington State Parks and Recreation Commission, 7150 Cleanwater Lane, P.O. Box 42650, Olympia, WA 98504; (360) 902-8844; www.parks.wa.gov.

Finding the trailhead: From US 101 in Astoria, exit north onto the bridge across the Columbia River, following signs to Ilwaco and Long Beach. At the end of the bridge, turn left onto US 101 toward Ilwaco and Long Beach. Go 11.5 miles north on US 101 to Ilwaco. In downtown Ilwaco, continue straight (left) toward Fort Canby State Park. Travel south on Fort Canby Road for 3.6 miles and turn left into a gravel parking area and trailhead signed for the Coastal Trail.

The Hike

Just a short drive north of Astoria is 1,882-acre Fort Canby State Park, located on the scenic Long Beach Peninsula in southwest Washington. This state park boasts 7 miles of hiking trails, two unique lighthouses, a large campground, and the Lewis and Clark Interpretive Center.

You'll start this route on Coastal Trail loops through a large grove of old-growth Sitka spruce trees carpeted with abundant sword fern, blue-berried salal, and wood sorrel. After 0.8 mile you'll arrive at a viewpoint of Baker Bay. Here you can see Ilwaco to the north and a small wetland area filled with a variety of ducks and geese. After getting warmed up on the Coastal Trail, you'll walk up the campground

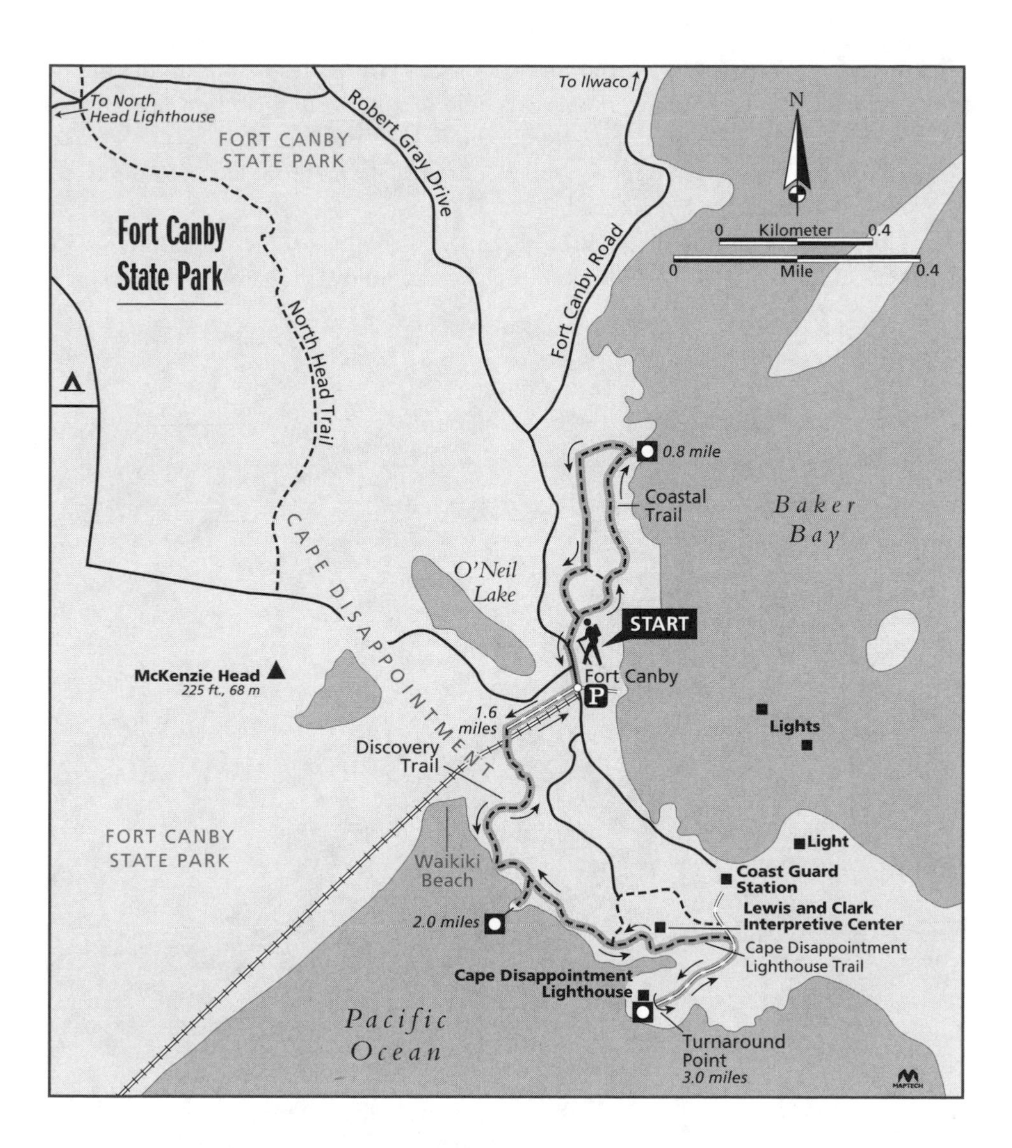

entrance road to the start of the Discovery Trail. This trail starts by climbing a short hill to a secluded, rocky cove called Waikiki Beach and continues another 0.5 mile through a woodsy setting along a high bluff to the Lewis and Clark Interpretive Center. The interpretive center is open 10:00 A.M. to 5:00 P.M. daily and has a suggested donation of $2.00. The center has displays chronicling the journey of the Lewis and Clark Expedition, information on the building of the Cape Disappointment Lighthouse, and exhibits describing the maritime history of this area, which is known as the "Graveyard of the Pacific" due to the hundreds of ships that were lost when attempting to cross the treacherous Columbia Bar (the mouth of the Columbia River). Large windows provide excellent views of the Cape Disappointment

Lighthouse, the Pacific Ocean, and the Columbia River. After exploring the interpretive center, you'll continue another 0.8 mile to a viewpoint of the Cape Disappointment Lighthouse. This impressive lighthouse was put into service on October 15, 1856, and it marks the entrance to the Columbia River. From here you'll retrace the same route back to the trailhead.

While you are visiting the park, be sure to visit the North Head Lighthouse. To get there from the Coastal trailhead, turn right and follow the paved park entrance

Cape Disappointment Lighthouse

road to the junction with Fort Canby Road (Road 100). Turn left and continue to the junction with North Head Lighthouse Road. Turn left and continue 0.5 mile to the trailhead. Walk 0.3 mile to the impressive light-keeper's houses and North Head Lighthouse located on the windblown North Head. The light-keeper's houses are available for rent (for more information call 360–642–3078). The North Head Lighthouse was built in 1898 as an additional navigation aid for ships entering the Columbia River from the north.

Miles and Directions

0.0 Start hiking on the signed Coastal Trail. Turn right at the next trail junction to begin the loop portion of the hike.

0.7 Turn right and walk down a side trail to a viewpoint of Baker Bay and a wetland area.

0.8 Arrive at the viewpoint. After enjoying the views turn around and head back to the main trail.

0.9 Turn right on the main loop trail.

1.2 Go right where a sign indicates RETURN TRAIL.

1.4 Turn right at the trail junction.

1.5 Arrive at the trailhead and the end of the Coastal Trail. To continue to the Discovery Trail, cross the park entrance road and walk along the paved campground entrance road.

1.6 Start hiking on the signed Discovery Trail, located on the left side of the campground entrance road.

1.7 Enjoy views of a secluded cove called Waikiki Beach.

2.0 Turn right and walk up a set of concrete stairs to a viewpoint of the Cape Disappointment Lighthouse and the Columbia River. After enjoying the views head back to the main trail and continue straight.

2.2 Arrive at the Lewis and Clark Interpretive Center. Turn right on the paved path that circles the interpretive center and watch for the signed Cape Disappointment Lighthouse Trail. Continue on the Cape Disappointment Lighthouse Trail to view the historic lighthouse.

2.5 Turn right at the trail junction.

2.7 Turn right on a paved path that heads uphill toward the Cape Disappointment Lighthouse.

3.0 Arrive at the lighthouse. Retrace the same route back to the trailhead.

4.5 Arrive at the trailhead.

Hike Information

Local Information

Long Beach Peninsula Visitors Bureau, P.O. Box 562, Long Beach, WA 98631; (800) 451-2542; www.funbeach.com.

Local Events/Attractions

Sand Sculpture Contest, held in July, Fort Canby State Park; (360) 642-3078.

Jazz & Oysters, held in August, Fort Canby State Park; (360) 642-3078.

Local Outdoor Retailers

Coast Fitness, 1230 Marine Drive, Astoria; (503) 325-1815.

2 Cathedral Tree to Astoria Column

This route explores a unique coastal forest right in the heart of Astoria. You'll get to view a 300-year-old Sitka spruce tree and climb to the top of the historic, 125-foot Astoria Column. From the top of the column, you'll have gorgeous views of downtown Astoria and the Columbia River.

Start: Cathedral Tree trailhead, located in downtown Astoria on Irving Avenue.
Distance: 3 miles out and back.
Approximate hiking time: 1 to 1.5 hours.
Difficulty: Moderate due to amount of elevation gain and steep climb to the top of the Astoria Column.
Total climbing: 540 feet.
Trail surface: Forest path, steps, wooden ramps.
Lay of the land: This route takes you through an inviting Sitka spruce forest to view the 300-year-old Cathedral Tree. It then ascends at a moderate pace through a woodsy setting to the top of Coxcomb Hill and the Astoria Column.
Seasons: Year-round.
Other trail users: None.
Canine compatibility: Leashed dogs permitted. (Dogs are not permitted in the Astoria Column.)
Land status: County park.
Nearest town: Astoria.
Fees and permits: No fees or permits are required.
Map: Maptech map: Astoria, Oregon.
Trail contact: Astoria/Warrenton Chamber of Commerce, 111 West Marine Drive, Astoria, OR 97103; (800) 875-6807.

Finding the trailhead: From U.S. Highway 101 in Astoria, turn south onto Sixteenth Street toward the Astoria Column. Travel 0.3 mile and turn left onto Irving Avenue. Continue 0.8 mile and park in a small, gravel parking area on the right side of the road. *Delorme: Oregon Atlas & Gazetteer:* Page 70, C3.

The Hike

As the oldest settlement west of the Rocky Mountains, Astoria is dotted with historical Victorian homes and has several museums dedicated to preserving its history. The town is named after John Jacob Astor, who helped to establish Fort Astoria in 1811. The area began to grow when settlers, many of whom were of Scandinavian descent, arrived in the area in the 1840s. The town is located on the south side of the Columbia River not far from the Columbia Bar (the mouth of the Columbia River). This location was perfect for taking advantage of the huge salmon runs that were present on the Columbia River at that time. Salmon canneries, shipbuilding, and logging became the basis for Astoria's growth, and by the 1870s the community grew to be the second-largest city in Oregon.

You can learn more about Astoria's history at the Maritime Museum located at 1792 Marine Drive. This 37,000-square-foot facility celebrates the seafaring history of the Astoria area. The museum has seven galleries that include displays about the

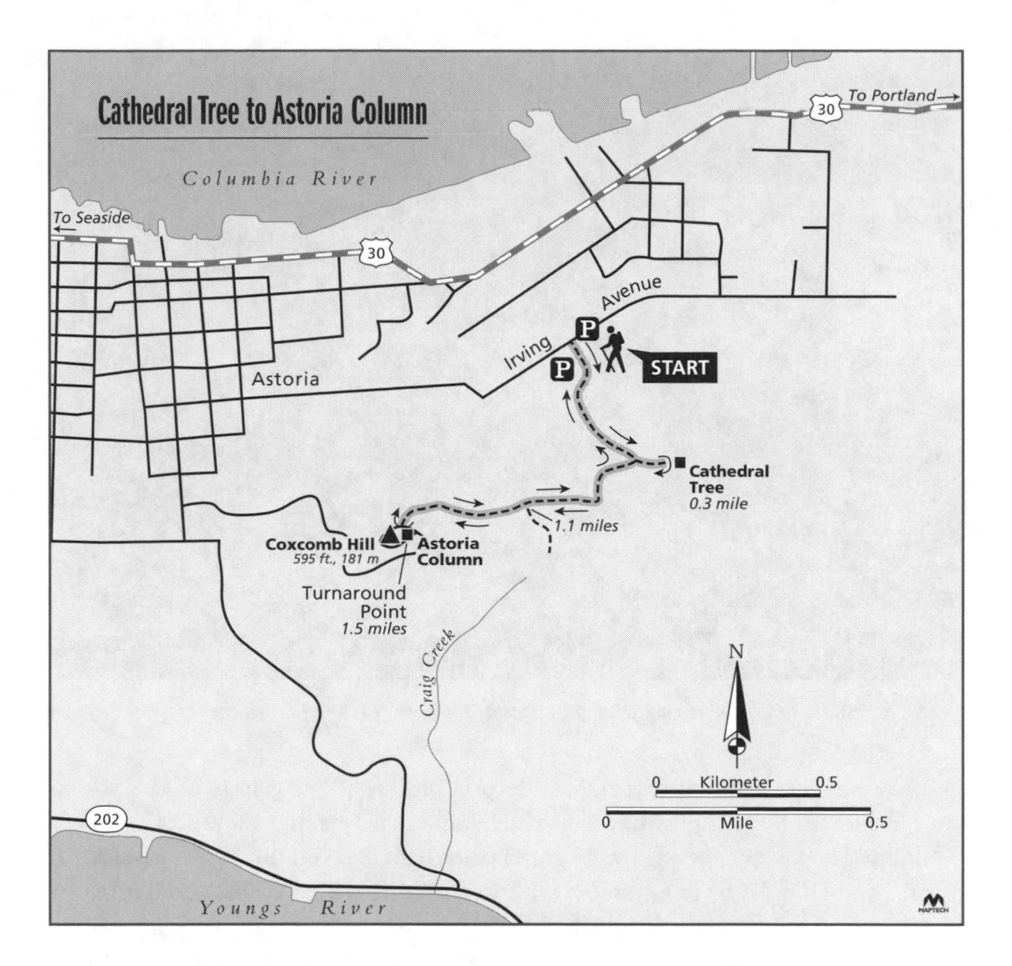

history of the salmon-packing industry, specifics on different types of boat design, and artifacts from the *Peter Iredale* shipwreck, which occurred near the mouth of the Columbia in 1906. This museum also has some modern maritime artifacts from the *New Carissa,* a wood-chip freighter that ran aground off Coos Bay in February 1999. The museum is open 9:30 A.M. to 5:00 P.M. daily.

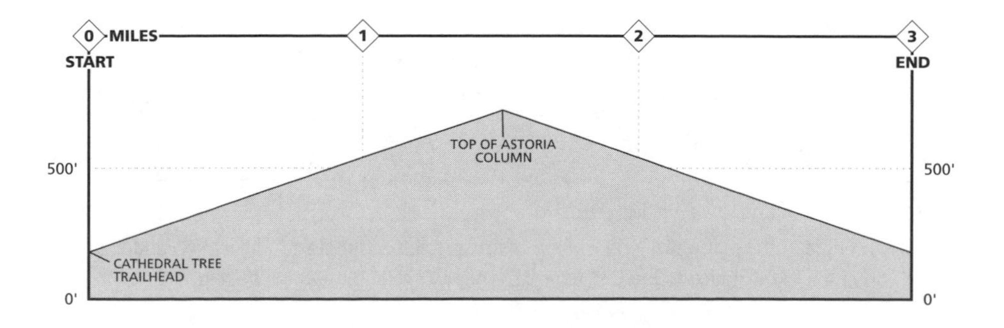

View of Astoria and Youngs Bay from the Astoria Column. Photo: Ken Skeen

You can get back to nature right in Astoria on this hiking tour that leads you to an old-growth Sitka spruce tree called the Cathedral Tree and the historic Astoria Column. The hike begins on a wide gravel path that takes you through a mossy Sitka spruce and Douglas fir forest dotted with sword fern. After 0.7 mile you'll arrive at the 300-year-old Cathedral Tree, which is more than 200 feet high, 8.5 feet in diameter, and has a circumference of 27.5 feet. The inside of the tree is hollowed out, making it appear as a natural cathedral. After viewing this grand old tree, you'll continue your tour with a moderate ascent for 0.8 mile to the Astoria Column, which is located on the top of Coxcomb Hill. This 125-foot-tall monument was completed in 1926 and was built by the Great Northern Railroad and Vincent Astor (great-grandson of Jacob Astor). Climb to the top of the column on a steep, narrow 166-step spiral staircase. Once you reach the top, you'll have outstanding views of the mouth of the Columbia River where it meets the Pacific Ocean, Mount St. Helens, Youngs Bay, downtown Astoria, and the Astoria bridge, which links Oregon and Washington. From here you'll retrace the same route back to your starting point.

Miles and Directions

0.0 Start walking on a wide gravel path.

0.3 Turn right and begin walking on a wood ramp. Turn left at the next trail junction and continue a short distance to the Cathedral Tree. After viewing the tree go back to the last trail junction and continue straight up a series of stairs. (FYI: Watch for blue-and-white circular trail markers placed on different trees marking the route.)

1.1 Turn right and continue toward the signed Astoria Column.

1.5 Arrive at the Astoria Column. Climb the narrow, spiral staircase to the top of the 125-foot tower. Enjoy the views from the top and then retrace the same route back to your starting point.

3.0 Arrive at the trailhead.

Hike Information

Local Information

Astoria/Warrenton Chamber of Commerce, 111 West Marine Drive, Astoria, OR 97103; (800) 875-6807.

Local Events/Attractions

Columbia River Maritime Museum, 1792 Marine Drive, Astoria; (503) 325-2323; www.crmm.org.

Fort Clatsop National Memorial, 92343 Fort Clatsop Road, Astoria; (503) 861-2471, ext. 214; www.nps.gov/focl.

Flavel House, 441 Eighth Street, Astoria; (503) 325-2203.

Local Outdoor Retailers

Coast Fitness, 1230 Marine Drive, Astoria; (503) 325-1815.

3 Fort Stevens State Park

Shipwrecks, sandy beaches, and wetlands filled with wildlife await those who wander on trails and beachfront in Fort Stevens State Park. You can view the skeleton hull of the *Peter Iredale* shipwreck, watch abundant bird life at the mouth of the Columbia, watch for migrating gray whales, take a stroll around scenic Coffenbury Lake, and learn about the area's history at the Military Museum located inside the park.

Start: Fort Stevens State Park is located 9 miles southwest of Astoria and about 15 miles northwest of Seaside off U.S. Highway 101.
Distance: Varies depending on trails selected.
Approximate hiking time: Varies depending on trails selected.
Difficulty: Easy.
Total climbing: None. Elevation profiles are not provided for hikes with less than 250 feet of elevation gain.
Trail surface: Paved path, sand, dirt path, and wooden ramp.
Lay of the land: A variety of hiking opportunities is available at the park, ranging from dirt paths to paved paths and sandy beach.
Seasons: Year-round.
Other trail users: Cyclists.
Canine compatibility: Leashed dogs permitted.
Land status: State park.
Nearest town: Astoria.
Fees and permits: $3.00 day-use fee.
Map: Maptech map: Warrenton, Oregon.
Trail contact: Oregon State Parks and Recreation, 1115 Commercial Street NE, Suite 1, Salem, OR 97301; (800) 551-6949; www.oregonstateparks.org/park_179.php.

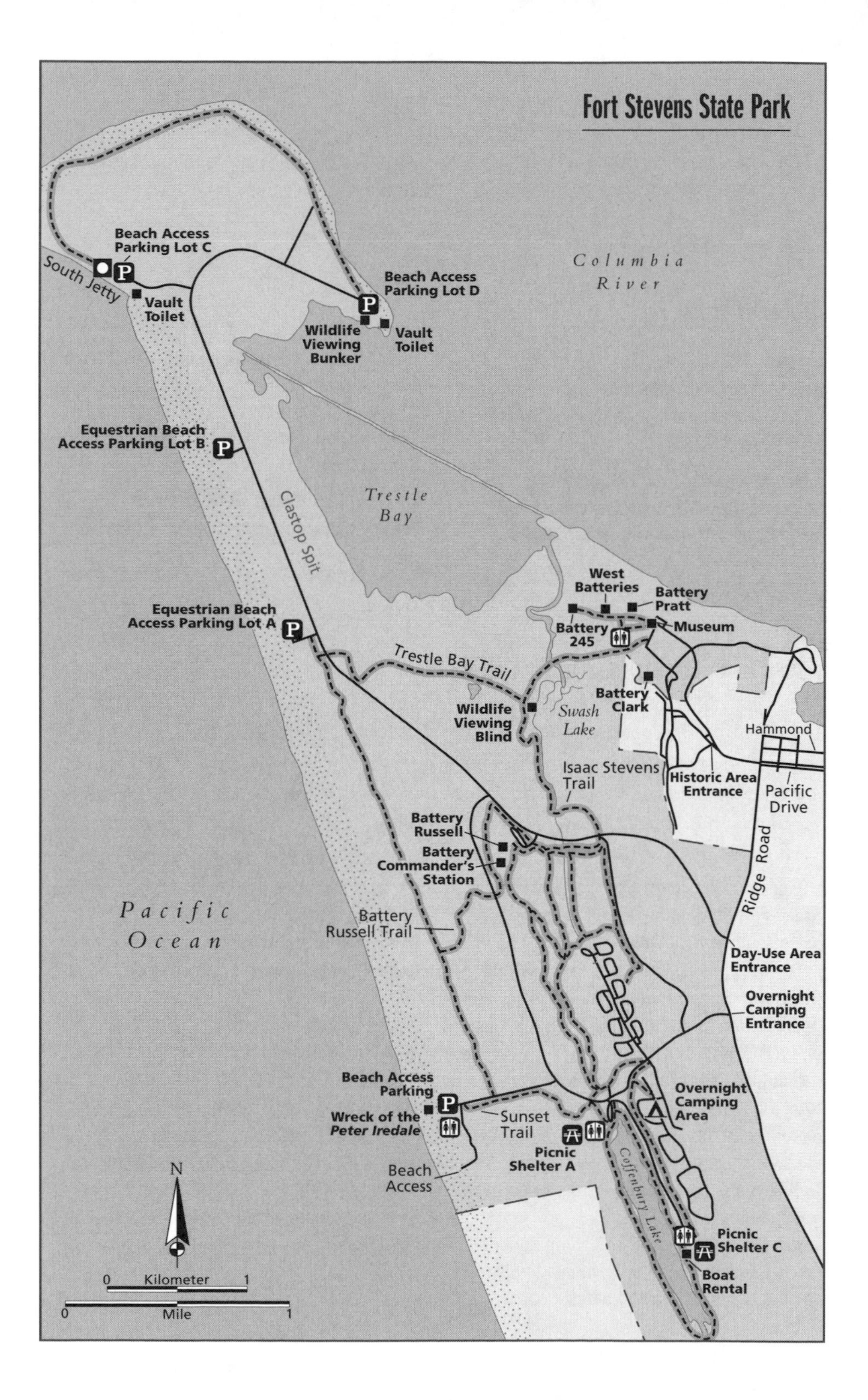

Fort Stevens State Park
Columbia River
Beach Access Parking Lot C
South Jetty
Vault Toilet
Beach Access Parking Lot D
Wildlife Viewing Bunker
Vault Toilet
Equestrian Beach Access Parking Lot B
Trestle Bay
Clastop Spit
Equestrian Beach Access Parking Lot A
West Batteries
Battery Pratt
Battery 245
Museum
Trestle Bay Trail
Battery Clark
Wildlife Viewing Blind
Swash Lake
Hammond
Isaac Stevens Trail
Historic Area Entrance
Pacific Drive
Battery Russell
Battery Commander's Station
Ridge Road
Pacific Ocean
Battery Russell Trail
Day-Use Area Entrance
Overnight Camping Entrance
Beach Access Parking
Wreck of the Peter Iredale
Sunset Trail
Overnight Camping Area
Picnic Shelter A
Beach Access
Coffenbury Lake
Picnic Shelter C
Boat Rental
N
0 Kilometer 1
0 Mile 1

Finding the trailhead: To get to Fort Stevens State Park, travel about 4 miles south of Astoria (or 9 miles north of Seaside) on US 101 and turn west and follow signs for 4.5 miles to the park. See the Miles and Directions section for detailed directions to different hiking opportunities in the park. *DeLorme: Oregon Atlas & Gazetteer:* Page 70, C2.

The Hike

Fort Stevens State Park encompasses 3,763 acres and offers a coastal habitat with a wonderful mix of shallow lakes, wetlands, coastal forest, and sandy beach, as well as a large campground. The park has an interesting history that dates from 1863, when it was established by President Lincoln during the Civil War in an effort to calm western military leaders' fears of increasing conflict with unionist states and territories. Luckily, the fort never saw any military action. In the early 1900s Fort Stevens served as a strategic garrison to protect trade and transportation routes. And during World War II, 2,500 soldiers stationed at Fort Stevens served under constant fear of attack from the Japanese navy. These fears were realized when a Japanese submarine approached the mouth of the Columbia River on the night of June 21, 1942, and fired on the fort. The seventeen fired shells did no damage, and no fire was returned because the submarine was out of range. The fort was decommissioned after World War II and used by the reserves and the Coast Guard until 1975, when it was turned into a state park.

Today this park offers 5 miles of hiking trails, a large campground, and unlimited beach access. You can hike 2.4 miles around scenic Coffenbury Lake, which is popular for fishing, swimming, and boating.

If you want to see an old shipwreck, check out the wreck of the *Peter Iredale*. In 1906 the four-masted British freighter was on its way from Australia to Astoria, Oregon, to pick up its next cargo. It was a very foggy, windy day and, as the ship approached the Columbia Bar, it became lost. Imagine the crews' frustration and fright when a strong gust of wind steered the ship aground onto Clatsop Spit. The crew survived, but the ship was so damaged it had to be abandoned and left to fate. The rusty frame of this ship, buried deep in the sand, serves as a stark reminder of the brutal storms and merciless seas that have plagued sailors of both the past and present along this stretch of Pacific Coast. Also known as the "Graveyard of the Pacific" because of storms, rough seas, and fog, this area has caused more than 2,000 ships to wreck while trying to cross the Columbia Bar (the entrance to the Columbia River).

If you want to go whale watching, head to the viewing tower located in parking lot C at the north end of the park. Whales usually can be seen in December and March. Also be on the lookout for sea lions and harbor seals. This parking area also gives you access to miles of sandy beach.

You can watch for abundant bird life by heading to parking lot D. A wood ramp leads you to a viewing platform overlooking Trestle Bay, which houses a large estuary where you may see great blue herons, long-billed dowitchers, cormorants, and western grebes. From this same parking area, you can walk north along Clatsop Spit and watch ships trying to cross the Columbia Bar. Look for the trail on the north side of the parking area. Follow the trail for about 2.2 miles as it heads around the north end of Clatsop Spit to its ending point at the South Jetty.

You may also want to explore the abandoned gun batteries of the Fort Stevens Military Reservation, which guarded the mouth of the Columbia River from the Civil War until World War II. You can view military artifacts and interpretive displays at the Fort Stevens Military Museum (503–861–2000), located off of Ridge Road adjacent to the park and open from 10:00 A.M. to 6:00 P.M. from June through September and from 10:00 A.M. to 4:00 P.M. the rest of the year. The Oregon Coast Hiking Trail also passes through the park and, if you are backpacking on this trail, hiker/biker campsites are available at Fort Stevens.

Miles and Directions

To hike 2.4 miles around Coffenbury Lake turn west at the campground entrance (the first park entrance) and go 0.3 mile to Picnic Area A at Coffenbury Lake.

To explore the wreck of the *Peter Iredale* as well as miles of sandy beach, turn left at the campground entrance (the first park entrance) and follow signs to a parking area near the shipwreck.

To watch for whales, sea lions, and other bird life, head to Parking Area C. Turn west into the Day-Use Entrance (the second park entrance) and follow it to Parking Area C, on the left side of the road.

To walk around the tip of Clatsop Spit and to view bird lie and ships crossing the Columbia Bar, head to Parking Area D. You can access the parking area by turning west into the Day-Use Entrance (the second park entrance) and continuing to the road's end at Parking Area D.

Hike Information

Local Information

Astoria/Warrenton Chamber of Commerce, 111 West Marine Drive, Astoria, OR 97103; (800) 875-6807.

Local Events/Attractions

Columbia River Maritime Museum, 1792 Marine Drive, Astoria; (503) 325-2323; www.crmm.org.

Fort Clatsop National Memorial, 92343 Fort Clatsop Road, Astoria; (503) 861-2471, ext. 214; www.nps.gov/focl.

Local Outdoor Retailers

Coast Fitness, 1230 Marine Drive, Astoria; (503) 325-1815.

Lodging

Grandview B&B, 1574 Grand Avenue, Astoria, OR 97103; (800) 488-3250; www.grandviewbedandbreakfast.com.

Officers' Inn B&B, 540 Russell Place, Hammond, OR 97121; (800) 377-2524; www.officersinn.net.

4 Ecola State Park to Indian Beach

Located in scenic Ecola State Park, this classic coastal route offers a winding single-track trail through a dense coastal forest with awesome ocean views, and a picturesque beach for a finale.

Start: The trailhead is located on the north side of the main parking lot in Ecola State Park, which is located about 2.5 miles north of Cannon Beach.
Distance: 3 miles out and back.
Approximate hiking time: 1 to 1.5 hours.
Difficulty: Easy due to well-graded trail.
Total climbing: 175 feet. Elevation profiles are not provided for hikes with less than 250 feet of elevation gain.
Trail surface: Dirt path.
Lay of the land: This trail begins in Ecola State Park and takes you through a beautiful coastal forest to Indian Beach.
Seasons: Year-round. The trail can be muddy during the winter months.
Other trail users: None.
Canine compatibility: Leashed dogs permitted.
Land status: State park.
Nearest town: Cannon Beach.
Fees and permits: A $3.00 day-use fee is required and can be obtained at the entrance booth to the park.
Map: Maptech map: Tillamook Head, Oregon.
Trail contact: Oregon State Parks and Recreation, 1115 Commercial Street NE, Suite 1, Salem, OR 97301; (800) 551-6949; www.oregonstateparks.org/park_188.php.

Finding the trailhead: From U.S. Highway 101 at the north end of Cannon Beach, exit west at the ECOLA STATE PARK sign. Travel about 0.25 mile and turn right at a small sign for the park. Go 2.3 miles on a narrow, windy road to a large parking area and the trailhead. *DeLorme: Oregon Atlas & Gazetteer:* Page 64, A1.

The Hike

Ecola State Park covers 1,304 acres and displays breathtaking views from several different viewpoints. For a warm-up be sure to head toward the ocean on a short paved trail that leads to expansive viewpoints looking south toward Cannon Beach and Haystack Rock. From this vantage point you may see the spouts of gray whales during their semiannual migration. These amazing marine mammals migrate south during December and January and north during March and April. During Whale Watch Week, held the last week in December and the last week in March, trained volunteers can help you spot the whales (see the Hike Information section).

This route begins on the north side of the main parking area and follows the Oregon Coast Trail north for 1.5 miles through mystical coastal forest of Sitka spruce and western hemlock to Indian Beach. Along the way you'll pass three spectacular viewpoints. Once you reach Indian Beach, you can beachcomb and watch surfers and boogie boarders catching waves offshore. From Indian Beach you'll have great views of the 62-foot-high Tillamook Rock Lighthouse, which rests on a large chunk of basalt rock located more than a mile offshore from Tillamook Head. This lighthouse was built in 1881 and acted as a lifesaving beacon for ships headed for the

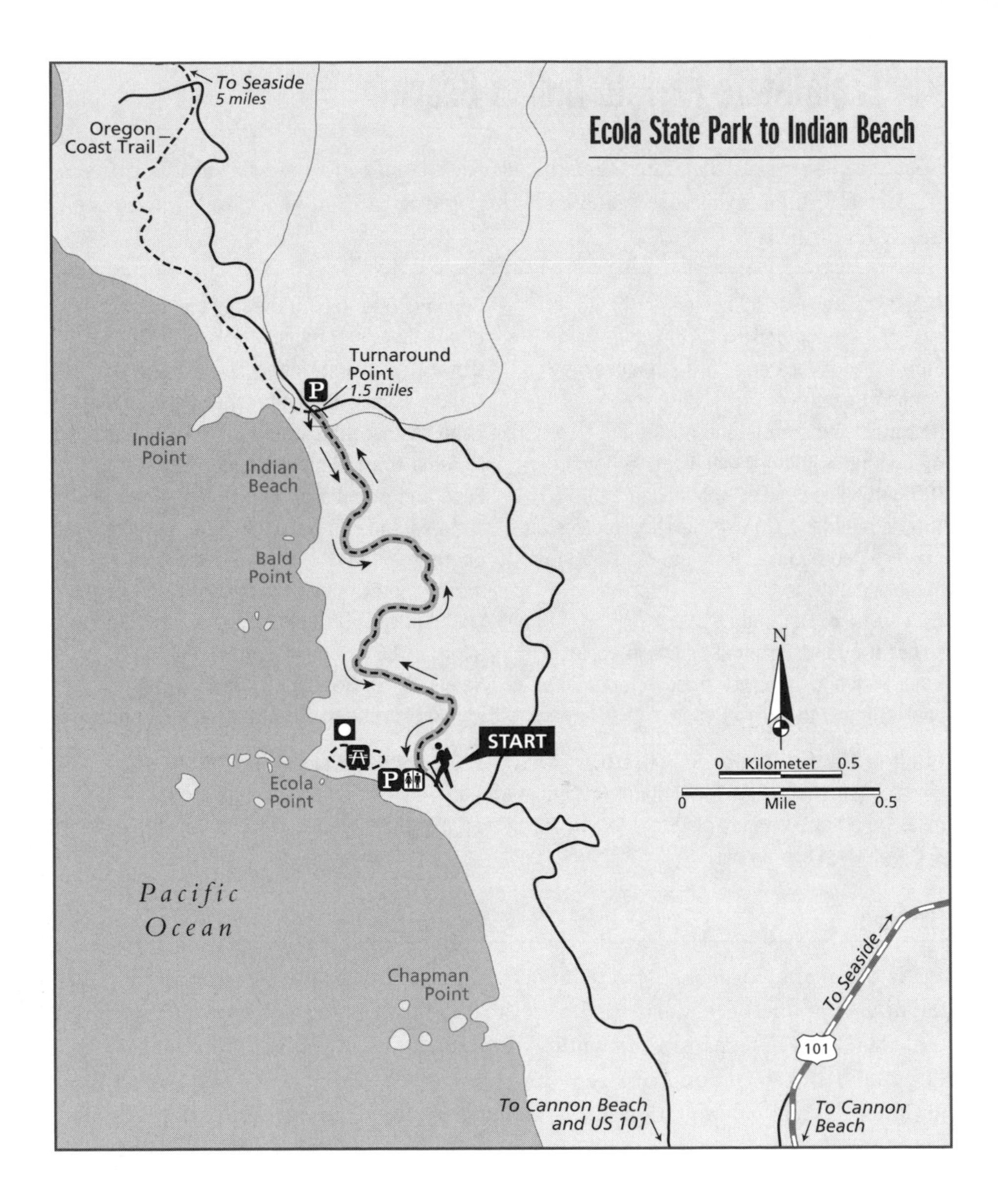

Columbia River. Nicknamed "Terrible Tilly" this lighthouse is privately owned and does not allow public access.

From Indian Beach you have the option of continuing north on the Oregon Coast Trail for about another 6 miles as it weaves through coastal forest and travels over Tillamook Head to Seaside. If you are backpacking this section of the Oregon Coast, there is a backpackers' camping area located 1.5 miles north of Indian Beach. To leave a vehicle at the northern trailhead in Seaside, travel about 10 miles north on U.S. Highway 101. In Seaside turn left (west) onto U Avenue and go 0.1 mile and turn left onto Edgewood Avenue. Continue for about 1.1 miles (this turns into Sunset Avenue) to the end of the road and the trailhead.

Miles and Directions

0.0 Look for a small trailhead sign on the north side of the parking lot. Pick up the singletrack trail as it winds through a dense forest.

1.5 Turn left at the fork and continue to secluded Indian Beach (your turnaround point). From here, retrace the same route back to the starting point. **Option:** You can continue 6 miles north on the Oregon Coast Trail to Seaside. Look for the trailhead on the right side of the Indian Beach day-use parking area.

3.0 Arrive at the trailhead.

Hike Information

Local Information

Cannon Beach Chamber of Commerce and Information Center, Second Street and Spruce Street, Cannon Beach, OR 97110; (503) 436-2623; www.cannonbeach.org.

Local Events/Attractions

Sandcastle Day, held in June, Cannon Beach; (503) 436-2623.

Whale Watch Week, held the last week in December and the last week in March,

Ecola State Park

Cannon Beach; (541) 563-2002; www.whalespoken.org.

Lodging

Tolovana Inn, 3400 South Hemlock Street, Tolovana Park, OR 97145; (800) 333-8890; www.tolovanainn.com.

Restaurant

Bill's Tavern & Brewhouse, 188 North Hemlock Street, Cannon Beach; (503) 436-2202.

5 Cannon Beach

This beach trek starts in the quaint town of Cannon Beach and heads south on a spacious sandy beach where you'll pass by 235-foot Haystack Rock. This distinct rock promontory is designated as part of the Oregon Islands Wildlife Refuge and is an important nesting spot for puffins, pelagic cormorants, pigeon guillemots, and western gulls. At low tide you can explore the tide pools at the base of Haystack Rock and then continue your beach journey to the turnaround point at Tolovana Wayside.

Start: Public parking area in downtown Cannon Beach at Second and Spruce Street.
Distance: 4 miles out and back.
Approximate hiking time: 1.5 to 2 hours.
Difficulty: Easy.
Total climbing: 10 feet. Elevation profiles are not provided for hikes with less than 250 feet of elevation gain.
Trail surface: Sidewalk, sandy beach.
Lay of the land: This beach route begins in downtown Cannon Beach and heads south past Haystack Rock to the Tolovana Beach Wayside.
Seasons: Year-round.
Other trail users: Cyclists.
Canine compatibility: Leashed dogs permitted.
Land status: Public beach.
Nearest town: Cannon Beach.
Fees and permits: No fees or permits required.
Map: Maptech map: Tillamook Head, Oregon.
Trail contact: Cannon Beach Chamber of Commerce and Information Center, Second Street and Spruce Streets, Cannon Beach, OR 97110; (503) 436-2623; www.cannonbeach.org.

Finding the trailhead: Head about 73 miles west of Portland on U.S. Highway 26 to the intersection with US 101. Turn south onto U.S. Highway 101 and take the Cannon Beach exit. Continue driving south through downtown Cannon Beach to a public parking area located at the intersection of Second and Spruce Streets. *DeLorme: Oregon Atlas & Gazetteer:* Page 64, A1.

The Hike

The hamlet of Cannon Beach, located approximately 73 miles northwest of Portland, is a popular tourist destination and home to famous Haystack Rock. Tourists who come here can stroll through the town's art galleries and boutiques, relax at its

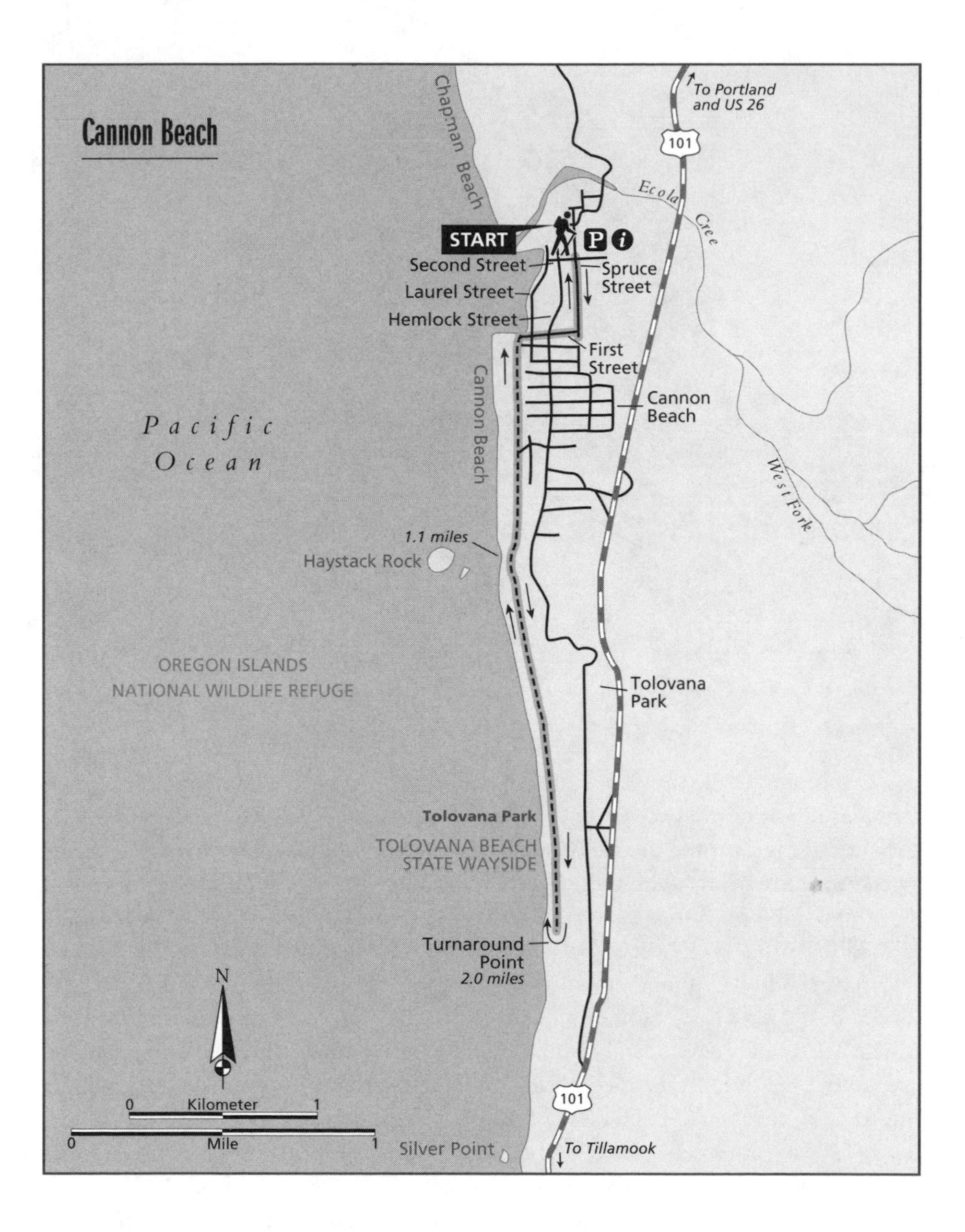

quaint cafes, and walk along the broad, sandy beach to see the prominent 235-foot Haystack Rock. The town is well-known for attracting artists and has more than a dozen art galleries that feature water colors, oil painting, ceramics, photography, fiber arts, bronze works, and blown glass. The town is also host to the annual Sandcastle Day (held in June), which features amazing sand sculptures by some of the best sandcastle builders on the West Coast.

Haystack Rock at Cannon Beach

Lewis and Clark traveled to the Cannon Beach area in January 1806 when Native Americans told them about a whale that has washed up on the beach. The whale was found at the mouth of a creek. Clark named the creek "Ecola," which is the Native American term for "whale."

Cannon Beach earned its name after a series of events that took place in the mid-1800s. In 1846 the U.S. survey schooner *Shark* sank near the mouth of the Columbia River. Within a month three cannons from this wreckage washed up on the beach near Arch Cape, south of present-day Cannon Beach. The cannons later vanished and legends developed regarding their disappearance. When Arch Cape built a post office in 1891, they named it Cannon Beach. As the area's population grew, four more post offices were built, three of which were designated with the name Ecola. In 1922 residents voted to change the name of the post offices from Ecola to Cannon Beach, and the name has stayed ever since.

You'll enjoy this 4-mile out-and-back beach trek, which starts at the parking lot next to the Chamber of Commerce Information Center in downtown Cannon Beach. If you want to take along a lunch, stop at Osburn's Grocery Store and Delicatessen, at Hemlock Street just north of Second Street. Once you reach the beach, you'll turn south and arrive at 235-foot Haystack Rock after 1.1 miles. The origin of Haystack Rock began with a series of eruptions some seventeen million years ago that poured molten rock over the Columbia Plateau. The eruptions continued for more than ten million years, spreading lava over 78,000 square miles of earth. Some of these lava flows reached to the ocean, which was 25 miles inland from its present-day location. When the lava invaded the soft marine sediments of the coast, different knobs, sheets, and fingers of rock began to form. As the rock cooled, it turned into basalt. Over millions of years these basalt formations have eroded away to form the rocky cliffs and headlands that are present today along the coast of Oregon. Haystack Rock is one such result of this erosion process. Designated as part of the Oregon Islands Wildlife Refuge, Haystack Rock is also an important nesting spot for puffins, pelagic cormorants, pigeon guillemots, and western gulls. At the base of Haystack Rock, you'll also find tide pools filled with such colorful creatures as sea anemones, starfish, mussels, and hermit crabs. From Haystack Rock the route continues another 0.9 mile south to your turnaround point at Tolovana Wayside.

Miles and Directions

0.0 From the public parking area, turn left onto Spruce Street.

0.1 Turn right onto First Street.

0.2 Cross Hemlock Street and continue west toward the beach. Cross Laurel Street and then pick up the sandy path that takes you to the beach. Once you reach the beach, turn left (south) and enjoy a fun trek on the long, flat sandy beach.

1.1 You'll pass 235-foot Haystack Rock on your right. Check out the tide pools at the base of this rocky promontory.

2.0 Arrive at Tolovana Wayside (your turnaround point). Retrace the same route back to your starting point.

4.0 Arrive at the public parking area and your starting point.

Hike Information

Local Information

Cannon Beach Chamber of Commerce and Information Center, Second Street and Spruce Street, Cannon Beach, OR 97110; (503) 436-2623; www.cannonbeach.org.

Local Events/Attractions

Sandcastle Day, held in June, Cannon Beach; (503) 436-2623.

Whale Watch Week, held the last week in December and the last week in March, Cannon Beach; (541) 563-2002; www.whalespoken.org.

Lodging

Tolovana Inn, 3400 South Hemlock Street, Tolovana Park, OR 97145; (800) 333-8890; www.tolovanainn.com.

Restaurant

Bill's Tavern & Brewhouse, 188 North Hemlock Street, Cannon Beach; (503) 436-2202.

6 Saddle Mountain

This trail to the top of 3,283-foot Saddle Mountain, the highest point in the northern Coastal Mountains, begins in a thickly wooded expanse of alder forest. It then climbs through a beautiful Douglas fir forest with a thick understory of wood sorrel, trillium, western columbine, coast penstemon, and many other unique wildflowers. Eventually the trail becomes rocky and eroded and necessitates some careful navigation, but the effort is worth it, for those who make it to the top are rewarded with magnificent views.

Start: From the Saddle Mountain State Park trailhead located about 65 miles west of Portland (and 17 miles northeast of Cannon Beach) off U.S. Highway 26.
Distance: 5.2 miles out and back.
Approximate hiking time: 2 to 3 hours.
Difficulty: Difficult due to loose rocks and dirt on steep terrain. In winter the trail can be very icy and treacherous.
Total climbing: 1,623 feet.
Trail surface: The first half is an easy and well-maintained dirt path; the final 1.5 miles are very eroded but include cables, walkways, and stairs to aid travel.
Lay of the land: Climbs through alder forests and open, alpinelike landscape to the summit where you can enjoy breathtaking views of the Coast Range on a clear day.
Seasons: Year-round.
Other trail users: None.
Canine compatibility: Leashed dogs permitted.
Land status: State park.
Nearest town: Cannon Beach.
Fees and permits: No fees or permits required.
Map: Maptech map: Saddle Mountain, Oregon.
Trail contact: Oregon State Parks and Recreation, 1115 Commercial Street NE, Suite 1, Salem, OR 97301; (800) 551-6949; www.oregonstateparks.org/park_197.php.

Finding the trailhead: From Portland travel 65 miles west on US 26 to a sign for Saddle Mountain State Park. Turn right (north) onto Saddle Mountain Road and continue 7 miles to the trailhead.

From Cannon Beach travel 10 miles east on US 26 and turn left (north) onto Saddle Mountain Road. Continue 7 miles to the trailhead. *DeLorme: Oregon Atlas & Gazetteer:* Page 64, A3.

The Hike

As one of the highest peaks in Oregon's northern Coast Mountain Range, Saddle Mountain rises 3,283 feet above sea level. The gray monolith juts its basalt head above its neighbors and stands testament to its volcanic beginnings. The peak is the eroded remnant of the Columbia basalt flows that poured through the area approximately fifteen million years ago. The massive flows originated more than 250 miles away in eastern Washington. When the lava came into contact with an ancient sea that covered the area, it cooled rapidly and formed fragmented layers. When North America pushed its way under the old Pacific seafloor, Saddle Mountain was born.

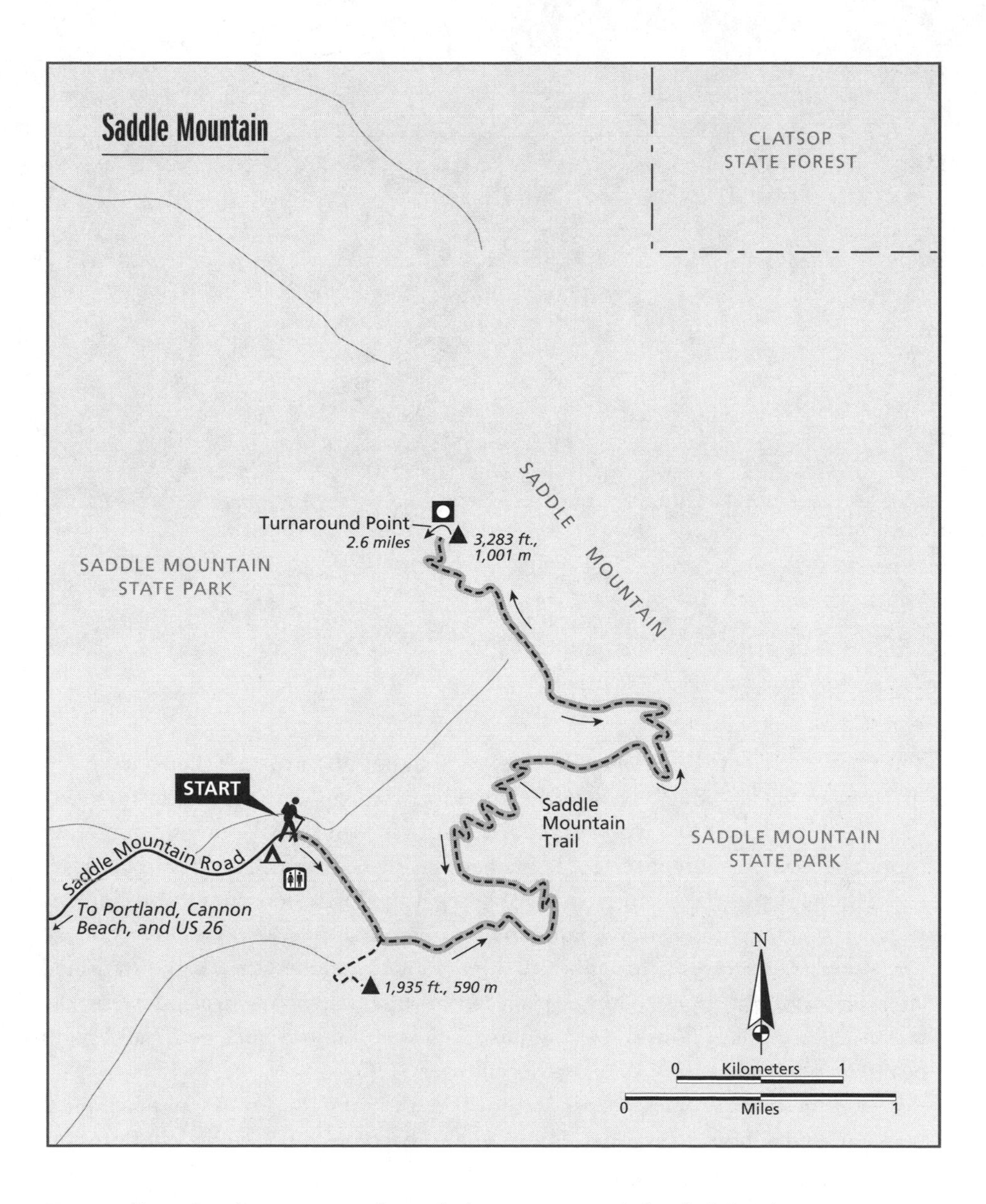

Eventually soft sedimentary rock eroded away to reveal the dark basalt mountaintop visible today.

To see Saddle Mountain up close, try this strenuous 5.2-mile out-and-back trek to the summit. The trailhead is located at the base of the mountain, as are water, rest room facilities, and ten primitive campsites. The trail's first mile slips through a thick, secondary-growth forest of red alder that thrives in the moist environment. Red alders can be found at elevations up to 3,000 feet and are easily identified by their grayish white bark. They're often covered with a mottled coat of moss and lichen.

Scenic views from the Saddle Mountain Trail

The coastal Indian tribes steeped the tree's bark in hot water to cure rheumatic fever. (It contains salicin, which even today is used in prescription medication for treatment of this disease.) The wood of the tree also was used to make utensils and other tools. The lower section of this route is a haven for wildflowers. The cloverlike leaves and delicate white flowers of wood sorrel carpet the forest floor. You'll also find triangular trillium, pink western columbine, and blue coast penstemon. Other botanical delights scattered throughout the woods include the hairy-stemmed checker-mallow, a high-stemmed plant with large, daisylike purple flowers; the tooth-leafed monkey flower, a yellow, tubular flower with toothlike petals; and goat's beard, recognizable by its white, feathery flowers.

Soon the trail becomes steeper and the forest canopy thins to reveal many great views around almost every bend. The path also becomes more eroded and precipi-

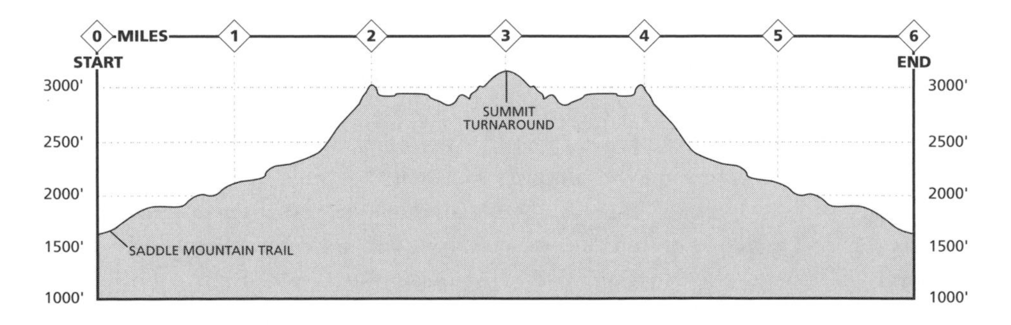

tous and requires some careful footwork over rocky ledges. (Notice the firm grasp the thick red stems of Oregon stonecrop have on the ledges, and wish you had the same.) In an attempt to make navigating easier, stairs and walkways have been built over the more difficult sections of trail. The walkways also protect the wildflower meadows of blue iris, Indian paintbrush, meadow chickweed, phlox, and larkspur.

After about 2 miles the trail crosses a narrow saddle then climbs to the domelike summit. The push to the top is somewhat treacherous. The trail is steep and filled with loose rocks. Fortunately, stairs and cables are in place to make things easier. Still, these devices are not always reliable—some are loose and can be dangerous. At the broad, flat summit there are grand views of Nehalem Bay to the southwest, the Columbia River to the northwest, and the snowcapped Cascade peaks of Mount Jefferson and Mount Hood to the east.

Summertime crowds on this popular trek—especially at the summit—can be fierce. If you want solitude come here on a weekday or on an off-season weekend in the spring or fall.

Miles and Directions

0.0 Start at the trailhead at the Saddle Mountain State Park parking lot. (FYI: There are rest rooms and water here. The trail begins with a climb through an alder forest.)

1.5 (Note: The trail becomes steeper and, in parts, rocky and eroded.)

1.7 (FYI: Several bridges cross an alpinelike landscape of wildflowers. Look for blue iris, Indian paintbrush, white meadow chickweed, chocolate lily, phlox, and larkspur.)

2.2 Hike across a narrow saddle before climbing to the summit. (Note: The final stretch includes loose rocks and is very steep–use the stairs, walkways, and cables to ensure you don't slip.)

2.6 Arrive at the 3,283-foot summit where you'll enjoy magnificent views of Nehalem Bay to the southwest, the Columbia River to the northwest, and snowcapped Cascade peaks to the east. Retrace the same route back to the trailhead.

5.2 Arrive at the trailhead.

Hike Information

Local Information

Cannon Beach Chamber of Commerce and Information Center, Second Street and Spruce Street, Cannon Beach, OR 97110; (503) 436-2623; www.cannonbeach.org.

Local Events/Attractions

Sandcastle Day, held in June, Cannon Beach; (503) 436-2623.

Whale Watch Week, held the last week in December and the last week in March, Cannon Beach; (541) 563-2002; www.whalespoken.org.

Lodging

Tolovana Inn, 3400 South Hemlock Street, Tolovana Park, Oregon 97145; (800) 333-8890; www.tolovanainn.com.

Restaurant

Bill's Tavern & Brewhouse, 188 North Hemlock Street, Cannon Beach; (503) 436-2202.

7 Oswald West State Park–Short Sand Beach

Take an amazing walk through a grove of old-growth coastal forest along the banks of Short Sand Creek to Short Sand Beach and Smugglers Cove in Oswald West State Park. Enjoy a day at the beach watching surfers and boogie boarders riding the waves, exploring tide pools, and enjoying gorgeous coastal scenery.

Start: Oswald West State Park parking area located 14.8 miles south of Cannon Beach on U.S. Highway 26.
Distance: 1 mile out and back (with longer options).
Approximate hiking time: 1 hour.
Difficulty: Easy due to well-graded path and minimal elevation gains.
Total climbing: 100 feet. Elevation profiles are not provided for hikes with less than 250 feet of elevation gain.
Trail surface: Paved path and gravel path.
Lay of the land: This easy hike travels next to picturesque Neyacarni Creek through a spectacular old-growth forest of red cedar, Sitka spruce, and Douglas fir trees and ends at Short Sand Beach.
Seasons: Year-round (the driest months are June through October).
Other trail users: None.
Canine compatibility: Leashed dogs permitted.
Land status: State park.
Nearest town: Cannon Beach.
Fees and permits: No fees or permits required.
Map: Maptech map: Arch Cape, Oregon.
Trail contact: Oregon State Parks and Recreation, 1115 Commercial Street NE, Suite 1, Salem, OR 97301; (800) 551-6949; www.oregonstateparks.org/park_195.php.

Finding the trailhead: From the junction of U.S. Highways 26 and 101, turn south and travel 14.8 miles to a parking area on the left (east) side of the road in Oswald West State Park.

The Hike

Oswald West State Park covers 2,474 acres and encompasses some of the most beautiful landscapes on the Oregon Coast. It houses Neahkahnie Mountain, Arch Cape, Cape Falcon, Smugglers Cove, and Short Sand Beach. The park was named after Governor Oswald West, who was in office from 1911 to 1915. The state park features many hiking trails and a walk-in campground. The sites are first-come, first-served, and the campground fills up rapidly on summer weekends.

This route takes you on an amazing walk through a giant stand of old-growth Sitka spruce, red cedar, and Douglas fir trees along the banks of picturesque Short Sands Creek. Start your journey at the wood trailhead sign located on the north side of the parking lot. Walk on the paved path as it leads you under the highway and follow it as it descends at a gradual pace next to Short Sand Creek. Most likely you'll share the trail with surfers and boogie boarders who are heading to Short Sand Beach and Smugglers Cove to spend the day riding waves. Enjoy the soothing

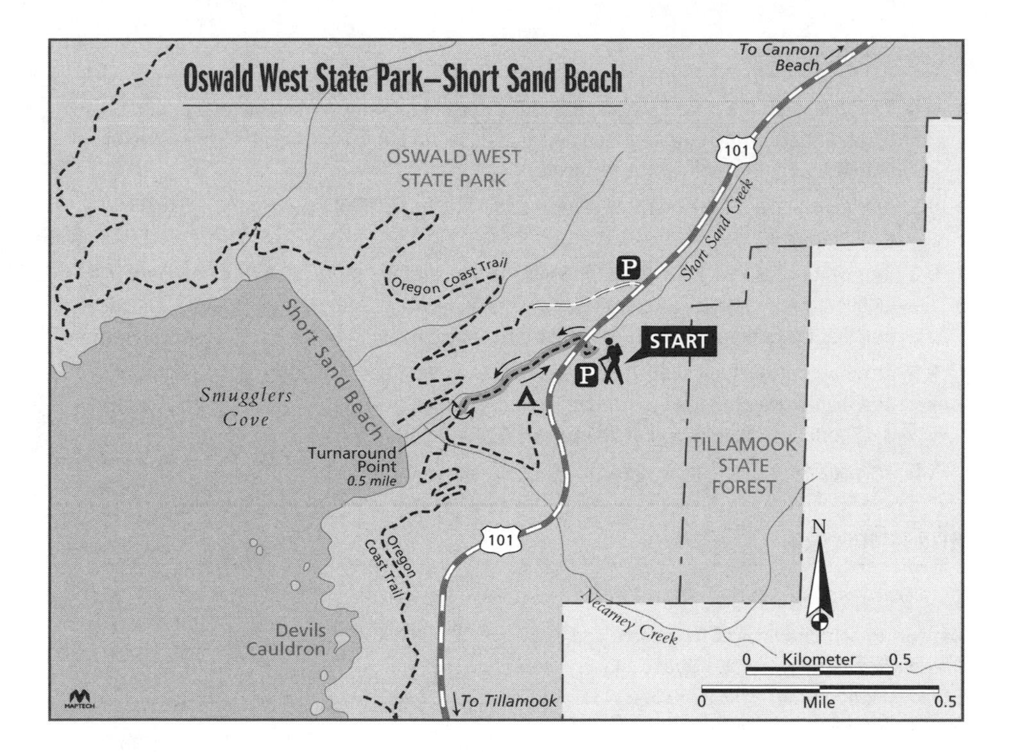

sounds of the creek and the lush greenery of huckleberry, salmonberry, and salal bushes that line the creek. Huckleberries have round red berries that are about one centimeter in diameter; salmonberries are shaped like a raspberry and can range in color from yellow to light reddish-pink in color; salal berries are bluish-purple, round-shaped, and grow in thick clusters. All three of these berries were an important food source for coastal Native Indian tribes. Salmonberries were mixed with fat and salmon to create a high-calorie food that was an important energy source during the harsh winter months. They also dried and mashed salal berries and huckleberries and made cakes out of them to be stored for later use. The leaves of the salal plant were applied to burns and cuts as a first-aid remedy. In addition, the leaves of the plant were also brewed as a tea and used to treat coughs, heartburn, and tuberculosis.

After a short 0.5-mile walk next to the creek, you'll arrive at a picturesque picnic area shaded by towering Douglas fir trees. A short trail leads down a flight of steps from the picnic area to Short Sand Beach and Smugglers Cove, which is flanked by Point Illga to the south and Cape Falcon to the north. On summer weekends this beautiful beach is filled with sunbathers, surfers, boogie boarders, families, and dogs. If you are looking for a longer hike, you can head 2 miles north from the picnic area on the Oregon Coast Trail to Cape Falcon.

Miles and Directions

0.0 Start hiking on the signed paved path at the north end of the parking area. The path continues under the highway and then begins paralleling Short Sand Creek. (FYI: Rest rooms and water are available at the trailhead.)

0.1 Turn right where a sign indicates BEACH ACCESS. (FYI: The trail that goes right is signed for the campground.)

0.3 Turn right at the trail fork signed for beach access and the picnic area. Not long after this junction, you'll cross a footbridge over the creek. After crossing the bridge look for a side trail that leads down to the creek and a deep rocky pool.

0.5 Arrive at a picnic area shaded by stately Sitka spruce trees. Walk through the picnic area and then arrive at the beach. **Option:** From the picnic area you have the option of continuing north 2 miles one way on the Oregon Coast Trail to Cape Falcon.

1.0 Arrive at the public parking area and your starting point.

Hike Information

Local Information

Cannon Beach Chamber of Commerce and Information Center, Second Street and Spruce Street, Cannon Beach, OR 97110; (503) 436-2623; www.cannonbeach.org.

Local Events/Attractions

Sandcastle Day, held in June, Cannon Beach; (503) 436-2623.

Whale Watch Week, held the last week in December and the last week in March, Cannon Beach; (541) 563-2002; www.whalespoken.org.

Lodging

Tolovana Inn, 3400 South Hemlock Street, Tolovana Park, OR 97145; (800) 333-8890; www.tolovanainn.com.

Restaurant

Bill's Tavern & Brewhouse, 188 North Hemlock Street, Cannon Beach; (503) 436-2202.

8 Neahkahnie Mountain

This route takes you on a journey to the 1,631-foot summit of Neahkahnie Mountain, where local legend says buried treasure still exists. From the top you'll have stunning ocean views (on a clear day) for 50 miles in every direction.

Start: On Forest Road 38555 off U.S. Highway 101 parking area located 17.2 miles south of Cannon Beach off U.S. Highway 26.
Distance: 3.2 miles out and back.
Approximate hiking time: 1.5 hours.
Difficulty: Difficult due to the large amount of elevation gain and the rough trail at the summit.
Total climbing: 741 feet.
Trail surface: Singletrack and a small section of doubletrack road.
Lay of the land: This route takes you through a mystical coastal forest to the summit of Neahkahnie Mountain and palatial ocean views.
Seasons: Year-round (the driest months are June through October).
Other trail users: Hikers only.
Canine compatibility: Dogs permitted.
Land status: State park.
Nearest town: Cannon Beach.
Fees and permits: No fees or permits required.
Map: Maptech map: Arch Cape, Oregon.
Trail contact: Oregon State Parks and Recreation, 1115 Commercial Street NE, Suite 1, Salem, OR 97301; (800) 551-6949; www.oregonstateparks.org.

Finding the trailhead: From the junction of US 26 and US 101 (just north of Cannon Beach), travel 17.2 miles south on US 101 (or 28 miles north of Tillamook) to the junction with gravel FR 38555, marked by a brown hiker sign (this turn is difficult to see!). Turn left (east) and continue on FR 38555 for 0.6 mile and park in a pullout on the left. *DeLorme: Oregon Atlas & Gazetteer:* Page 64, C1.

The Hike

Some of the most breathtaking views of the northern Oregon coast can be seen from the top of 1,631-foot Neahkahnie Mountain. Back in the seventeenth century, it was fairly common to see Spanish sailing vessels along this stretch of coast, many of which carried cargoes of beeswax (used in candle making), a common item for trade at the time. Ten tons of beeswax have since been found along the northern Oregon coast, some pieces of which have elaborate carvings of crucifixes and other designs. Some of the waxen pieces found are kept at the Tillamook Pioneer Museum (see Hike Information).

The Tillamook Pioneer Museum is also home to a unique set of inscribed rocks found by a farmer at the southern base of Neahkahnie Mountain in the 1890s. These rocks have carvings thought to reveal the hiding place for a buried treasure near Neahkahnie Mountain. Treasure hunters believe, based on the rocks found and by stories told by the Tillamook and Clatsop Indians, that this treasure is buried some-

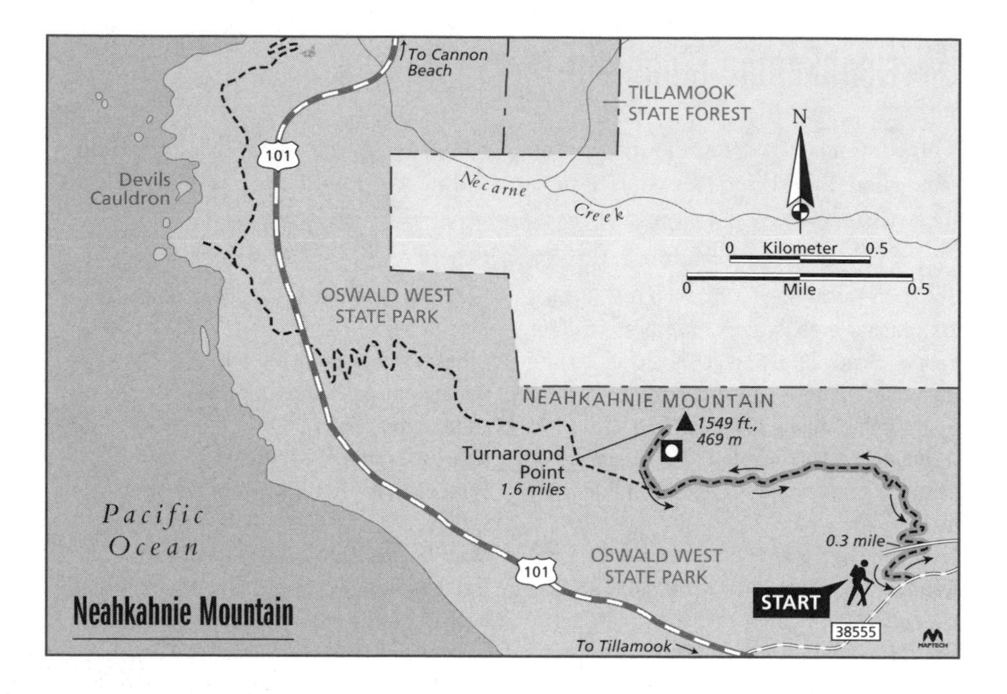

where near the mountain. For the past one hundred years, fortune seekers have sought this legendary treasure, but with no luck.

The story begins in the mid-1700s when a Spanish galleon sailing off the coast was caught in a storm and blown ashore at Cape Foulweather, near the base of Neahkahnie Mountain. The ship's crew came ashore and, in desperation, buried a large chest filled with valuables. Some accounts of the story say that a crewman was shot to death, then buried on top of the chest. Native Americans who witnessed this murder abandoned the site out of fear that the spirit of the murdered man would haunt them forever.

This route immediately begins ascending the south side of the mountain and is lined with salal, Oregon grape, foxglove, and wild raspberries. Watch for garter snakes slithering across the trail and rabbits hopping through the thick underbrush. Take heart, this sparse forest progressively becomes more interesting as you climb. After about 0.5 mile the trail enters a thicker forest corridor filled with big Sitka spruce. After 1.5 miles you'll emerge from the forest and arrive at a junction with a rough trail on your right. This short and extremely steep trail takes you to the rocky spine of the windblown summit, which has stunning views (on a clear day) looking north toward Cannon Beach and south toward Manzanita.

Scenic views from the summit of Neahkanhnie Mountain ▶

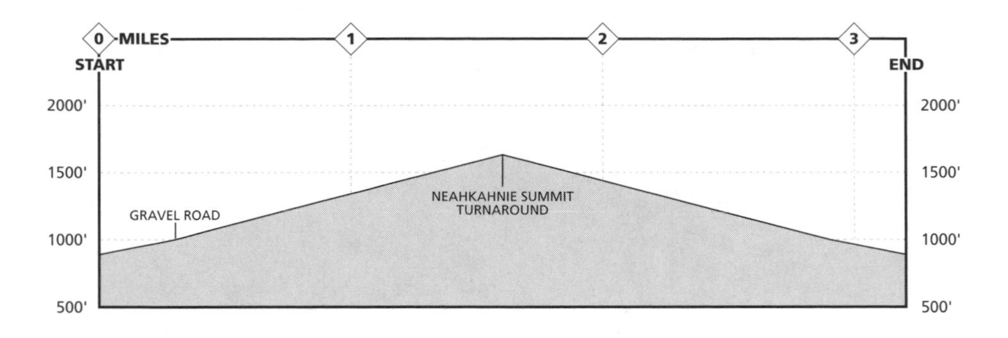

Miles and Directions

0.0 Start by walking about 15 feet up the gravel road and turning left on a singletrack trail marked with a brown trail sign. You'll immediately begin climbing very steeply.

0.3 (FYI: Pass a spectacular viewpoint looking south toward Nehalem Bay.) Cross a gravel road and continue hiking on the singletrack trail.

1.3 (FYI: Pass a bench and a viewpoint looking north toward Cannon Beach.)

1.5 As you round a sharp bend to the right (before emerging out of the trees), look for a rough trail that heads steeply uphill to the right. Turn right and ascend on this rough, rocky trail to the summit viewpoint.

1.6 Arrive at the 1,631-foot summit viewpoint. Return to the trailhead on the same route.

3.2 Arrive at the trailhead.

Hike Information

Local Information

Cannon Beach Chamber of Commerce and Information Center, Second Street and Spruce Street, Cannon Beach, OR 97110; (503) 436-2623; www.cannonbeach.org.

Local Events/Attractions

Sandcastle Day, held in June, Cannon Beach; (503) 436-2623.

Whale Watch Week, held the last week in December and the last week in March, Cannon Beach; (541) 563-2002; www.whalespoken.org.

Lodging

Tolovana Inn, 3400 South Hemlock Street, Tolovana Park, OR 97145; (800) 333-8890; www.tolovanainn.com.

Restaurant

Bill's Tavern & Brewhouse, 188 North Hemlock Street, Cannon Beach; (503) 436-2202.

9 Cape Meares State Park

Cape Meares, located in Cape Meares State Park, is one of three scenic capes along the Three Capes Scenic Highway—the other two capes are Cape Lookout and Cape Kiwanda. A hike here includes numerous opportunities to view seabirds and migrating gray whales. Other attractions include the Cape Meares Lighthouse, which was built in 1890; old-growth Sitka spruce trees; spectacular ocean views; and abundant wildlife and coastal forestland. Plan on spending the better part of a day here and be sure to bring your binoculars.

Start: From the state park parking area approximately 11 miles west of Tillamook off the Three Capes Scenic Loop Highway.
Distance: Varies depending on the trails selected.
Approximate hiking time: 30 minutes to 1 hour.
Difficulty: Easy due to the flat terrain and well-maintained trails.
Total climbing: None. Elevation profiles are not provided for hikes with less than 250 feet of elevation gain.
Trail surface: The Cape Meares Lighthouse and Octopus Tree Trails are paved, wheelchair-accessible out and backs; the Big Spruce Tree Trail is a level, forested-path loop.
Lay of the land: Trails lead to a historic lighthouse and scenic viewpoints on the tip of a magnificent headland. Within the park you will also find spectacular ocean views, abundant wildlife, and a coastal forest.
Seasons: Year-round. The best months are May through October.
Other trail users: Hikers only.
Canine compatibility: Leashed dogs permitted.
Land status: State park.
Nearest town: Tillamook.
Fees and permits: No fees or permits required.
Map: Maptech map: Netarts, Oregon.
Trail contact: Oregon State Parks and Recreation, 1115 Commercial Street NE, Suite 1, Salem, OR 97301; (800) 551-6949; www.oregonstateparks.org/park_181.php.

Finding the trailhead: From U.S. Highway 101 in Tillamook: Follow the signs to Cape Lookout Loop Road (the Three Capes Scenic Highway). Drive approximately 10 miles west on the Three Capes Scenic Highway to the Cape Meares State Park sign. To proceed to the main parking area in the park, turn right (west) onto the Park Road and drive 0.6 mile to a parking area.

From Pacific City: Drive 26 miles north on Cape Lookout Road (the Three Capes Scenic Highway) to the Cape Meares State Park sign. Turn left (west) and drive 0.6 mile on the Park Road to the parking area.

If you want to view the Big Spruce Tree, turn right into a pullout right before the Cape Meares State Park turnoff. A short loop trail will take you by the Big Spruce Tree.

DeLorme: Oregon Atlas & Gazetteer: Page 58, A1.

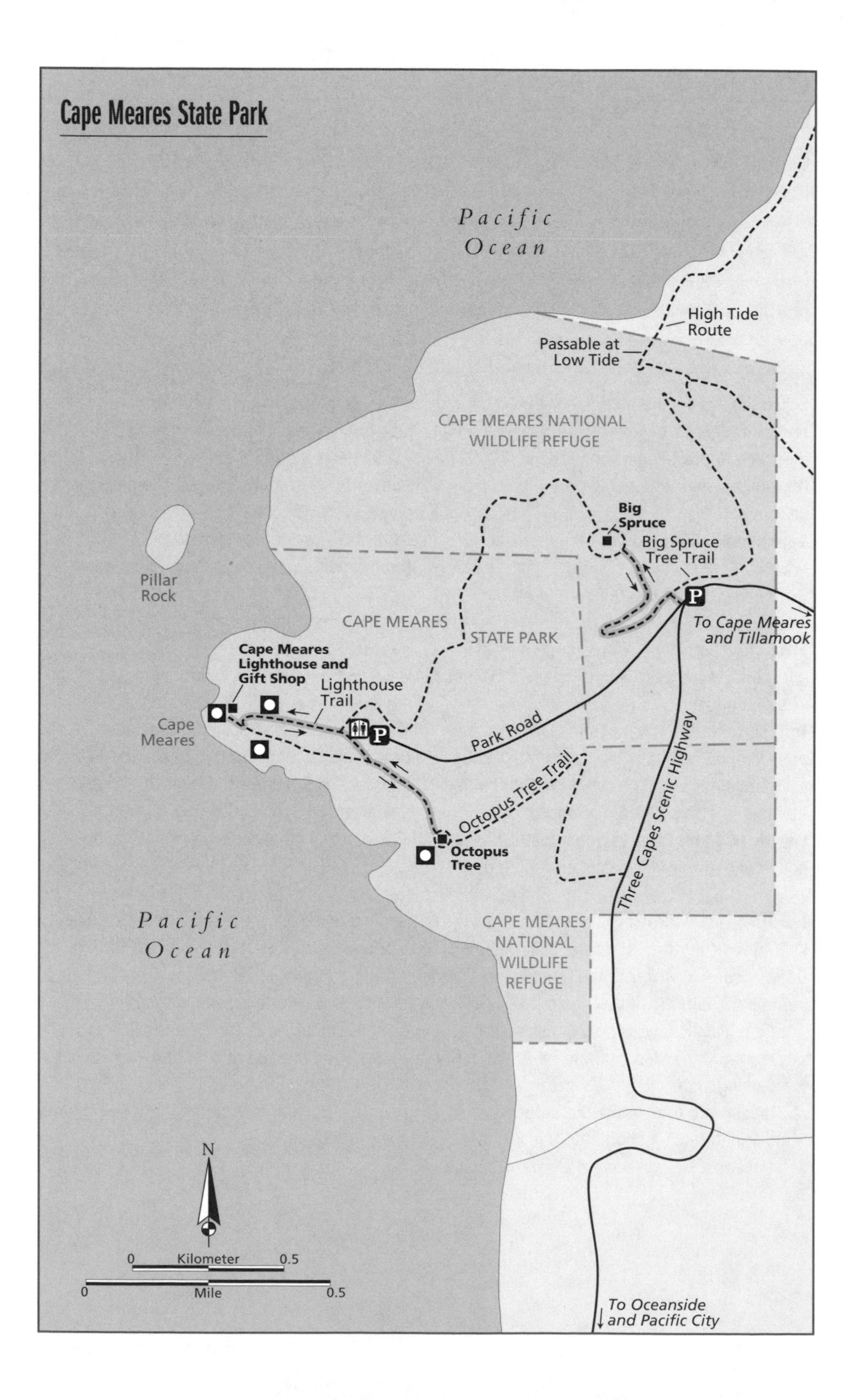
Cape Meares State Park
Pacific Ocean
High Tide Route
Passable at Low Tide
CAPE MEARES NATIONAL WILDLIFE REFUGE
Big Spruce
Big Spruce Tree Trail
Pillar Rock
CAPE MEARES
STATE PARK
To Cape Meares and Tillamook
Cape Meares Lighthouse and Gift Shop
Lighthouse Trail
Cape Meares
Park Road
Three Capes Scenic Highway
Octopus Tree Trail
Octopus Tree
Pacific Ocean
CAPE MEARES NATIONAL WILDLIFE REFUGE
N
0 Kilometer 0.5
0 Mile 0.5
To Oceanside and Pacific City

The Hike

The 233-acre Cape Meares State Park is a must-see stop for anyone traveling along the North Oregon Coast. This scenic cape is well-known for its large concentration of nesting seabirds and its historic lighthouse.

You can start your exploration by walking down the 0.4-mile, out-and-back, paved Cape Meares Lighthouse Trail to the 40-foot-tall Cape Meares Lighthouse. Along the way you'll pass seabird colonies nesting on the sheer, 200-foot rocky cliffs. Bring binoculars for close-up views of these feathered cape residents, which include double-crested cormorants, Brandt's cormorants, pelagic cormorants, pigeon guillemots, common murres, and tufted puffins. Bald eagles and peregrine falcons also have been spotted in the area.

In 1886 the U.S. Army Corp of Engineers sent a representative to survey the Cape Meares site and the Cape Lookout site, located south of Cape Meares, to see which would be more suitable for a lighthouse. After several days of surveying, the engineers picked the Cape Meares site because of its lower elevation, which would allow light to travel farther in foggy weather.

Additionally, it had a spring nearby that could provide fresh water and was more accessible than the Cape Lookout site. In 1887 Congress passed a bill that provided funding to begin construction on the lighthouse. A road was built to the site, and construction finally commenced in the spring of 1889. The interior walls were built with bricks made at the construction site, the exterior walls from sheet iron shipped in from Portland. In November 1889 the lighthouse was complete. At the time, the light consisted of a five-wick oil lamp turned by a 200-pound lead weight. The lens is a first-order Fresnel lens that was shipped from Paris via Cape Horn and up the

BIRD IDENTIFICATION 101 There are many bird species living along the cliffs and offshore islands of this scenic cape. Following are descriptions of just a few.

- Pelagic cormorants are solid black with a white patch on their flank during breeding season. These birds nest predominantly on the south side of the cape.
- Brandt's cormorants have a buff-colored patch adjacent to a blue throat patch and solid black coloring with a sprinkling of fine white feathers on the back and neck.
- Double-crested cormorants have bright yellow and orange markings on their throat and face and have a crooked neck in flight.
- Tufted puffins have a stocky black body, white facial mask, yellow feather tufts on their head, and bright orange feet.
- Common murres are dark brown on the head, back, and wings. They also have a white breast patch and dark yellow feet. They nest on the cliff faces on the north side of the cape.

west coast to Cape Meares. The lens itself has eight sides, four primary lenses, and four bull's-eye lenses covered with red panels.

To view the intricate Fresnel lens, climb a series of steps to the top of the lighthouse tower. A gift shop in the lower section of the lighthouse is open daily May through September and on the weekends in March, April, and October. If visiting the lighthouse isn't enough, check out another amazing attraction at this park—the Octopus Tree. A short, 0.2-mile, out-and-back, wheelchair-accessible trail leads from the main parking area to an ancient Sitka spruce whose low-slung branches truly resemble an octopus. The spruce was used as a burial tree in Native American ceremonies; its octopus-shaped arms held canoes, where the bodies of the tribe's dead were placed. It is speculated that Native Americans, who lived along the northern Oregon coast for nearly 30,000 years, bent the younger tree's more pliable branches outward into a horizontal position. Eventually the tree's branches would take shape and continue to grow. The Octopus Tree is one such specimen that is thought to have endured this ritual when it was very young, surviving to grow old and maintaining its odd shape.

To view another old-growth Sitka spruce, drive 0.6 mile to the park entrance and park in a dirt pullout on the north side of the road. A 0.4-mile, out-and-back loop trail leads to a magnificent 400-year-old tree. As you walk the path, be on the lookout for odd-looking banana slugs. These interesting, slow-moving creatures eat plant matter and recycle the material back to the soil. They also secrete a thin coat of mucus that helps them travel over the forest floor.

Miles and Directions

The Cape Meares Lighthouse Trail and the Octopus Tree Trail start from the main parking area. The Big Spruce Tree Trail begins in a dirt pullout on the north side of the park road just before the entrance to the park.

Hike Information

Local Information

Tillamook Chamber of Commerce, 3705 Highway 101 North, Tillamook, OR 97141; (503) 842-7525; www.tillamookchamber.org.

Local Events/Attractions

Tillamook Cheese Factory, 4175 Highway 101 North, Tillamook; (503) 815-1300; www.tillamookcheese.com.

Local Outdoor Retailers

Tillamook Sporting Goods, 2205 North Main Street, Tillamook; (503) 842-4334.

◀ *Cape Meares Lighthouse*

10 Cape Lookout

This easy ramble through a lush coastal forest of rare old-growth Sitka spruce leads to the end of scenic Cape Lookout in Cape Lookout State Park. Along the way there are magnificent views of Cape Meares to the north and Cape Kiwanda to the south. Gray whales can be seen in December, January, March, and April as they near the cape on their semiannual migrations.

Start: The trailhead is located 13 miles southwest of Tillamook and 16 miles north of Pacific City on the Three Capes Scenic Highway.
Distance: 5 miles out and back.
Approximate hiking time: 2 to 3 hours.
Difficulty: Moderate due to elevation gain.
Total climbing: 400 feet.
Trail surface: Well-maintained dirt path through a thick Sitka spruce forest with occasional roots and rocks and wooden ramps over muddy sections of the trail.
Lay of the land: Hike on a forest path through a shady Sitka spruce forest along some exposed cliffs to the tip of Cape Lookout.
Seasons: Year-round. The best months are June through October.
Other trail users: Hikers only.
Canine compatibility: Leashed dogs permitted.
Land status: State park.
Nearest town: Tillamook.
Fees and permits: A $3.00 day-use pass is required. You can purchase a pass at the self-pay machine at Cape Lookout State Campground located north of the trailhead off the Three Capes Scenic Highway.
Map: Maptech map: Sand Lake, Oregon.
Trail contact: Oregon State Parks and Recreation, 1115 Commercial Street NE, Suite 1, Salem, OR 97301; (800) 551-6949; www.oregonstateparks.org/park_186.php.

Finding the trailhead: From U.S. Highway 101 in Tillamook, head 15.5 miles southwest on the Three Capes Scenic Highway to the signed Cape Lookout trailhead on the right side of the highway.

From the intersection of Oregon Highway 18 and US 101 in Lincoln City, turn north on US 101. Travel 14.6 miles north on US 101 and turn left (west) onto Brooten Road where a sign states CAPE KIWANDA RECREATION AREA/PACIFIC CITY. Go 2.8 miles west on Brooten Road and then turn left onto Pacific Avenue toward "Netarts/Oceanside." Continue 0.3 mile on Pacific Avenue and then turn right onto Kiwanda Drive. Go 15.3 miles to the signed Cape Lookout trailhead on the left side of the highway. *DeLorme: Oregon Atlas & Gazetteer:* Page 58, B1.

The Hike

Cape Lookout, part of the 2,000-acre Cape Lookout State Park (host to a campground, scenic Netarts Spit, and a variety of plants and animals), is a spectacular headland made up of a series of lava flows fifteen to twenty million years old. Jutting into the ocean like an arrowhead, its 400-foot cliffs are regularly pounded and carved by rhythmic waves and currents. The scenic cape is popular among whale

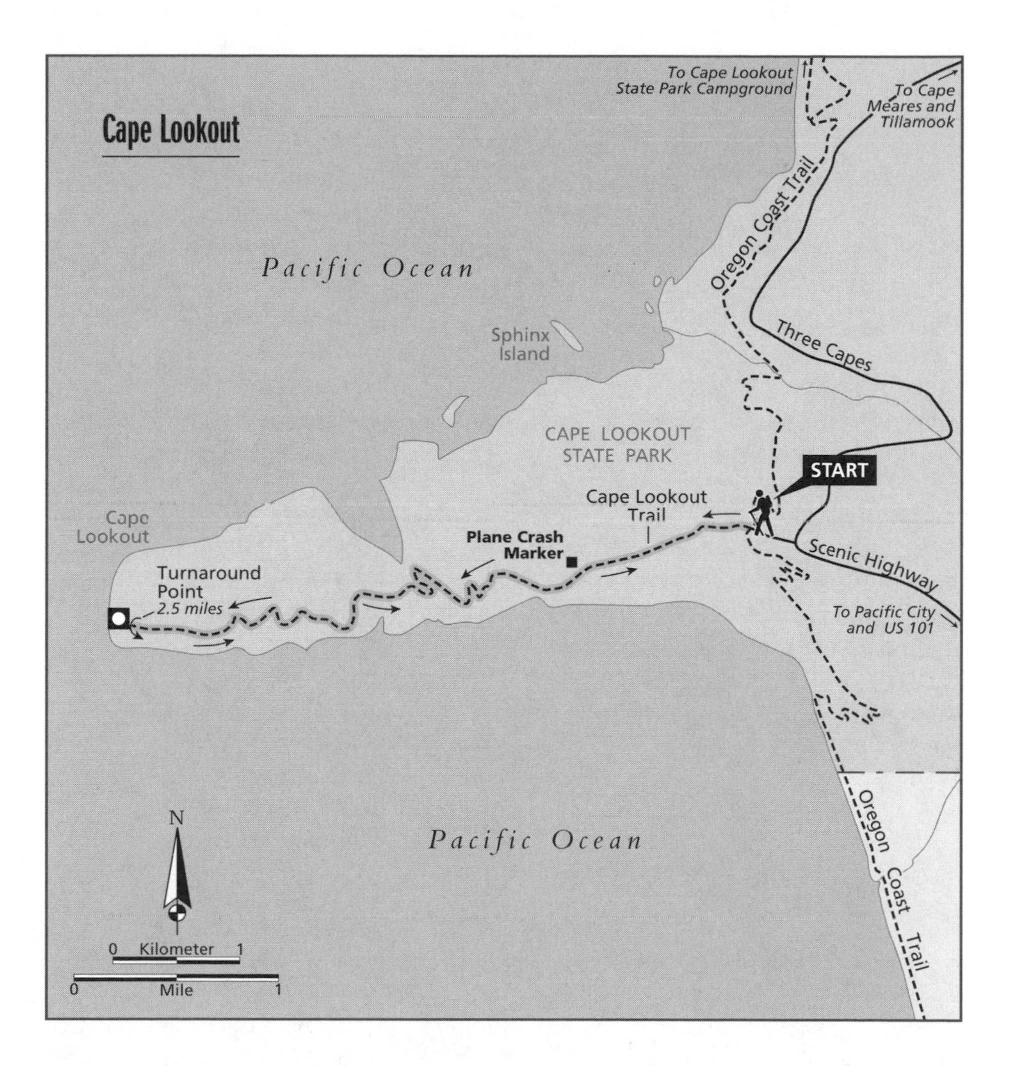

watchers, who come to observe gray whales during their semiannual migrations—epic 10,000-mile round-trip journeys from breeding lagoons in Baja California, Mexico, to the rich Arctic Ocean and back again. The whales migrate south during

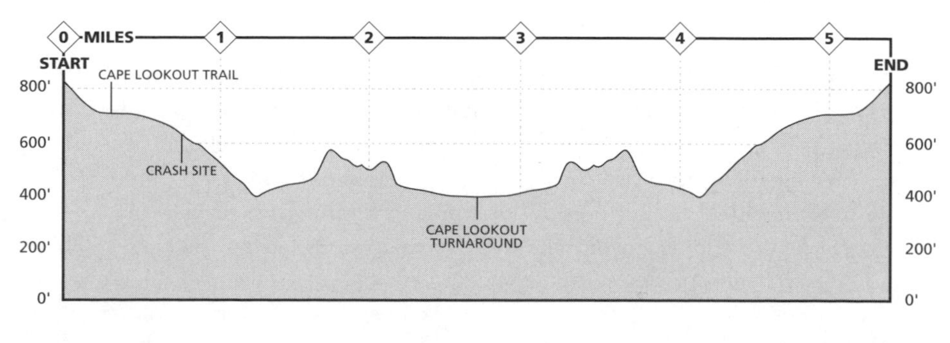

Enjoying the ocean view from the tip of Cape Lookout

the months of December and January and north from March through April. Mature gray whales are 35 to 45 feet long and weigh anywhere from 22 to 35 tons. Females are larger than males and can live for fifty years—some males reach the ripe old age of sixty. The gentle giants feed on shrimplike amphipods by scraping mud from the ocean bottom and then filtering unwanted material through their baleen.

To reach the tip of the cape, take the trail that travels left just past the trailhead sign. The path begins by descending a series of switchbacks through a thick grove of

Sitka spruce. These tough, stout trees are often referred to as "tideland spruce," and they thrive in the moist, cool temperatures that are characteristic of their coastal home. The Sitka spruce ranks with the Douglas fir and western red cedar as one of the largest tree species in the Northwest—only redwoods and sequoias are bigger.

Just over half a mile from the trailhead, the path arrives at a commemorative marker honoring an air force crew that perished in a nearby plane crash in August 1943. From here there are also views of Cape Kiwanda and Cascade Head to the south.

Continuing on, the trail includes several convenient wooden boardwalks over the seemingly endless mire of mud. Up to 90 inches of rain falls annually along this stretch of the coast. The resulting foliage is striking—notice the bright green leaves of salal and salmonberry and the feathery fans of sword and maidenhair fern that cover the forest floor. After a while the trail reveals views of Netarts Bay, Three Arch Rocks, and Cape Meares. The sandy, flat bottom of Netarts Bay makes it a perfect environment for shellfish such as oysters, razor clams, butter clams, and crabs. The last half mile of the path is lined with Indian paintbrush, delicate wild iris, white yarrow, and bushy thimbleberry. The trail ends at a sharp point; if you look off the edge, you'll see the frothy Pacific pounding its huge swells against the rocky cliffs below. A convenient wooden bench has been placed at this classic viewpoint. Stay for a while and admire the view before heading back to the trailhead.

Miles and Directions

0.0 Start at the trailhead in the southwest corner of the Cape Lookout parking area. Take the trail that goes left. (FYI: The trail to the right heads north to Cape Lookout Campground.) Bear right at the first junction, just a few yards up the trail. (FYI: A left here will lead you along the Oregon Coast Trail to Sand Lake.) Descend through a thick grove of statuesque spruce trees.

0.5 Turn right at the trail fork.

0.6 (FYI: A commemorative marker honors the crew of an air force plane that crashed 500 feet west of this site on August 1, 1943.)

1.4 (FYI: Enjoy a good view of the northern coastline and Cape Meares.)

2.5 Arrive at the end of the official trail and your turnaround point. Retrace the same route back to the trailhead.

5.0 Arrive at the trailhead.

Hike Information

Local Information

Tillamook Chamber of Commerce, 3705 Highway 101 North, Tillamook, OR 97141; (503) 842-7525; www.tillamookchamber.org.

Local Events/Attractions

Tillamook Cheese Factory, 4175 Highway 101 North, Tillamook; (503) 815-1300; www.tillamookcheese.com.

Local Outdoor Retailers

Tillamook Sporting Goods, 2205 North Main Street, Tillamook; (503) 842-4334.

11 Munson Creek Falls

Take an easy ramble among spectacular old-growth red cedar and Sitka spruce to a viewpoint of Munson Falls—Oregon's second-highest waterfall.

Start: This route is located 8.9 miles southeast of Tillamook off U.S. Highway 101.
Distance: 0.6 mile out and back.
Approximate hiking time: 30 minutes to 1 hour.
Difficulty: Easy.
Total climb: 100 feet. Elevation profiles are not provided for hikes with less than 250 feet of elevation gain.
Trail surface: Gravel path.
Lay of the land: This route travels along the banks of Munson Creek through a stately corridor of old-growth western red cedar and big leaf maple to a viewpoint of Munson Falls.
Seasons: Year-round.
Other trail users: None.
Canine compatibility: Leashed dogs permitted.
Land status: State natural area.
Nearest town: Tillamook.
Fees and permits: No fees or permits required.
Map: Maptech map: Beaver, Oregon.
Trail contact: Oregon State Parks and Recreation, 1115 Commercial Street NE, Suite 1, Salem, OR 97301; (800) 551-6949; www.oregonstateparks.org/park_245.php.

Finding the trailhead: From the intersection of the Three Capes Scenic Highway and US 101 in Tillamook, travel 7.4 miles south on US 101 to the signed Munson Creek Falls State Natural Site turnoff on the left side of the road. Turn left (east) on Munson Creek Road and go 1.5 miles to a circular parking lot and the trailhead. *DeLorme: Oregon Atlas & Gazetteer:* Page 58, A2.

The Hike

This short hike takes you along rambling Munson Creek, which is draped with bigleaf maple, old-growth western red cedar, and Sitka spruce. This small state natural site harbors what is thought to be one of the country's tallest remaining Sitka spruce trees at 260 feet. As you hike the short path, enjoy the soothing sounds of the creek and look for edible salmonberries in midsummer. After 0.3 mile you'll arrive at a small picnic area and a viewpoint of the beautiful tiered cascade of 319-foot Munson Creek Falls—the highest in the Coast range.

Munson Creek Falls is not far from the friendly coastal city of Tillamook. The original inhabitants of the Tillamook area were three Native American tribes: the Nehalems, Nestuccas, and Tillamooks. These tribes were expert canoe builders and were often referred to as the "Canoe Indians." The first white settler in the Tillamook area was Joseph Champion, who arrived on the scene in 1851. Interestingly, he made his home in a giant spruce tree. During the next three years more settlers arrived in the Tillamook Valley. As a result of this growth, Tillamook County was established December 15, 1853, and Thomas Stillwell laid out the town of Tillamook in 1861. The growing community thrived on fishing, lumber, and raising dairy cattle.

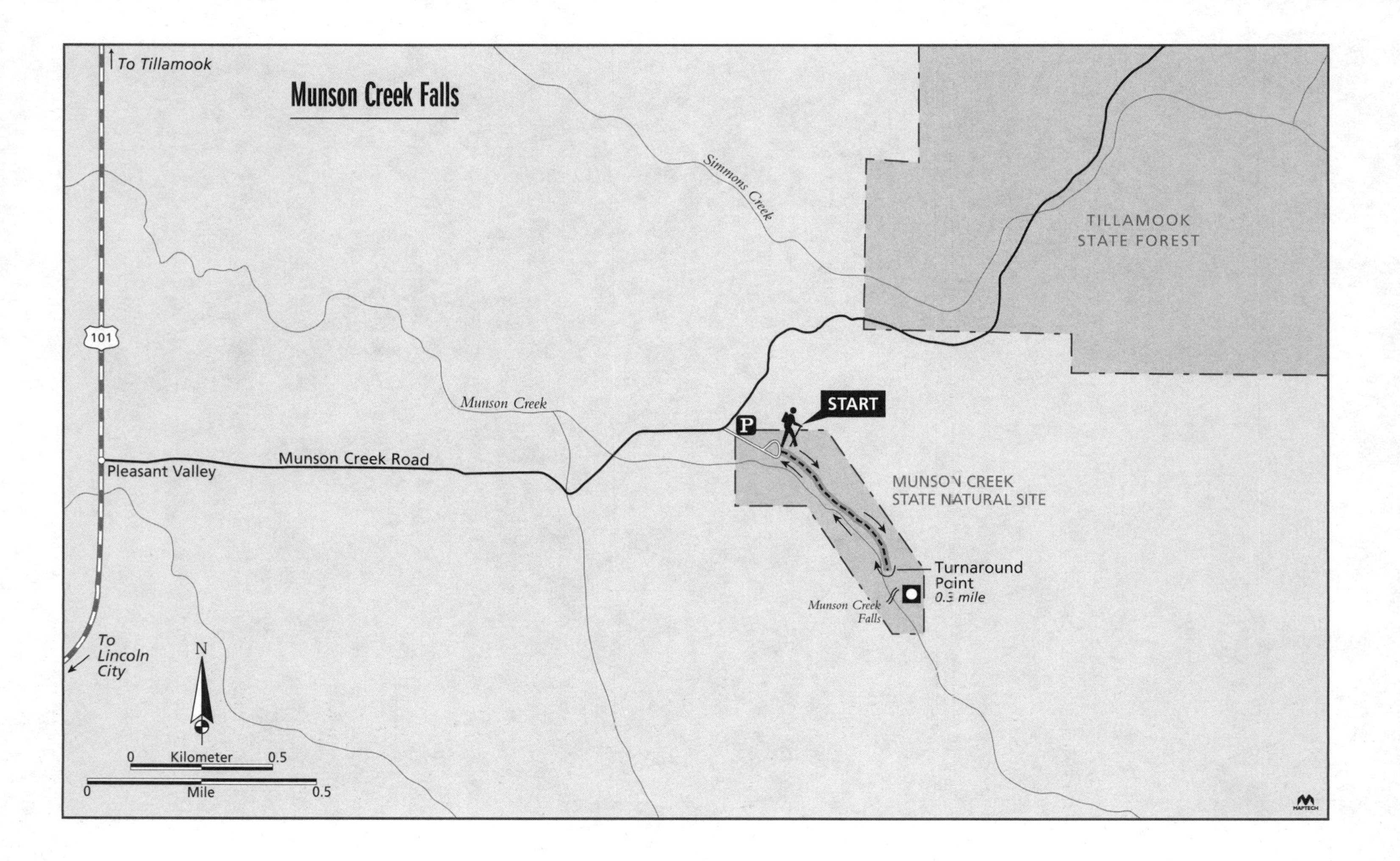
Munson Creek Falls
To Tillamook
101
Pleasant Valley
Munson Creek Road
Munson Creek
Simmons Creek
TILLAMOOK
STATE FOREST
START
P
MUNSON CREEK
STATE NATURAL SITE
Turnaround
Point
0.3 mile
Munson Creek
Falls
To
Lincoln
City
N
0
Kilometer
0.5
0
Mile
0.5
MAPTECH

The wet climate (over 90 inches per year) and rich soils in the Tillamook Valley provide an excellent environment for raising dairy cattle. The Tillamook Valley is home to more than 150 dairy farms that raise more than 26,000 dairy cattle and produce in excess of $85 million worth of cheese and dairy products per year. You can experience the cheese-making process firsthand at the Tillamook Cheese Factory Visitor's Center, located 2 miles north of Tillamook on US 101. At the visitor center you can learn about the cheese-making process by watching workers make cheese, watching educational videos, and touring many different interpretive displays. The cheese factory also has a cafe and gift store, so you can taste different cheeses, ice cream, and other tantalizing items. The visitor center is open daily and admission is free.

Miles and Directions

0.0 Begin walking on the signed gravel path.

0.3 Arrive at a viewpoint of 319-foot Munson Creek Falls. Retrace the same route back to the trailhead.

0.6 Arrive at the trailhead.

Hike Information

Local Information

Tillamook Chamber of Commerce, 3705 Highway 101 North, Tillamook, Oregon 97141; (503) 842-7525; www.tillamookchamber.org.

Local Events/Attractions

Tillamook Cheese Factory, 4175 Highway 101 North, Tillamook; (503) 815-1300; www.tillamookcheese.com.

Local Outdoor Retailers

Tillamook Sporting Goods, 2205 North Main Street, Tillamook; (503) 842-4334.

Hiking with your dog is a fun way to explore the Oregon Coast.
Photo: Ken Skeen

12 Cape Kiwanda State Natural Area

The route takes you on a beach trek and then to the top of Cape Kiwanda in Pacific City. You can explore tide pools, play in the surf, and enjoy spectacular views of Haystack Rock, Nestucca Bay to the south, and Cape Lookout to the north.

Start: The trailhead is located at the public parking area off Kiwanda Drive in Pacific City. Pacific City is about 28 miles south of Tillamook and 18 miles north of Lincoln City off U.S. Highway 101.
Distance: 1 mile out and back (with an 8.4-mile out-and-back option to the tip of Nestucca Spit).
Approximate hiking time: 1 hour (4 to 6 hours for the optional trek to Nestucca Spit).
Difficulty: Moderate.
Total climbing: 100 feet. Elevation profiles are not provided for hikes with less than 250 feet of elevation gain.
Trail surface: Sand.
Lay of the land: This route travels north on Cape Kiwanda Beach and then heads to the summit of the Cape Kiwanda sand dune in Pacific City.
Seasons: Year-round.
Other trail users: None.
Canine compatibility: Leashed dogs permitted.
Land status: State park.
Nearest town: Pacific City.
Fees and permits: No fees or permits required.
Map: Maptech map: Nestucca Bay, Oregon.
Trail contact: Oregon State Parks and Recreation, 1115 Commercial Street NE, Suite 1, Salem, OR 97301; (800) 551-6949; www.oregonstateparks.org/park_180.php.

Finding the trailhead: From the intersection of Oregon Highway 18 and US 101 in Lincoln City, turn north on US 101. Travel 14.6 miles north on US 101 and turn left (west) onto Brooten Road where a sign states CAPE KIWANDA RECREATION AREA/PACIFIC CITY. Go 2.8 miles west on Brooten Road and then turn left onto Pacific Avenue toward "Netarts/Oceanside." Continue 0.3 mile on Pacific Avenue and then turn right onto Kiwanda Drive. Go 1 mile and then turn left into the Cape Kiwanda public parking area adjacent to the Pelican Pub and Brewery Restaurant.

From Tillamook travel 25 miles south on US 101 and turn right (west) onto Brooten Road where a sign states CAPE KIWANDA RECREATION AREA/PACIFIC CITY. Go 2.8 miles west on Brooten Road and then turn left onto Pacific Avenue toward "Netarts/Oceanside." Continue 0.3 mile on Pacific Avenue and then turn right on Kiwanda Drive. Go 1 mile and then turn left into the Cape Kiwanda public parking area adjacent to the Pelican Pub and Brewery Restaurant. *DeLorme: Oregon Atlas & Gazetteer:* Page 58, C1.

The Hike

Pacific City is a coastal hamlet nestled next to the Nestucca River and is home to striking Cape Kiwanda—a golden sandstone headland sculptured by the relentless ocean swells of the Pacific. This small coastal town is well-known for its fleet of dory boats. Dory boats are flat-bottomed fishing boats, which can be launched off the flat sandy beach at the base of Cape Kiwanda. A local fleet still launches these boats into

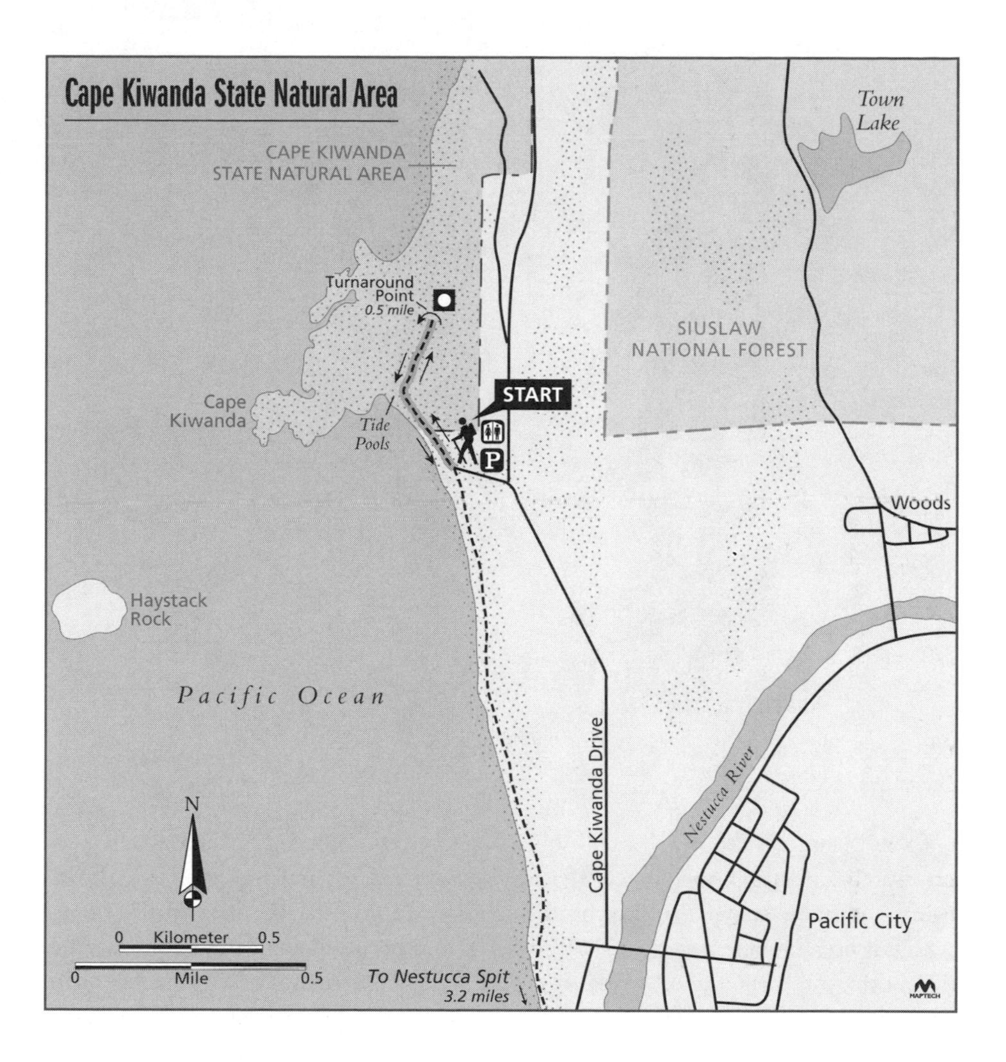

the calm morning surf to fish for halibut, lingcod, rock cod, and other commercial fish species that are plentiful around offshore Haystack Rock.

Local artifacts indicate that Pacific City (originally known as Ocean Park) began as a Native American village at the mouth of the Nestucca River. In the late 1800s settlers moved into the area and developed the land for farming and built a sawmill. Settlers also fished the rich Pacific waters. When a toll road was built from the Willamette Valley in 1880, visitors began traveling to this inviting coastal area. As the summer crowds began to swell so did commerce. By 1895 the area hosted a campground, general store, and hotel. Visitors gained access to the beach via ferry, which was eventually replaced by much-needed bridges. In 1909 a post office was built and the name of the town officially became Pacific City. Not long afterward a school was erected, and the area became a well-known resort destination.

Surfers check out the waves at Cape Kiwanda in Pacific City.

You'll start this fun beach trek by heading north on Kiwanda Beach, where you can watch surfers and boogie boarders playing in the waves and anglers in dory boats fishing offshore. After 0.3 mile stop to explore tide pools at the base of the dune, which is home to anemones, sea stars, mussels, and hermit crabs. After exploring the tide pools, you'll get a good workout on the steep and strenuous 0.2-mile ascent to the top of Cape Kiwanda. From the top you'll have spectacular views of Haystack Rock, Nestucca Bay to the south, and Cape Lookout to the north. For a longer beach adventure, you can head south from the parking area and hike 4.2 miles one way to the end of Nestucca Spit. If you decide on this longer option, be sure to plan your hike at low tide.

Miles and Directions

0.0 From the parking area, turn right (north) and walk on the beach to the base of Cape Kiwanda sand dune. **Option:** You can also turn left and hike 4.2 miles one way to the tip of Nestucca Spit.

0.3 Begin your 0.2-mile ascent of the Cape Kiwanda sand dune. (FYI: Check out tide pools at the base of Cape Kiwanda.)

0.5 Arrive at the top of Cape Kiwanda. Retrace the same route back to the trailhead.

1.0 Arrive back at your starting point.

Hike Information

Local Information

Pacific City/Woods Chamber of Commerce, P.O. Box 331, Pacific City, OR 97135; (888) 549-2632; www.pacificcity.net.

Local Events/Attractions

Reach the Beach, held in mid-May, American Lung Association of Oregon, 7420 SW Bridgeport Road, Suite 200, Tigard, OR 97224; (503) 924-4094; www.reachthebeach.org.

Restaurant

Pelican Pub & Brewery, 33180 Cape Kiwanda Drive, Pacific City; (503) 965-7007; www.pelicanbrewery.com.

13 Pheasant Creek Falls and Niagara Falls

This easy forest trek leads you into a canyon to a viewpoint of Pheasant Creek Falls and Niagara Falls. Other pleasant trailside distractions include the opportunities to view black-tail deer and elk, taste salmonberries and thimbleberries, and wade in bouldery Pheasant Creek.

Start: The trailhead is located about 31 miles southeast of Tillamook and 44 miles northeast of Lincoln City in the Siuslaw National Forest.
Distance: 2 miles out and back.
Approximate hiking time: 1 hour.
Difficulty: Easy.
Total climbing: 380 feet.
Trail surface: Dirt path.
Lay of the land: This isolated route descends into a scenic forested canyon that houses Pheasant Creek Falls and Niagara Falls in the Siuslaw National Forest.
Seasons: Year-round. The trail can be muddy during the winter months.
Other trail users: None.
Canine compatibility: Dogs permitted.
Land status: National forest.
Nearest town: Tillamook.
Fees and permits: No fees or permits required.
Map: Maptech map: Beaver, Oregon.
Trail contact: Siuslaw National Forest, Hebo Ranger District, 31525 Highway 22, Hebo, OR 97122; (503) 392-3961; www.fs.fed.us/r6/siuslaw.

Finding the trailhead: From the intersection of the Three Capes Scenic Highway and U.S. Highway 101 in Tillamook, drive 15 miles south on US 101 (or 28 miles north of Lincoln City) to the small town of Beaver. Just past milepost 80 turn left (east) toward the Nestucca Recreation Area and Blaine. Continue 6.7 miles to Blaine. In Blaine continue as the road veers right where a sign indicates TO BIBLE CREEK ROAD. Go 5.1 miles and turn right toward Niagara Falls (this turn is easy to miss!). Travel 4.4 miles (the paved road turns to gravel after 0.3 mile) to an unsigned road junction. Turn right and continue 0.7 mile to a large gravel parking area. *DeLorme: Oregon Atlas & Gazetteer:* Page 58, A2.

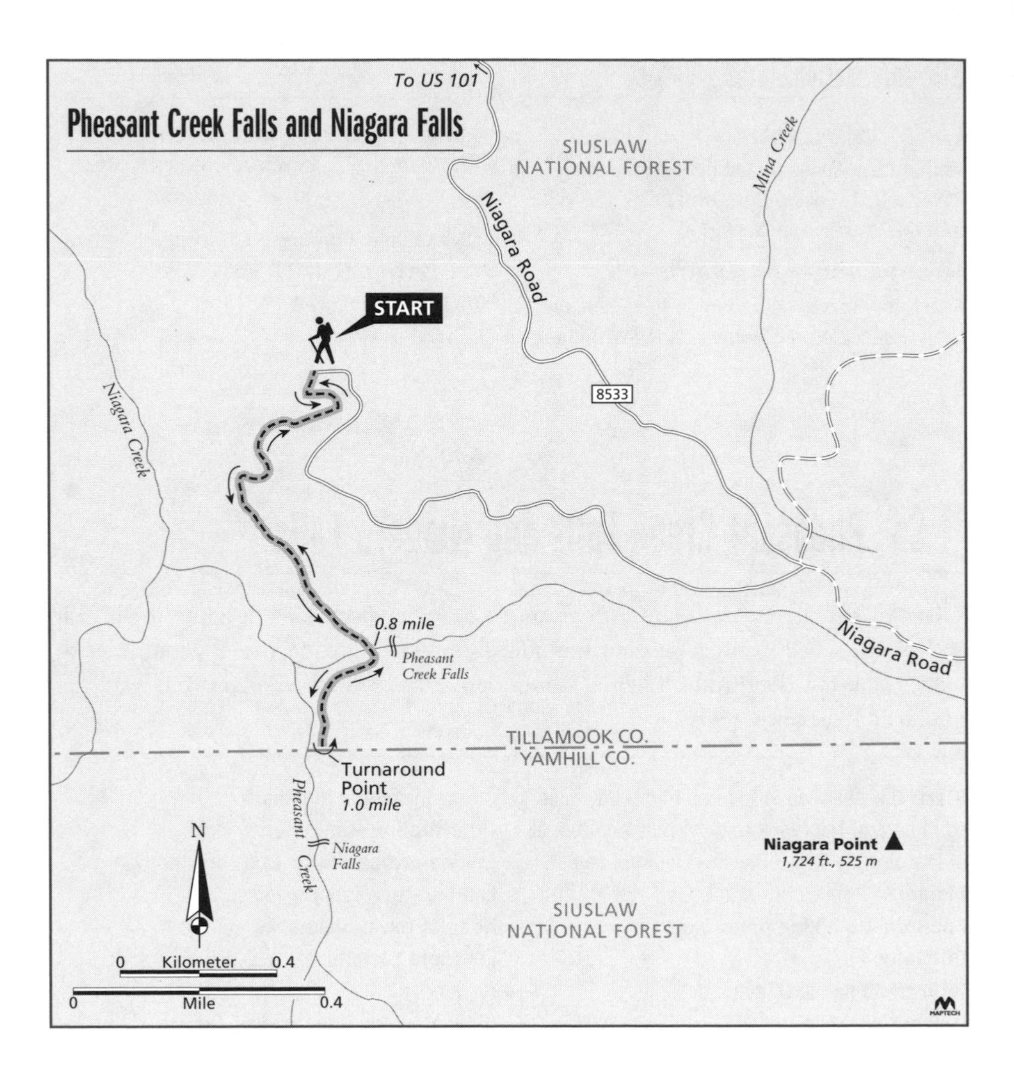

The Hike

If you love waterfalls you'll enjoy this easy stroll to a viewpoint of Pheasant Creek Falls and Niagara Falls in the Siuslaw National Forest. You'll begin by walking on a well-graded forest path that descends through a second-growth forest of Douglas fir and red alder carpeted with vine maple, sword fern, and the delicate triangular blooms of trillium. Watch for elk or black-tail deer darting across the path or the loud calls of Steller's jays. Squirrels can also be seen scurrying from branch to branch. Wood benches are present at different intervals along the route, allowing you to sit and enjoy the sights and sounds of the forest.

After 0.8 mile you'll cross a bridge and arrive at a viewpoint of the splashing cascade of 100-foot Pheasant Creek Falls. From this spot you can also see the feathery

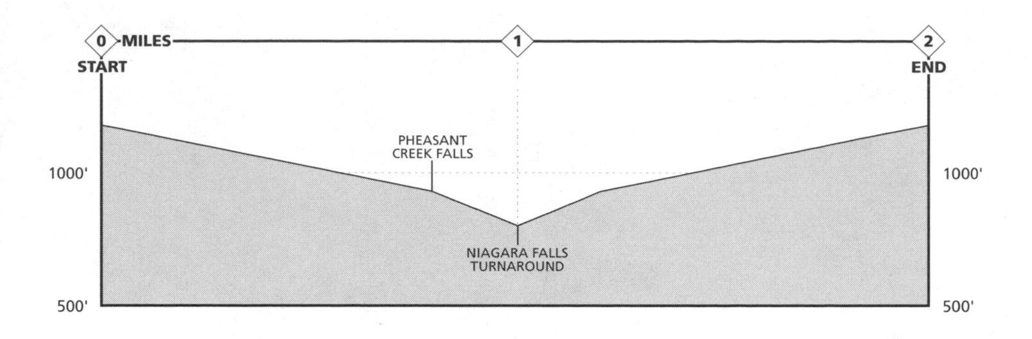

cascade of 130-foot Niagara Falls as it spills over a basalt ledge into a deep rock bowl. After another 0.2 mile you'll arrive at a picnic table and the trail's end next to picturesque Pheasant Creek. Look for edible yellow-colored salmonberries and red thimbleberry (a member of the raspberry family) that line the trail. Not only is the fruit of this plant edible but also the leaves and flowers are high in vitamins and minerals and can be dried to make a wonderful-tasting tea. It is important to note that this tea should be made with only completely fresh or dried leaves. During the wilting stage the leaves develop mildly toxic properties and should not be used. Another fun distraction on this route is the opportunity to wade in the cool, bouldery creek.

Miles and Directions

0.0 Start hiking on trail 1379 where a sign indicates ONE MILE TO NIAGARA FALLS TRAIL.

0.8 (FYI: Enjoy views of Pheasant Creek Falls on the left.)

1.0 Pass a picnic table on your left. Walk past the picnic table to a viewpoint of Niagara Falls at the trail's end next to the creek. After admiring the falls retrace the same route back to the trailhead.

2.0 Arrive at the trailhead.

Hike Information

Local Information

Tillamook Chamber of Commerce, 3705 Highway 101 North, Tillamook, OR 97141; (503) 842-7525; www.tillamookchamber.org.

Local Events/Attractions

Tillamook Cheese Factory, 4175 Highway 101 North, Tillamook; (503) 815-1300; www.tillamookcheese.com.

Local Outdoor Retailers

Tillamook Sporting Goods, 2205 North Main Street, Tillamook; (503) 842-4334.

14 Kiwanda Beach to Porter Point

This beautiful beach trek heads north to the mouth of the Nestucca River. Beach combing and wildlife watching are favorite activities on this route.

Start: The trailhead is located about 3 miles north of the small community of Neskowin.
Distance: 1.8 miles out and back.
Approximate hiking time: 1 hour.
Difficulty: Easy due to flat beach walking and no elevation gain.
Total climbing: None. Elevation profiles are not provided for hikes with less than 250 feet of elevation gain.
Trail surface: Sandy beach.
Lay of the land: This hike travels north on a flat sandy beach to the mouth of the Nestucca River.
Seasons: Year-round.
Other trail users: None.
Canine compatibility: Leashed dogs permitted.
Land status: State park.
Nearest town: Neskowin.
Map: Maptech map: Nestucca Bay, Oregon.
Fees and permits: No fees or permits required.
Trail contact: Oregon State Parks and Recreation, 1115 Commercial Street NE, Suite 1, Salem, OR 97301; (800) 551-6949; www.oregonstateparks.org.

Finding the trailhead: From the junction of the Three Capes Scenic Highway and U.S. Highway 101 in Tillamook, travel south for 28.6 miles (or 14 miles north of Lincoln City) to the junction with Winema Road. Turn right (west) onto Winema Road and continue 0.6 mile to the road's end. *DeLorme: Oregon Atlas & Gazetteer:* Page 58, C1.

The Hike

This peaceful beach hike travels north on a long sandy beach to the mouth of the Nestucca River. Look for sand dollars and other seashells as you hike north. Sand dollars are close cousins to sea stars and sea urchins. They have a pancakelike body, thousands of tube feet, velvety, densely packed spines, and move through the sand picking up small edible particles. When alive the animal can be colored gray, red, or purple.

Watch for brown pelicans flying above the waves and loud calls of glaucous-winged gulls circling high above. You also may see western sandpipers running back and forth along the tide line, feeding on insects and small crustaceans. You can identify western sandpipers by their long black bill, reddish colored head and shoulders, light colored breast, and black legs.

After 0.4 mile you'll walk through a narrow opening between some large sandstone rocks that are covered with thousands of tiny barnacles. These tiny animals

◀ *Niagara Falls. Photo: Ken Skeen*

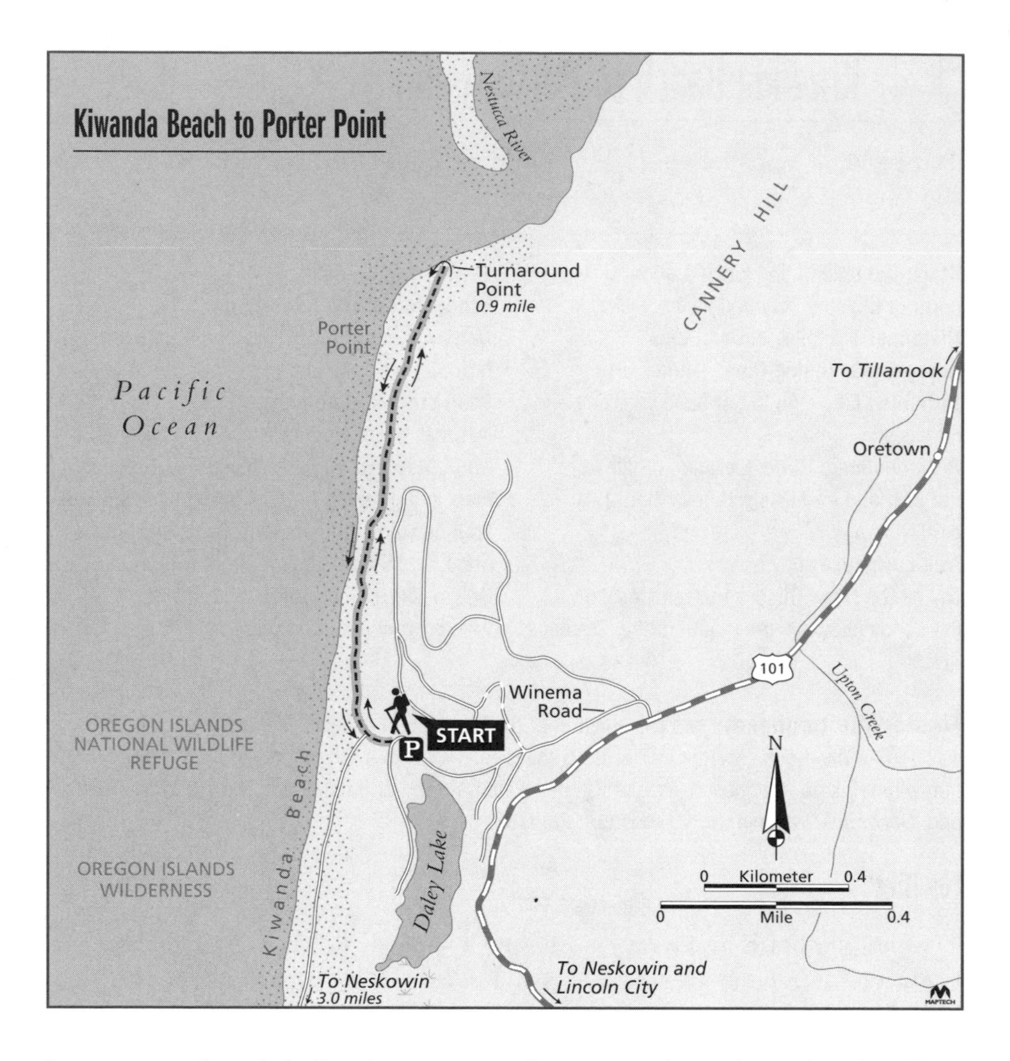

have a cone-shaped shell and are cemented permanently to the rocks. They filter plankton out of the water with a featherlike appendage.

As you continue the beach becomes wilder and more mystical with its frequent blanket of fog, salty ocean wind, crashing waves, and scattered piles of driftwood. After 0.9 mile you'll arrive at your turnaround point at the edge of the Nestucca River and Porter Point. Watch for sea lions swimming in the mouth of the river and resting on the sandy shore. From here you'll retrace the same path back to your starting point.

If you are interested in a longer hike, you can hike south from the trailhead along the beach for 3.3 miles to explore Proposal Rock, located in the small beach community of Neskowin. Neskowin Creek skirts the rock and offers plenty of fun wading opportunities.

Enjoying the solitude on Kiwanda Beach

Miles and Directions

0.0 Begin by walking on a short path that leads from the parking area to the beach. Once you reach the beach, turn right and walk north. **Option:** You can turn left (south) and walk 3.3 miles to Neskowin.

0.4 Walk through a narrow passage between a group of large sandstone rocks.

0.9 Arrive at the mouth of the Nestucca River and your turnaround point. Retrace the same route back to your starting point. (FYI: Look for sea lions and harbor seals swimming in the river mouth and resting on the river's sandy shoreline.)

1.8 Arrive at the trailhead.

Hike Information

Local Information

Lincoln City Visitor and Convention Bureau, 801 SW Highway 101, Suite 1, Lincoln City, OR 97367; (800) 452-2151; www.oregoncoast.org.

Local Events/Attractions

North Lincoln County Museum, 4907 SW Highway 101, Lincoln City; (541) 996-6614.

Local Outdoor Retailers

Eddie Bauer, 1552 SE East Devils Lake Road, Lincoln City; (541) 994-2220.

15 Harts Cove

This forest trail travels through a western hemlock and old-growth Sitka spruce forest to a dramatic cliff-top viewpoint overlooking Harts Cove. From this high perch you can see sea lions offshore and watch magnificent waves crashing into offshore rocks.

Start: The trailhead is located about 8.5 miles northwest of Lincoln City off U.S. Highway 101.
Distance: 5.4 miles out and back.
Approximate hiking time: 2.5 to 3.5 hours.
Difficulty: Moderate due to elevation gain.
Total climbing: 1,390 feet.
Trail surface: Well-maintained forest path with wooden bridges.
Lay of the land: This route descends a series of switchbacks through a young western hemlock forest and then traverses through an old-growth stand of Sitka spruce to an open, grassy headland above Harts Cove.
Seasons: Open July 16 through December 31. The trail can be muddy during the winter months.
Other trail users: None.
Canine compatibility: Leashed dogs permitted.
Land status: National forest.
Nearest town: Lincoln City.
Fees and permits: No fees or permits required.
Map: Maptech map: Neskowin, Oregon.
Trail contact: Siuslaw National Forest, Hebo Ranger District, P.O. Box 235, Hebo, OR 97122; (503) 392-3161; www.oregoncoast.com/hebord.

Finding the trailhead: From the junction of Oregon Highway 18 and US 101 in Lincoln City, head north on US 101 for 4.1 miles to the junction with gravel Forest Road 1861. Go left and continue 4.3 miles (after 3.3 miles you'll pass the upper trailhead to the Nature Conservancy preserve on the left) to the road's end and trailhead. *DeLorme: Oregon Atlas & Gazetteer:* Page 58, D1.

The Hike

This forest trail begins by descending on a series of switchbacks through a monochrome stand of 40-year-old western hemlock. After 0.7 mile you'll cross a wood footbridge over picturesque Cliff Creek. The soothing sounds of this bubbling creek mixed in with the far-off sound of sea lions and ocean wind blowing through the trees gives you a sense of anticipation as you continue your descent toward Harts Cove. After this creek crossing the forest opens up and comes alive with giant 250-year-old Sitka spruce trees at center stage. These rare gentle giants thrive in coastal areas and feature stout trunks with dozens of limbs that shoot outward from the base of the tree. This tree can grow more than 200 feet tall and can have a 12-foot-thick trunk. It is one of the Northwest's largest trees, along with the western red cedar and the Douglas fir. You can easily identify these trees from other coastal species by their reddish brown to purplish-colored bark that is patterned in large, loose scales. The needles are also flat and prickly and do not roll easily between your fingers. Mixed in with the Sitka giants are large western hemlock trees. These trees are very prolific

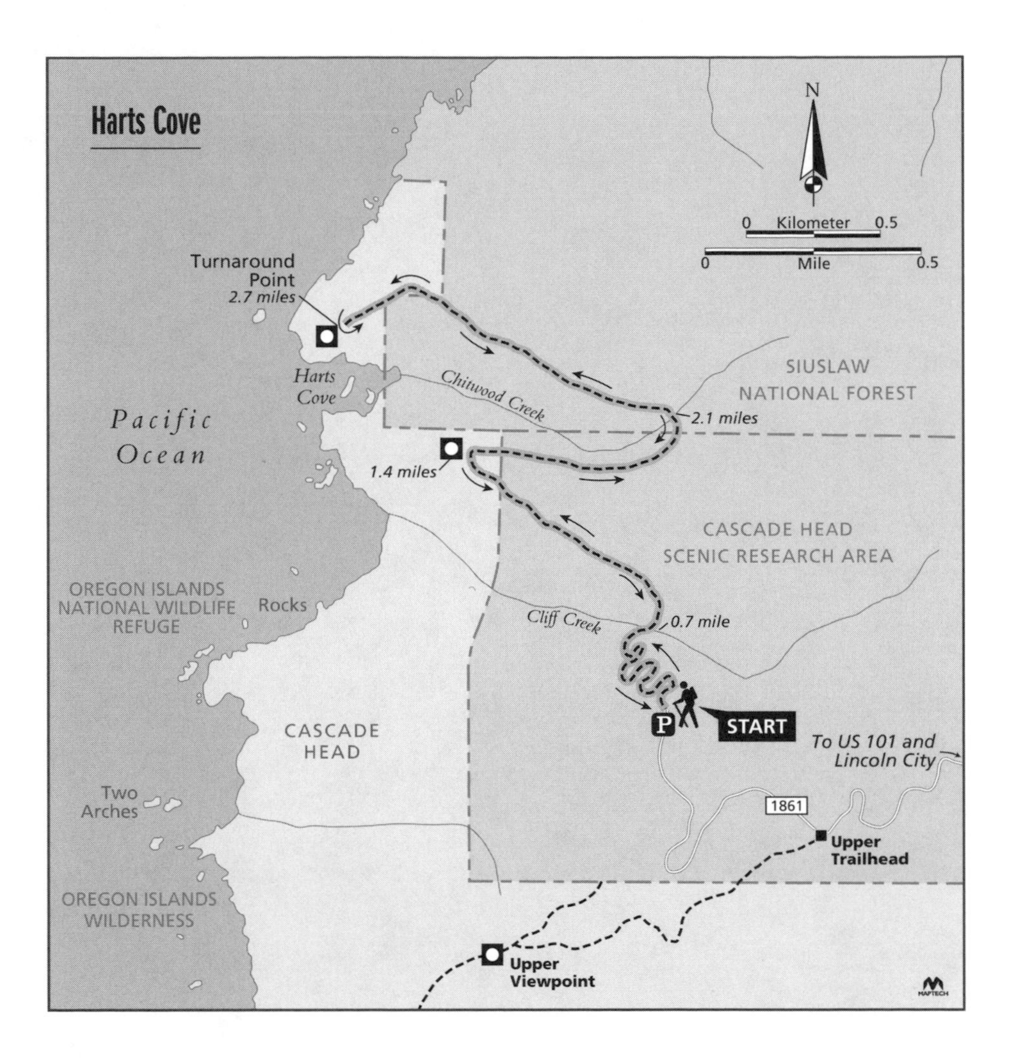

because the seedlings have the ability to grow in dense shady areas. You can recognize this tree by its short, blunt needles that are unequal in length. The branches of the tree also have a delicate, fanlike appearance. The cones are about an inch long and grow in large clusters. The tops of smaller western hemlock trees also tend to droop.

As you continue your journey, you'll pass a rest bench at 1.4 miles with a viewpoint of the distant headland. As you continue to descend, the sounds of crashing waves and the raucous calls of sea lions beckon you through a maze of green filled with wood sorrel, sword fern, lady fern, and candy flower. You'll also notice mushrooms of all shapes and sizes clinging to the bases of trees and old logs. After 2.1 miles you'll cross charming Chitwood Creek and in another 0.4 mile you'll exit out of the trees and enter an open grassy meadow atop a dramatic bluff. Continue as the trail descends through a beautiful meadow made up of red fescue, wild rye, coastal

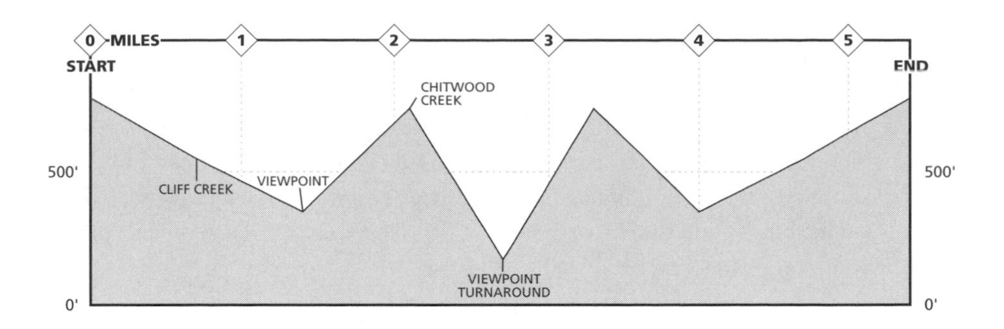

paintbrush, wild iris, yarrow, and goldenrod. You'll arrive at a dramatic viewpoint overlooking Harts Cove to the south (your turnaround point). From here look for pods of sea lions riding the waves offshore and watch huge breakers crash into rocky cliffs.

Miles and Directions

0.0 Begin walking on the dirt path as it heads down a set of steep switchbacks.

0.7 Cross Cliff Creek on a wood footbridge.

1.4 Pass a rest bench and viewpoint on the left. Continue your descent on the main trail.

2.1 Cross Chitwood Creek on a wood footbridge.

2.5 Exit out of the trees and enter an open grassy meadow atop a dramatic bluff above Harts Cove.

2.7 Arrive at a spectacular viewpoint above Harts Cove (your turnaround point). Retrace the same route back to the trailhead. (Note: Don't be tempted to head down to the exposed rocks above the shoreline. Nothing grows here because sneaker waves routinely break in this region.)

5.4 Arrive at the trailhead.

Hike Information

Local Information

Lincoln City Visitor and Convention Bureau, 801 SW Highway 101, Suite 1, Lincoln City, OR 97367; (800) 452-2151; www.oregoncoast.org.

Local Events/Attractions

North Lincoln County Museum, 4907 SW Highway 101, Lincoln City; (541) 996-6614.

Local Outdoor Retailers

Eddie Bauer, 1552 SE East Devils Lake Road, Lincoln City; (541) 994-2220.

Wild, rocky coastline at Harts Cove

16 Cascade Head

This route takes you on a trek through the Cascade Head National Scenic Research Area, which harbors one of the six remaining populations of the threatened Oregon silverspot butterfly and rare wildflowers. You'll take a journey through coastal forest where you may see Roosevelt elk or black-tail deer and then arrive on the top of the open, windy summit of Cascade Head.

Start: The trailhead is located 4 miles north of Lincoln City off U.S. Highway 101.
Distance: 4.2 miles out and back (with longer options).
Approximate hiking time: 2.5 to 3.5 hours.
Difficulty: Difficult due to the large amount of elevation gain.
Total climbing: 1,150 feet.
Trail surface: Dirt path, wood-chip path, wood ramps, wooden bridges, and stairs.
Lay of the land: This hike climbs steeply through a Sitka spruce and cedar forest to a dramatic viewpoint in a beautiful meadow in the Cascade Head Scenic Research Area.
Seasons: Open from July 16 through December 31. The trail can be muddy during the winter months.
Other trail users: None.
Canine compatibility: Dogs are not permitted.
Land status: Scenic Research Area.
Nearest town: Lincoln City.
Fees and permits: No fees or permits required.
Map: Maptech map: Neskowin, Oregon.
Trail contact: Cascade Head Scenic Research Area, The Nature Conservancy of Oregon, 821 SE Fourteenth Avenue, Portland, OR 97215; (503) 230-1221; www.nature.org.

Finding the trailhead: From the junction of Oregon Highway 18 and US 101, travel north on US 101 for 1.3 miles to the junction with Three Rocks Road. Turn left and continue 2.5 miles to a parking area on the left side of the road at Knight County Park. *DeLorme: Oregon Atlas & Gazetteer:* Page 58, D1.

The Hike

Established in 1974, the Cascade Head National Scenic Research Area covers 270 acres and protects rare native grasses, wildflowers, and the federally threatened Oregon silverspot butterfly. In the early 1960s this unique headland was under the threat of development. Volunteers purchased the property and gave it to the Nature Conservancy to oversee and protect.

You'll begin your exploration by following a wood-chip trail for 0.4 mile as it travels next to the highway through private land and national forest. Over the next 0.7 mile, the trail climbs steeply through a stand of 50- to 150-year-old western hemlock and Sitka spruce trees, with an understory of lady fern, sword fern, candy flower, wood sorrel, and edible red huckleberries and salmonberries. Keep a close eye out for the swift movements of Roosevelt elk and black-tail deer.

After a mile you'll emerge from the forest as the trail continues ascending through an open grassland made up of many native plant species, including red fes-

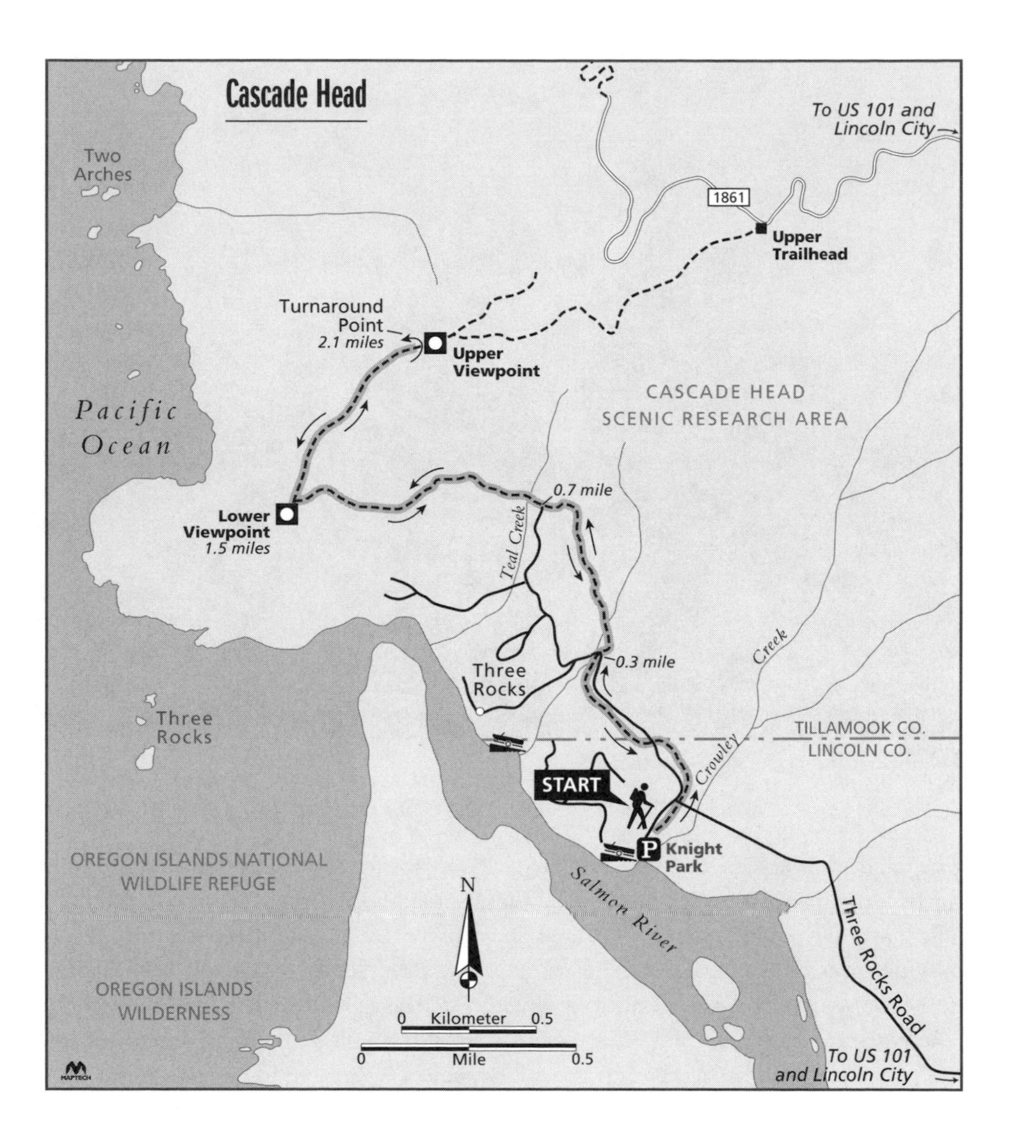

cue, wild rye, goldenrod, coastal paintbrush, wild iris, blue violet, lupine, Indian thistle, coyote bush, and yarrow. The yarrow plant can be identified by its flat-topped flower heads made up of small white flowers and feathery leaves. The dried leaves and flowers of this plant are often used as an ingredient in cold remedies, where it acts as an analgesic and expectorant. You'll soon arrive at the lower viewpoint at 1.5 miles, where you'll have great views of the Salmon River Estuary and Lincoln City to the south.

This open meadow ecosystem is haven to the threatened Oregon silverspot butterfly and is one of six remaining areas where this butterfly is found. Its current range is along the northern California coast, the Washington coast, and the Oregon coast.

Hiking at Cascade Head. Photo: Ken Skeen

The biggest threats to the butterfly are fire suppression, land development, introduction of non-native plant species, and the decline of open-meadow environments. The butterfly prefers coastal meadows surrounded by forest. The open meadows provide protection for the caterpillars, nectar for the adults, and wind protection. The butterflies move into the surrounding forest areas to find shelter from the wind. The best time to see the butterfly is from August through September, when it is in the adult stage. Adults lay eggs on the tall grasses in August and September and the caterpillar emerges in early spring. The caterpillar forms a cocoon in early summer and reaches the adult butterfly stage in midsummer. The butterfly is about 1 inch

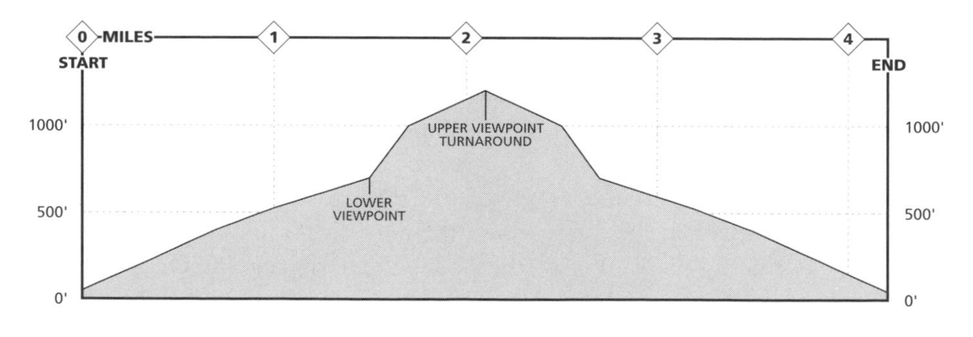

wide and has orange and brown markings on the top of the wings and silver spots under the wings. Bald eagles, northern harriers, and red-tail hawks are often seen flying over this open-meadow ecosystem.

After 2.1 miles you'll arrive at the upper viewpoint (your turnaround point), where you'll have more magnificent views of the mouth of the Salmon River and Siletz Bay looking south and Cape Lookout to the north.

Miles and Directions

0.0 Start hiking on the wood-chip trail that begins next to an interpretive sign. Go about 50 yards and cross Three Rocks Road and continue on the wood-chip trail on the other side.

0.2 Cross a paved road and continue on the wood-chip trail on the other side.

0.3 Turn right and cross a paved road. Arrive at a wood trail sign and continue climbing steeply on a series of wooden steps. Look for yellow trail signs marking the route.

1.5 Arrive at the lower viewpoint.

2.1 Arrive at the upper viewpoint (your turnaround point). Retrace the same route back to your starting point. **Option:** You can continue on the trail for 1 mile to the upper trailhead.

4.2 Arrive at the trailhead.

Hike Information

Local Information

Lincoln City Visitor and Convention Bureau, 801 SW Highway 101, Suite 1, Lincoln City, OR 97367; (800) 452-2151; www.oregoncoast.org.

Local Events/Attractions

North Lincoln County Museum, 4907 SW Highway 101, Lincoln City; (541) 996-6614.

Local Outdoor Retailers

Eddie Bauer, 1552 SE East Devils Lake Road, Lincoln City; (541) 994-2220.

17 Drift Creek Falls

This forest path that descends 340 feet takes you on a fun tour through a thick coastal forest and across a magnificent suspension bridge over Drift Creek. From the bridge you'll have a grand view of the shimmering cascade of Drift Creek Falls.

Start: The trailhead is located about 12 miles southeast of Lincoln City off U.S. Highway 101.
Distance: 3 miles out and back.
Approximate hiking time: 1 to 1.5 hours.
Difficulty: Easy due to well-graded path and minimal elevation gain.
Total climbing: 260 feet.
Trail surface: Well-maintained dirt path, and suspension bridge.
Lay of the land: This tourist trail descends into a forested creek canyon and leads you across an extravagant suspension bridge to a viewpoint of the feathery cascade of Drift Creek Falls in the Siuslaw National Forest.
Seasons: Year-round.
Other trail users: None.
Canine compatibility: Leashed dogs permitted.
Land status: National forest.
Nearest town: Lincoln City.
Fees and permits: $5.00 Northwest Forest Pass. You can purchase a pass on-line at www.fs.fed.us/r6/feedemo, or by call calling (800) 270-7504.
Map: Maptech map: Devils Lake, Oregon.
Trail contact: Siuslaw National Forest, Hebo Ranger District, P.O. Box 235, Hebo, OR 97122; (503) 392-3161; www.oregoncoast.com/hebord.

Finding the trailhead: From US 101 just past milepost 119 in Lincoln City, turn left (east) onto Drift Creek Road. Go 1.6 miles on Drift Creek Road to the junction with South Drift Creek Road and turn right. Go 0.4 mile and turn left onto Drift Creek Camp Road. Continue 0.9 mile to another road junction signed DRIFT CREEK FALLS TRAIL and turn left. Continue about 9.8 miles (following signs to the Drift Creek Falls Trail) to a parking area on the right side of the road. *DeLorme: Oregon Atlas & Gazetteer:* Page 52, A1.

The Hike

You'll enjoy this popular forest trek, which begins by descending at a gentle pace on wide switchbacks through a second-growth Douglas fir forest carpeted with thick clusters of salal, sword fern, and edible salmonberries and bright red huckleberries. You'll also be treated to a few remaining old-growth trees hiding deep in the canyon.

After 1.3 miles you'll arrive at the extravagant expanse of the 240-foot-long Drift Creek Suspension Bridge. Built in 1997 the bridge is anchored to a rock face on one side and bolted to concrete anchors on the other side. Bridge materials were flown in by helicopter and the bridge span was assembled using a skyline cable rigging system that was suspended 100 feet from the canyon floor. The bridge is dedicated to trail builder Scott Paul, who died while working on the rigging for the bridge. You'll have fantastic views of 75-foot-tall Drift Creek Falls as it plunges over

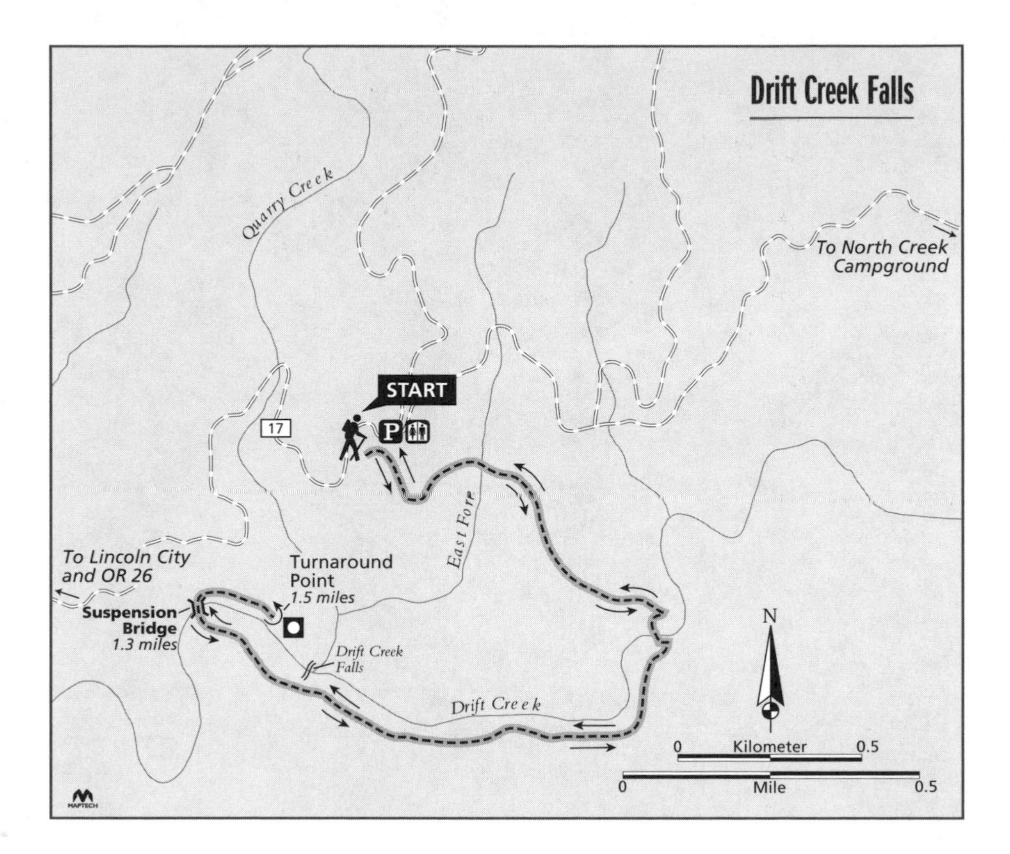

a basalt ledge to the creek below. After crossing the bridge you'll follow the trail another 0.2 mile as it descends to the edge of the creek. Wading in the creek during the hot summer months is a favorite activity. After cooling off in the creek, head back on the same route to your starting point.

Miles and Directions

0.0 Start walking on the signed trail that begins descending at a gentle pace from the parking area.

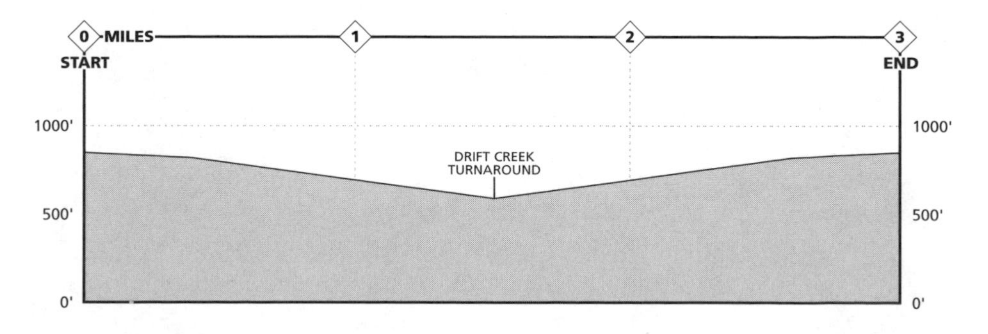

1.3 Cross a dramatic creek canyon on a high suspension bridge.

1.5 Arrive at the trail's end next to Drift Creek. Have fun wading in the creek and admiring the 75-foot cascade of Drift Creek Falls. Retrace the same route back to the trailhead.

3.0 Arrive at the trailhead.

Hike Information

Local Information

Lincoln City Visitor and Convention Bureau, 801 SW Highway 101, Suite 1, Lincoln City, OR 97367; (800) 452-2151; www.oregoncoast.org.

Local Events/Attractions

North Lincoln County Museum, 4907 SW Highway 101, Lincoln City; (541) 996-6614.

Local Outdoor Retailers

Eddie Bauer, 1552 SE East Devils Lake Road, Lincoln City; (541) 994-2220.

BERRY TRIVIA Huckleberries were an important part of the Coastal Indians' diet. They were used as bait to catch fish. They were also dried and mashed into cakes. The berry juice was used as a mouthwash and to stimulate the appetite. The leaves and bark were made into a liquid that was gargled to relieve sore throats.

◄ *The amazing 240-foot long suspension bridge that spans Drift Creek*

18 Devil's Punchbowl State Natural Area

Churning waves, offshore rocks, and an interesting sea cave are some of the many highlights on this fun coast hike. This route begins with a tour of Devil's Punchbowl, a collapsed sea cave, and then you'll take a stroll on Beverly Beach.

Start: Devil's Punchbowl State Natural Area is located about 9 miles north of Newport on the Otter Crest Scenic Loop off U.S. Highway 101.
Distance: 2.8 miles out and back.
Approximate hiking time: 1 hour.
Difficulty: Easy.
Total climbing: 95 feet. Elevation profiles are not provided for hikes with less than 250 feet of elevation gain.
Trail surface: Paved path, stairs, beach, and tide pools.
Lay of the land: This route offers outstanding views of a collapsed sea cave, takes you on a journey along picturesque Beverly Beach, and also gives you the opportunity to explore rocky tide pools.
Seasons: Year-round.
Other trail users: None.
Canine compatibility: Leashed dogs permitted.
Land status: State natural area.
Nearest town: Newport.
Fees and permits: No fees or permits required.
Map: Maptech map: Newport North, Oregon.
Trail contact: Oregon State Parks, 1115 Commercial Street NE, Suite 1, Salem, OR 97301; (800) 551-6949; www.oregonstateparks.org/park_217.php.

Finding the trailhead: From the junction of Oregon Highway 18 and US 101 in Lincoln City, travel south for 21.5 miles (or 8 miles north of Newport) and turn west at a sign for Devil's Punchbowl. Go 0.2 mile to a T-junction and stop sign. Turn left and continue to the junction with First Street. Turn right and go 0.2 mile to the road's end at the Devil's Punchbowl Day Use Area. *DeLorme: Oregon Atlas & Gazetteer:* Page 32, Inset 1, C1.

The Hike

This state natural area features dramatic rock formations and tide pools that can be explored at low tide. Begin by walking on the paved path that starts on the south side of the parking area next to the cliff's edge. When you look over the edge, you'll see waves frothing and churning in a collapsed sea cave that looks like a huge punch bowl. Wind, rain, and the wave action have eroded the soft, sandstone rock that makes up this unique rock formation. From this cliff-side viewpoint, you'll also have nice views of a large offshore sea stack called Gull Rock. Follow the paved path through a scenic picnic area sheltered by a thick grove of shore pine trees. The route continues along the sidewalk until you reach a set of stairs that descend through a small grove of Sitka spruce trees to Beverly Beach. Once you reach the beach, you'll walk 1.2 miles south to the entrance tunnel to Beverly Beach State Park (your turnaround point). This large state park is one of the busiest on the Oregon Coast and

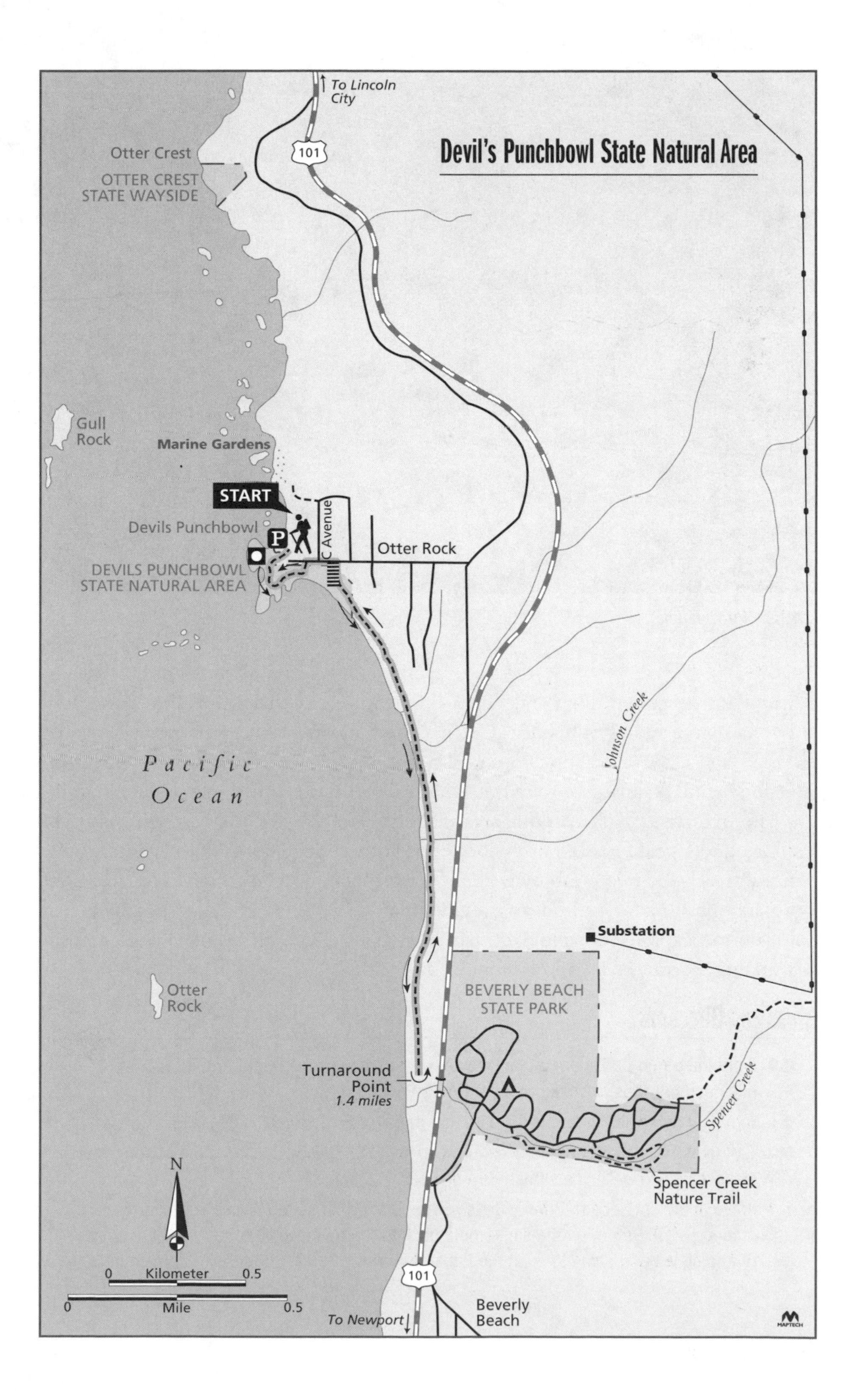

Devil's Punchbowl State Natural Area
To Lincoln City
101
Otter Crest
OTTER CREST STATE WAYSIDE
Gull Rock
Marine Gardens
START
Devils Punchbowl
C Avenue
Otter Rock
DEVILS PUNCHBOWL STATE NATURAL AREA
Johnson Creek
Pacific Ocean
Substation
BEVERLY BEACH STATE PARK
Otter Rock
Turnaround Point
1.4 miles
Spencer Creek
Spencer Creek Nature Trail
N
0 Kilometer 0.5
0 Mile 0.5
101
To Newport
Beverly Beach
MAPTECH

Devil's Punchbowl

features a large campground and a 0.75-mile nature trail that winds through coastal forest along the shores of Spencer Creek. (The trail can be accessed between campsites C3 and C5.) In addition to regular camping sites, this park has yurts you can rent for the night, a large covered meeting hall, a visitor center, and a playground.

After returning to the parking area at Devil's Punchbowl, you have the option of exploring rocky tide pools that are located a short distance north of the parking area. You can reach the tide pools by walking a few blocks up C Avenue and turning left onto an asphalt path that leads to the tide pools and a small, secluded beach. At low tide you can explore this abundant marine garden filled with bright orange starfish, sea urchins, hermit crabs, and sculpin fish.

Miles and Directions

0.0 From the paved parking area, walk south on the fenced paved path that hugs the cliff edge and provides dramatic views of Devil's Punchbowl.

0.1 Turn right and walk on the paved path that parallels First Street.

0.2 Turn right and walk down a long set of wood stairs to Beverly Beach. At the bottom of the stairs, continue walking south on Beverly Beach.

1.4 Arrive at the entrance to Beverly Beach State Park Campground on the left (your turnaround point). Return on the same route back to the trailhead. (FYI: You have the option of turning left and going through the tunnel to Beverly Beach State Park Campground, where you can access the 0.75-mile Spencer Creek Nature Trail, located between campsites C3 and C5.)

2.8 Arrive at the trailhead.

Hike Information

Local Information

Newport Chamber of Commerce, 555 SW Coast Highway, Newport, OR 97365; (800) 262-7844; www.newportchamber.org.

Local Events/Attractions

Oregon Coast Aquarium, 2820 SE Ferry Slip Road, Newport; (541) 867-3474; www.aquarium.org.

Local Outdoor Retailers

Fred Meyer, 150 NE 20th Street, Newport; (541) 265-4581.

North Coast Honorable Mentions

A Banks–Vernonia State Park Trail

You'll enjoy the smooth graded surface on this 20-mile multiuse trail that travels through a serene forest canopy. From the Buxton trailhead you have the option of hiking 14 miles north or 6 miles south as the trail follows the old rail line. This easy track gives you the freedom to enjoy a short leisurely hike or a longer adventure. You'll share the trail with mountain bikers and equestrians. To get there from I–405 in Portland, head west on U.S. Highway 26 toward "Beaverton–Ocean Beaches." After approximately 28 miles turn right onto Fisher Road. Go 0.7 mile, passing through the small town of Buxton. Turn right onto Bacona Road and proceed 0.7 mile to the entrance road to the Buxton trailhead, marked by a state park sign. Turn right and go another 0.1 mile to a large parking area and trailhead. For more information contact Oregon State Parks and Recreation, 1115 Commercial Street NE, Suite 1, Salem, OR 97301; (800) 551–6949; www.oregonstateparks.org/park_145.php. *DeLorme: Oregon Atlas & Gazetteer:* Page 65, C7.

B Gales Creek

This 10.8-mile out-and-back route takes you on a tour along the banks of Gales Creek in the Tillamook State Forest. Follow the trail as it ambles along the creek through a thick canopy of Douglas fir and big-leaf maple trees to your turnaround point at Bell Camp Road. To get there from I–405 and U.S. Highway 26 in Portland, head 20.5 miles west on US 26 to the junction with Oregon Highway 6. Head left (west) on OR 6 toward Banks and Tillamook to just before milepost 37, where you'll turn right toward Gales Creek Campground. Continue 0.7 mile to a large gravel parking lot on the left.

For more information contact Tillamook State Forest, Forest Grove; (503) 357–2191; www.odf.state.or.us/tsf/tsfhome.htm. Before you hike this trail, it is highly recommended that you obtain a Tillamook State Forest/Wilson River Highway Area map, available from the Tillamook State Forest, 801 Gales Creek Road, Forest Grove, OR 97116; (503) 357–2191; www.odf.state.or.us/tsf/tsfhome.htm. *DeLorme: Oregon Atlas & Gazetteer:* Page 65, C6.

C Hagg Lake

The 14.1-mile Hagg Lake Trail passes through open meadows and oak woodlands next to the shores of 1,113-acre Hagg Lake. Rewards along the way include prime blackberry picking, awesome swimming holes, and opportunities to view a variety of wildlife, including deer, coyotes, bobcats, osprey, hawks, bald eagles, songbirds, and a variety of waterfowl. To get there from Portland, head 21 miles west on U.S. Highway 26 to the junction with Oregon Highway 6. Turn left onto OR 6 (toward Banks, Forest Grove, and Tillamook) and go 2.5 miles to the intersection with Oregon Highway 47. Turn south and proceed 12.5 miles to the junction with Scoggins Valley Road. Turn right (west) onto Scoggins Valley Road and head 3.1 miles to the Henry Hagg Lake/Scoggins Valley Park entrance (there is an entrance fee of $4.00 during the summer months). Go 0.3 mile past the entrance booth to the junction with West Shore Drive. Turn left onto West Shore Drive and travel 3.9 miles to the Sain Creek Picnic Area on the right. From the picnic area you can hike in either direction on the scenic lake trail. For more information contact Washington County Parks, Facilities Management Division, Support Services Department, 111 SE Washington Street, Hillsboro, OR 97123; (503) 846–3692; www.co.washington.or.us/deptmts/sup_serv/fac_mgt/parks/hagglake.htm. *DeLorme: Oregon Atlas & Gazetteer:* Page 59, A7 and Page 65, D7.

D King Mountain

The 4.8-mile King Mountain Trail is a difficult, strenuous trek through a red alder and spruce forest to a viewpoint atop King Mountain, with spectacular 360-degree views of the Coast Range and Cascade Mountains. This hike will turn your thighs to noodles, but the view from the top is worth the effort. To get there from Portland, drive 30 miles west on U.S. Highway 26 to its junction with Oregon Highway 6. Exit and drive 27 miles west to a dirt pullout and the trailhead on the right (north) side of the road. For more information contact Tillamook State Forest, 801 Gales Creek Road, Forest Grove, OR 97116; (503) 357–2191; www.odf.state.or.us/tsf/tsfhome.htm. *DeLorme: Oregon Atlas & Gazetteer:* Page 64, C4.

E Arcadia Beach State Recreation Site

This nineteen-acre state recreation site features a long flat sandy stretch of beach that is sandwiched between Humbug Point to the north and Hug Point to the south. Picnicking, fishing, and beachcombing are popular activities here. This recreation site is located 3 miles south of Cannon Beach on U.S. Highway 101. For more information contact the Oregon State Parks and Recreation, 1115 Commercial Street NE, Suite 1, Salem, OR 97301; (800) 551–6949; www.oregonstateparks.org. *DeLorme: Oregon Atlas & Gazetteer:* Page 64, A1.

F Nehalem Bay State Park

This 890-acre state park is located on a sand spit between Nehalem Bay and the Pacific Ocean. It features a large campground if you want to stay for a few days. On one side of the campground is scenic Nehalem Bay, where kayaking is a popular activity. On the other side of the campground are sand dunes that lead to a 4-mile-long sandy beach that extends to the end of the Nehalem Bay Spit. You can walk on the 1.5-mile paved path that winds through open dunes adjacent to the bay and have opportunities to see deer, elk, and other wildlife. If you trek along the bay beachfront, watch for abundant bird life and seals. To get to the park from Manzanita, drive 3 miles south on U.S. Highway 101 to Carey Street. Turn west onto Carey Street and drive 1.5 miles to the park entrance. For more information contact the Oregon State Parks and Recreation, 1115 Commercial Street NE, Suite 1, Salem, OR 97301; (800) 551–6949; www.oregonstateparks.org. *DeLorme: Oregon Atlas & Gazetteer:* Page 64, C1.

G Oceanside Beach State Recreation Site

This 7.2-acre state recreation area is located in the small community of Oceanside. When you visit this area, you can walk on the beach and hunt for agates and check out the wildlife. A half mile offshore is Three Arch Rocks, home to thirteen species of seabirds including storm petrels, cormorants, gulls, common murres, and Oregon's largest colony of tufted puffins. It is also host to a breeding colony of Steller's sea lions. The rocks are designated wilderness and all animals that live here are protected. While you're visiting the Oceanside area, be sure to stop at Roseanna's Oceanside Cafe, 1490 Pacific Street, Oceanside; (503) 842–7351. This recreation site is located 11 miles west of Tillamook and about 23 miles north of Pacific City on the Three Capes Scenic Highway. For more information contact the Oregon State Parks and Recreation, 1115 Commercial Street NE, Suite 1, Salem, OR 97301; (800) 551–6949; www.oregonstateparks.org. *DeLorme: Oregon Atlas & Gazetteer:* Page 58, A1.

H Roads End State Recreation Site

Roads End covers 4.7 acres and is a great spot to walk on the beach and watch surfers, windsurfers, and boogie boarders catching waves offshore. A short trail leads to a beach that is nestled in a sheltered cove. From the beach you'll have views of Cascade Head to the north, and at low tide you can explore the tide pools that are located about 1 mile north at the base of a rocky headland. If you hike south the beach is more developed, with Chinook Winds Casino at center stage. From the intersection of U.S. Highway 101 and Oregon Highway 18 in Lincoln City, drive 2.7 miles south on US 101 to Logan Road. Turn west onto Logan Road and continue approximately 1 mile to the parking area. For more information contact the Oregon State Parks and Recreation, 1115 Commercial Street NE, Suite 1, Salem, OR 97301; (800) 551–6949; www.oregonstateparks.org. *DeLorme: Oregon Atlas & Gazetteer:* Page 58, D1.

I Gleneden Beach State Recreation Site

This 17.5-acre recreation area has a nice picnic area set against a backdrop of shore pine trees. A paved path leads to a sandy beach, where you can take a long stroll and watch for sea lions playing in the surf. Gleneden Beach is located 7 miles south of Lincoln City off U.S. Highway 101. For more information contact the Oregon State Parks and Recreation, 1115 Commercial Street NE, Suite 1, Salem, OR 97301; (800) 551–6949; www.oregonstateparks.org. *DeLorme: Oregon Atlas & Gazetteer:* Page 32, Inset 1, A1.

J Fogarty Creek State Recreation Area

This recreation area covers 142 acres and is haven to bubbling Fogarty Creek. You can enjoy a large grassy picnic area decorated with red cedar, Sitka spruce, and shore pine. You explore the park on paved paths that cross charming arched footbridges as well as head under the highway to explore a secluded beach. Fogarty Creek is located 2 miles north of Depoe Bay on U.S. Highway 101. For more information contact the Oregon State Parks and Recreation, 1115 Commercial Street NE, Suite 1, Salem, OR 97301; (800) 551–6949; www.oregonstateparks.org. *DeLorme: Oregon Atlas & Gazetteer:* Page 32, Inset 1, B1.

K Valley of the Giants

This 51-acre preserve is haven to a rare grove of old-growth 400- to 450-year-old Douglas fir and western hemlock trees, some of which have trunks that measure more than 20 feet in circumference. This area was protected as an Outstanding Natural Area by the Bureau of Land Management (BLM) in 1976. You can walk through this land of giant trees on a scenic 1.3-mile loop trail. Once on the trail you'll feel as if you're in a prehistoric place, with the mossy covered giants standing as sentinels in a fog-shrouded setting filled with ferns, trillium, and oxalis. To get there from Salem, travel west on Oregon Highway 22 to the junction with Oregon Highway 223. Turn south and continue to Falls City. Once in Falls City follow Falls City Road into town. Turn south onto Bridge Street and follow it as it turns into Valsetz Road and turns to gravel. Follow this road for about 14.8 miles and you'll arrive at the now-abandoned logging community of Valsetz. Follow the road as it veers to the left and then arrives at a T-junction. Turn right, and continue for 8.4 miles, and turn right at a road junction. Continue another 5.2 miles (keeping left at all junctions) to a bridge crossing the North Fork Siletz River. Travel about a mile after the bridge to a road junction and turn right for 0.5 mile to the signed trailhead. For more information contact the Bureau of Land Management, Salem District, 1717 Fabry Road SE, Salem, OR 97306; (503) 375–5646; www.or.blm.gov/salem. *DeLorme: Oregon Atlas & Gazetteer:* Page 52, A3.

L Finley National Wildlife Refuge

This 5,325-acre refuge provides a variety of habitats for a myriad of wildlife. It is composed of oak woodlands, marsh, croplands, and Douglas fir forest. It is haven to the Dusky Canada goose as well as great blue herons, egrets, long-billed marsh wrens, Canada geese, ducks, raptors, woodpeckers, black-tail deer, coyote, and beaver. The refuge has a series of trails that explore the different habitats in the park, giving you the opportunity to view a variety of wildlife. Note that some trails are closed from November 1 to April 30. To get there travel 11 miles south of Corvallis on Oregon Highway 99W to a signed turnoff for the Finley Wildlife Refuge. Turn right (west) and follow signs for about 3 miles to the refuge. For more information contact the William L. Finley National Wildlife Refuge, 26208 Finley Refuge Road, Corvallis, OR 97333; (541) 757–7236. *DeLorme: Oregon Atlas & Gazetteer:* Page 52, A3.

M Dan's Trail

Just outside the Corvallis city limits is the McDonald Dunn Research Forest, which has dozens of trails waiting to be explored. This difficult 8.2-mile out-and-back route gives you a good introduction to this scenic area. The hike starts in Chip Ross Park and climbs 780 feet through scenic forest to the summit of 1,495-foot Dimple Hill. From the summit you'll have awesome views of Corvallis and the surrounding Coast Mountain Range. To get there travel about 20 miles south of Salem on I–5 to exit 234B. At the end of the exit ramp, follow Pacific Boulevard southeast for a mile until it turns into U.S. Highway 20. Continue following US 20 west toward Corvallis. After about 10 miles turn right onto Conifer Boulevard. Proceed on Conifer Boulevard for 1.4 miles to Oregon Highway 99 West. Turn left onto OR 99 West and go 0.3 mile to the intersection with Walnut Boulevard. Turn right onto Walnut Boulevard and travel 1.1 miles to Northwest Highland Drive. Turn right onto Northwest Highland Drive and proceed 0.9 mile to Lester Avenue. Turn left onto Lester Avenue and go 0.9 mile to the trailhead at the road's end at Chip Ross Park. For more information contact Oregon State University, College of Forests, 8692 Peavey Arboretum Road, Corvallis, OR 97330; (541) 737–6702 or (541) 737–4434 (recorded message); www.cof.orst.edu/resfor/rec/purpose.sht. *DeLorme: Oregon Atlas & Gazetteer:* Page 53, D6.

Central Coast

The Central Oregon Coast has many trails that will appeal to all levels of hikers. Located on the north side of Yaquina Bay, Newport is a good place to start your exploration. You can begin by checking out the Yaquina Head Outstanding Natural Area. One of the main attractions in this natural area is the 93-foot-tall Yaquina Head Lighthouse. In addition you can hike on several different trails that lead to tide pools, beach, and scenic viewpoints. You can also learn more about the geology, plants, and history of this area by visiting the interpretive center, which is open in the summer months from 10:00 A.M. to 5:00 P.M. and in the winter months from 10:00 A.M. to 4:00 P.M. This is also one of the best places on the Oregon Coast to view seabirds nesting on offshore rocks (be sure to bring binoculars!). After visiting this natural area, your next stop should be the Yaquina Bay State Park and Lighthouse. Built in 1871, this lighthouse sits on a high bluff and offers outstanding views of Yaquina Bay and the Pacific Ocean. To get a closer view of Yaquina Bay and its amazing bird life, visit the Hatfield Marine Science Center Estuary Trail located 2.7 miles south of Newport. Once you've finished this short trail, visit the Hatfield Marine Science Center, which features touch tanks filled with anemones, starfish, and other tidal creatures; marine science films; and interpretive displays about the ocean, weather, and marine life. The Oregon Coast Aquarium is another must-stop if you are visiting Newport. Plan on spending the day at this amazing aquarium that has natural indoor and outdoor exhibits where you can see birds and marine mammals close-up. The aquarium is open from 9:00 A.M. to 6:00 P.M. daily (from Memorial Day through Labor Day) and from 10:00 A.M. to 5:00 P.M. the rest of the year.

The small community of Waldport, located 15 miles south of Newport on U.S. Highway 101, is located on the shores of Alsea Bay and is known for its world-class clamming and crabbing in Alsea Bay as well as its runs of salmon and steelhead in the Alsea River. When you visit Waldport stop by the Alsea Bay Interpretive Center (620 NW Spring Street, Waldport; 541–563–2002) to learn about the history of travel routes on the Oregon Coast, beginning with Native American trails and leading to road routes. A great place to view resident seabirds and rugged rocky coastline is at the Seal Rock State Recreation Area, located 5 miles north of Waldport. Elephant Rock dominates the beach scene and provides important nesting habitat for a variety of birds, including pigeon guillimots, tufted puffins, common murres, pelagic cormorants, and western and glaucous-winged gulls. Additional hikes you may want to visit when you are in the Waldport area include Alsea Falls and Green

Peak Falls (located about 49 miles east of Waldport off Oregon Highway 34) and Horse Creek—Harris Ranch (located in the spectacular Drift Creek Wilderness 21 miles northeast of Waldport).

The small hamlet of Yachats, located 9 miles south of Waldport on US 101, boasts beautiful coastal scenery and many hiking opportunities. A good introduction to this area is the Yachats 804 Trail. Located on the north edge of town, this short paved trail takes you past rugged, rocky coastline to a scenic beach. One of the most well-known hiking destinations on this part of the coast is Cape Perpetua. Located 3 miles south of Yachats, this 2,700-acre scenic area features ten trails that wind through coastal forest and along the rocky shoreline. Try the Saint Perpetua Trail, which ascends the south side of Cape Perpetua and rewards you with excellent views of Cape Foulweather to the north and Cape Blanco to the south. To explore tide pools and rocky shore, check out the Captain Cook Trail. Photography buffs will enjoy a visit to Heceta Head Lighthouse, which is nestled on the edge of the coastal protrusion Heceta Head. Built in 1894 this beautiful lighthouse and its picturesque surroundings are one of the most photographed scenes on the Oregon Coast. If you feel like staying overnight, the lighthouse keeper's quarters have been turned into a bed-and-breakfast (for information contact Heceta Head Lighthouse Bed and Breakfast, 92072 Highway 101 South, Yachats, OR 97498; 541–547–3696; www.hecetalighthouse.com).

There are many hikes located around Florence and Reedsport that explore coastal forest, lakes, sand dunes, and beach located in the Oregon Dunes National Recreation Area. Recommended destinations in this area are the Sutton Creek Recreation Area, Tahkenitch Creek, and Lake Marie. In addition, waterfall lovers will want to check out Sweet Creek Falls (located east of Florence) and Kentucky Falls and North Fork Smith River hikes, which are both located east of Reedsport.

19 Yaquina Head Outstanding Natural Area

The trails in the Yaquina Head Outstanding Natural Area take you through a rich coastal ecosystem, giving visitors an excellent opportunity to view seabirds, tide-pool creatures, harbor seals, and migrating gray whales. The other main attraction of this special ocean oasis is the 93-foot Yaquina Head Lighthouse—the tallest lighthouse in Oregon. It's recommended that you bring a pair of binoculars in order to get a close-up view of the abundance of wildlife this unique area has to offer.

Start: Trails at this natural area are located about 3 miles north of Newport off U.S. Highway 101.
Distance: Trails vary from 0.2 mile to 1 mile in length.
Approximate hiking time: 15 minutes to 1 hour depending on the trails selected.
Difficulty: Easy to moderate depending on the trails selected.
Total climbing: Varies depending on trail selected.
Trail surface: Paved walkways, dirt path, wooden steps, and rocky beach.
Lay of the land: The trails take you to a majestic lighthouse that sits atop a scenic headland. Yaquina Head is home to tide pools and a cobblestone beach. Its cliffs and offshore rocks are home to numerous species of seabirds and seals.
Seasons: Year-round.
Other trail users: None.
Canine compatibility: Dogs are not permitted.
Land status: Bureau of Land Management (BLM).
Nearest town: Newport.
Fees and permits: $5.00 entrance fee that is good for three consecutive days. You can also purchase an annual permit for $10.
Map: Maptech map: Newport North, Oregon.
Trail contact: Bureau of Land Management, 1717 Fabry Road SE, Salem, OR 97306; (541) 375-5646; www.or.blm.gov/salem/html/yaquina/index.htm.

Finding the trailhead: From Newport, drive 2 miles north on US 101. Turn left (west) onto Lighthouse Drive at the park sign. Drive 1 mile to the end of the road, where you'll reach a parking area. Be prepared to pay a $5.00 entrance fee at the entrance station. *Delorme: Oregon Atlas & Gazetteer:* Page 32, C1.

The Hike

Established in 1980 the Yaquina Head Outstanding Natural Area consists of 100 acres of rocky basalt cliffs, tide pools, rocky beaches, and grassy meadows that support a multitude of animal and aquatic life.

Managed by the Bureau of Land Management, this seaside oasis has many trails that lead you through different coastal life zones. It's recommended that you begin your tour of the area by stopping first at the interpretive center, located 0.7 mile from U.S. Highway 101 on Lighthouse Drive. The interpretive center has exhibits, video presentations, and hands-on displays about the geology and cultural and natural history of Yaquina Head. It's open in the summer months from 10:00 A.M. to 5:00 P.M. and in

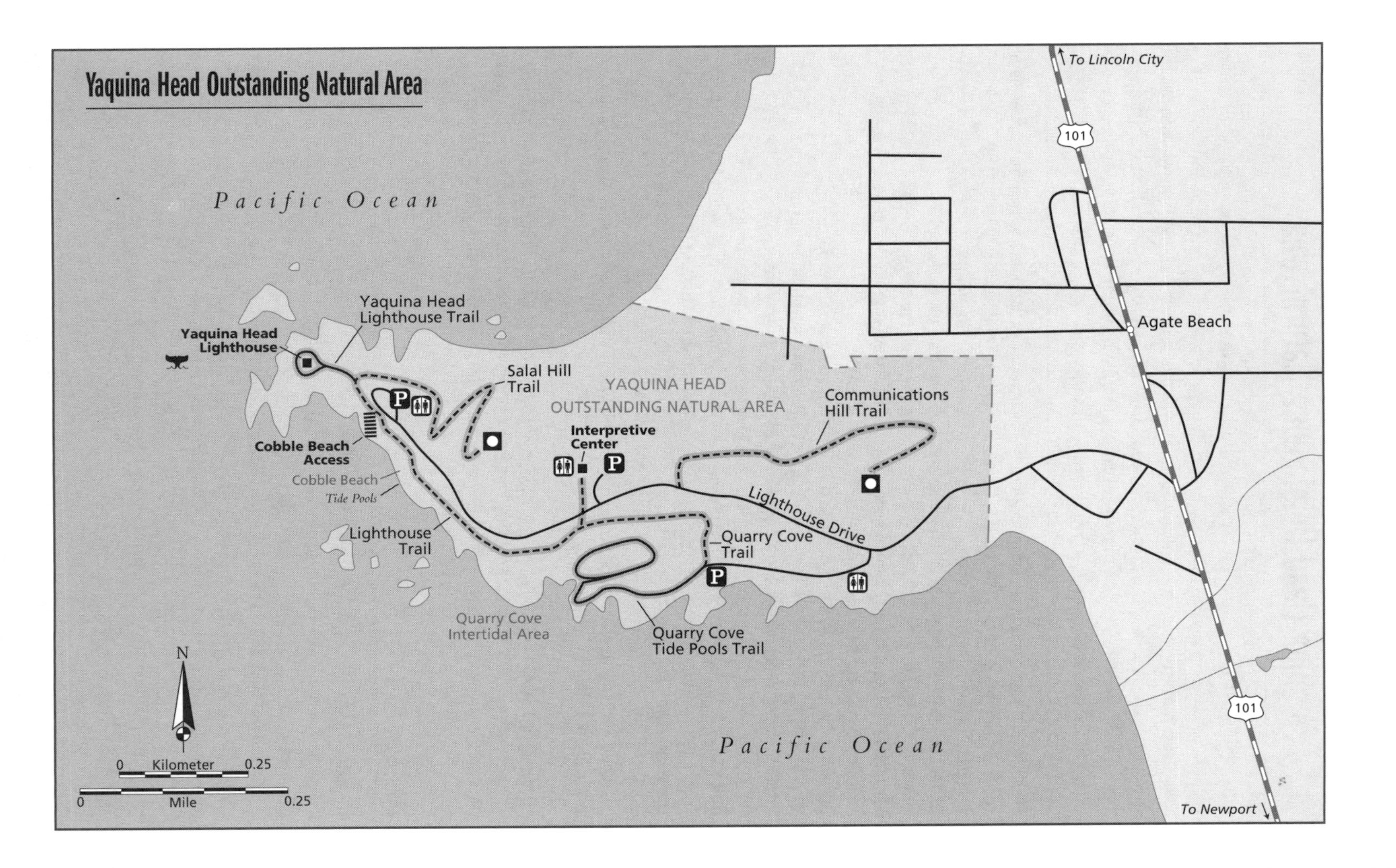
Yaquina Head Outstanding Natural Area
To Lincoln City
101
Pacific Ocean
Agate Beach
Yaquina Head
Lighthouse Trail
Yaquina Head
Lighthouse
Salal Hill
Trail
YAQUINA HEAD
OUTSTANDING NATURAL AREA
Communications
Hill Trail
Interpretive
Center
Cobble Beach
Access
Cobble Beach
Tide Pools
Lighthouse Drive
Lighthouse
Trail
Quarry Cove
Trail
Quarry Cove
Intertidal Area
Quarry Cove
Tide Pools Trail
N
0
Kilometer
0.25
0
Mile
0.25
Pacific Ocean
101
To Newport

the winter months from 10:00 A.M. to 4:00 P.M. Once you've filled up on facts at the interpretive center, turn right out of the interpretive center parking area and drive 0.3 mile to the end of Lighthouse Drive to the Yaquina Head Lighthouse Parking Area.

From the parking area take a leisurely walk over to the 93-foot-tall Yaquina Head Lighthouse. Construction on the classic seacoast tower began in the fall of 1871, taking two years to complete. Many of the building materials used for the lighthouse were shipped in from San Francisco and unloaded in Newport. They were then brought out to Yaquina Head by wagon over a crude, rough road along the coast. Amazingly, it took more than 370,000 bricks to build the tower. A two-story building was also constructed next door to house the lighthouse keepers and their families. In 1872 a Fresnel lens arrived in sections from France, and on August 20, 1873, Fayette Crosby, a lighthouse keeper, lit the lamp for the first time. In 1993 the lighthouse was refurbished by the Coast Guard and was officially named a part of the Yaquina Head Outstanding Natural Area. Tours of the lighthouse are available during the summer from noon to 4:00 P.M. Winter hours may vary depending on the weather. From the viewpoint at the lighthouse, you may have the opportunity to see gray whales during their winter migration from December through mid-February or during their spring migration, March through May.

After touring the lighthouse take a walk down a long series of steps to Cobble Beach. This rocky beach and the offshore rocks and islands are all part of the Oregon Islands National Wildlife Refuge. While you're on the beach, keep your eyes peeled, because you may spot black oyster catchers, easily recognized by their dark black plumage, gold eyes, bright red bills, and pink legs and feet. These birds feed on chitons, limpets, snails and other shellfish by picking the shellfish off the rocks with their long, sturdy beaks. In the rocky tide pools, you may see green anemones, prickly purple sea urchins, bright orange starfish, yellow sea lemons, oval-shelled mussels, volcano-shaped barnacles, turban snails, hermit crabs, and sculpin fish.

Looking toward the offshore islands you may spot some of the resident harbor seals. Your best chance at seeing harbor seal pups is during April and May. And a glance toward the offshore cliffs and islands will reveal multitudes of seabirds, comprised mainly of Brandt's cormorants, pelagic cormorants, tufted puffins, common murres, and pigeon guillemots. During the spring and summer, more than 24,000 birds nest on the cliffs and rocky islands surrounding Yaquina Head.

Once you're back at your vehicle, drive 0.5 mile on Lighthouse Drive and turn right into the Quarry Cove Parking Area. The Quarry Cove Tide Pools Trail is wheelchair accessible and takes you on a tour of an area once quarried for the hard basalt rock used to build roads. Today the area has evolved into a thriving intertidal ecosystem.

Miles and Directions

The Quarry Cove Parking Area is located on the left side of the road 0.5 mile from the intersection of Lighthouse Drive and US 101. From this parking area you can access the Quarry Cove Trail, Communications Hill Trail, and the wheelchair-accessible Quarry Cove Tide Pools Trail.

Yaquina Head Lighthouse

The interpretive center is located on the right side of the road 0.7 mile from the intersection of Lighthouse Drive and US 101. From this parking area you can access the Lighthouse Trail and the Quarry Cove Trail.

The Yaquina Head Lighthouse Parking Area is located 1 mile from the intersection of Lighthouse Drive and US 101. From this parking area you can access the paved trail to Yaquina Head Lighthouse, a stairway that takes you to Cobble Beach, and the Salal Hill Trail.

Hike Information

Local Information

Greater Newport Chamber of Commerce, 555 SW Coast Highway, Newport, OR 97365; (800) 262-7844; www.newportchamber.org.

Local Events/Attractions

Newport Seafood and Wine Festival, in February, Newport; (800) 262-7844.

Newport Microbrew Festival, in October, Newport; (800) 262-7844.

Newport Visual Arts Center, 777 NW Beach Drive, Newport; (541) 265-6540; www.coastarts.org/vac.

Oregon Coast Aquarium, 2820 SE Ferry Slip Road, Newport; (541) 867-3474; www. aquarium.org.

Local Outdoor Retailers

B-B Sport Center, 355 SW Coast Highway, Newport; (541) 265-7192.

20 Yaquina Bay State Park and Lighthouse

This route explores the Yaquina Bay Lighthouse, built in 1871. After exploring the lighthouse you'll take a stroll on a long sandy beach to the historic Nye Beach District in Newport, which is host to the Newport Visual Arts Center and fun shops.

Start: This recreation area is located 1 mile south of Newport on the west side of U.S. Highway 101.
Distance: 2.9 miles out and back.
Approximate hiking time: 1.5 to 2 hours.
Difficulty: Easy.
Total climbing: 90 feet. Elevation profiles are not provided for hikes with less than 250 feet of elevation gain.
Trail surface: Paved path, steps, sandy beach.
Lay of the land: This route starts with a tour of the Yaquina Bay Lighthouse and then heads north on a long sandy beach to the historic Nye Beach area in downtown Newport. Attractions at Nye Beach include the Newport Visual Arts Center and access to a historic shopping district.
Seasons: Year-round.
Other trail users: None.
Canine compatibility: Leashed dogs permitted.
Land status: State park.
Nearest town: Newport.
Fees and permits: No fees or permits required.
Map: Maptech map: Newport South, Oregon.
Trail contact: Oregon State Parks and Recreation, Suite 1, 1115 Commercial Street NE, Salem, OR 97301; (800) 551-6949; www.oregonstateparks.org/park_208.php.

Finding the trailhead: From the junction of U.S. Highways 101 and 20, travel 1 mile south on US 101 and turn right (west) at the Yaquina Bay State Park sign. This turn is just before you cross the Yaquina Bay Bridge. Continue 0.2 mile to a parking area on the left side of the road. *Delorme: Oregon Atlas & Gazetteer:* Page 32, Inset 1, C1.

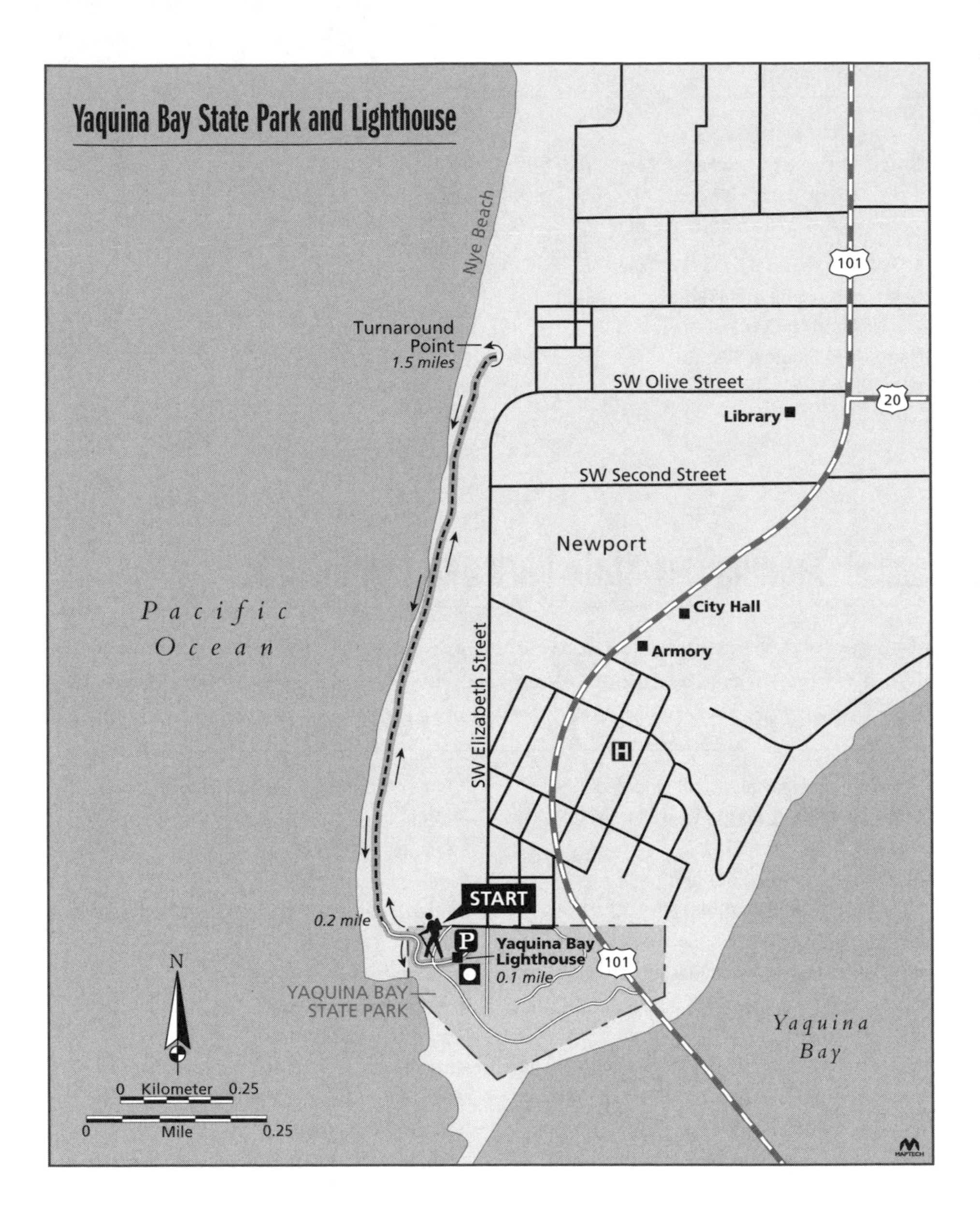

The Hike

The Yaquina Bay State Recreation Area covers thirty-six acres and is located on the north side of Yaquina Bay in Newport. This popular and often crowded park is filled with paved walking paths, picnic areas, and interpretive signs that describe the history of the area. From the parking area walk across the paved entrance road and climb a series of steps to the 40-foot-tall Yaquina Bay Lighthouse, perched at a high point on a short bluff. Built in 1871 the lighthouse served as the entrance light to Yaquina Bay and is the last wooden lighthouse remaining in Oregon. Charles Pierce was the original lighthouse keeper, and he made a salary of $1,000 per year. Charles, his wife, and seven children lived in the house. Water was collected in a cistern and hand pumped into the kitchen, and meals were cooked on a wood-burning stove. The lighthouse was decommissioned in 1874 because a new, brighter Yaquina Head Lighthouse was built 4 miles farther north in 1873. After the lighthouse was decommissioned, it fell into near ruin until the citizens of Newport and the Lincoln County Historical Society saved it from demolition in 1934. Since that time it has been fully restored, and you can tour the inside from 11:00 A.M. to 5:00 P.M. daily May through September and from noon to 4:30 P.M. October through April. After checking out the lighthouse, cross the paved entrance road and head down a series of steps through a thick stand of shore pine and salal, through some small sand dunes, to a long sandy beach. Before you descend, soak in the views of Yaquina Bay and the historic Yaquina Bay Bridge.

Once you reach the beach, you'll turn right (north) and walk on the beach for 1.3 miles to historic Nye Beach. As you hike this stretch of the route, keep your eye out for sandpipers and dunlins hunting for small crustaceans and worms along the shoreline and the far-off spouts of migrating gray whales (from December through June). Once your reach Nye Creek, you have the option of walking up a series of stairs and continuing to the Newport Visual Arts Center (777 NW Beach Drive). This center showcases the art of many northwest artists in the 1,000-foot Runyan Gallery and the 300-square-foot Upstairs Gallery. The Runyan Gallery is open from 11:00 A.M. to 6:00 P.M. Tuesday through Saturday, and the Upstairs Gallery is open from noon to 4:00 P.M. Tuesday through Saturday. After touring the galleries take time to stroll through the many fun shops and restaurants that are present in this historic district. From Nye Beach you'll retrace the same route back to your starting point.

Miles and Directions

0.0 From the parking area cross the entrance road and read interpretive signs under a white-roofed building located on the right side of stairs leading to the lighthouse. After reading the interpretive signs, head up the stairs to view the lighthouse.

0.1 Arrive at the lighthouse. After you are finished with your tour, head back down the stairs and cross the entrance road to the day-use parking area and walk down a set of stairs to the beach. (FYI: From the top of the stairs, you'll have great views of the Yaquina Bay Bridge, the north jetty, and Yaquina Bay.)

0.2 Arrive at the beach and turn right (north).

1.5 Arrive at historic Nye Beach, where Nye Creek empties into the ocean (your turnaround point). Retrace the same route back to the trailhead. **Option:** Turn right and explore the Newport Visual Arts Center and the shops in the Historic Nye District.

2.9 Arrive at the trailhead.

Yaquina Bay Bridge and Yaquina Bay in Newport

Hike Information

Local Information

Greater Newport Chamber of Commerce, 555 SW Coast Highway, Newport, OR 97365; (800) 262-7844; www.newportchamber.org.

Local Events/Attractions

Newport Seafood and Wine Festival, in February, Newport; (800) 262-7844.

Newport Microbrew Festival, in October, Newport; (800) 262-7844.

Newport Visual Arts Center, 777 NW Beach Drive, Newport; (541) 265-6540; www.coastarts.org/vac.

Oregon Coast Aquarium, 2820 SE Ferry Slip Road Newport; (541) 867-3474; www.aquarium.org.

Local Outdoor Retailers

B-B Sport Center, 355 SW Coast Highway, Newport; (541) 265-7192.

21 Hatfield Marine Science Center Estuary Trail

This hike takes you on a tour of the Yaquina Bay Estuary adjacent to the Hatfield Marine Science Center. Interpretive signs educate you on the plants and animals that inhabit this unique ecosystem. From the trail you'll have great views of the Yaquina Bay Bridge and Newport Harbor. After you complete this hike, be sure to explore the exhibits in the science center.

Start: This hike is located 2.7 miles south of Newport off U.S. Highway 101.
Distance: 1 mile out and back.
Approximate hiking time: 30 minutes to 1 hour.
Difficulty: Easy due to smooth paved surface and no elevation gain.
Total climbing: None. Elevation profiles are not provided for hikes with less than 250 feet of elevation gain.
Trail surface: Paved path, wooden ramps.
Lay of the land: This signed interpretive trail follows the edge of the Yaquina Bay Estuary in Newport.
Seasons: Year-round.
Other trail users: None.
Canine compatibility: Dogs are not permitted.
Land status: Hatfield Marine Science Center.
Nearest town: Newport.
Fees and permits: No fees or permits required.
Map: Maptech map: Newport South, Oregon.
Trail contact: Hatfield Marine Science Center, 2030 South Marine Science Drive, Newport, OR 97365; (541) 867-0271; www.hmsc.orst.edu/visitor.

Finding the trailhead: From the junction of U.S. Highways 101 and 20 in Newport, travel 1.8 miles south on US 101 to the sign for the Hatfield Marine Science Center. Turn onto OSU Drive and go 0.7 mile. Turn right at a sign for the Hatfield Marine Science Center Parking Area. Proceed 0.2 mile to the parking area. *Delorme: Oregon Atlas & Gazetteer:* Page 32, Inset 1, C1.

The Hike

This short paved trail explores the 3,900-acre Yaquina Estuary, located on the south side of Yaquina Bay in Newport. The nature trail is adjacent to the Hatfield Marine Science Center, which has a variety of displays that give you a closer look at the plants and animals that live on the Oregon Coast. You'll begin the hike by walking on the paved path next to the water's edge. After 0.2 mile you'll arrive at a wood picnic shelter where you can sit and observe a variety of birds as well as stay dry if it's raining. Watch for blue herons hunting for fish and small reptiles. Also be on the lookout for whimbrels using their long, probelike beaks to search for small crustaceans and worms along the muddy shoreline. Dunlins and sandpipers can also be seen probing the mudflats for food. Farther offshore you may see Brant's geese, which spend the winter in the estuary feeding on abundant, bright green eelgrass. These birds have a black head, neck, and breast; dark brown backs and undersides; and a white neckband and tail feathers. The geese arrive in mid-November and stay

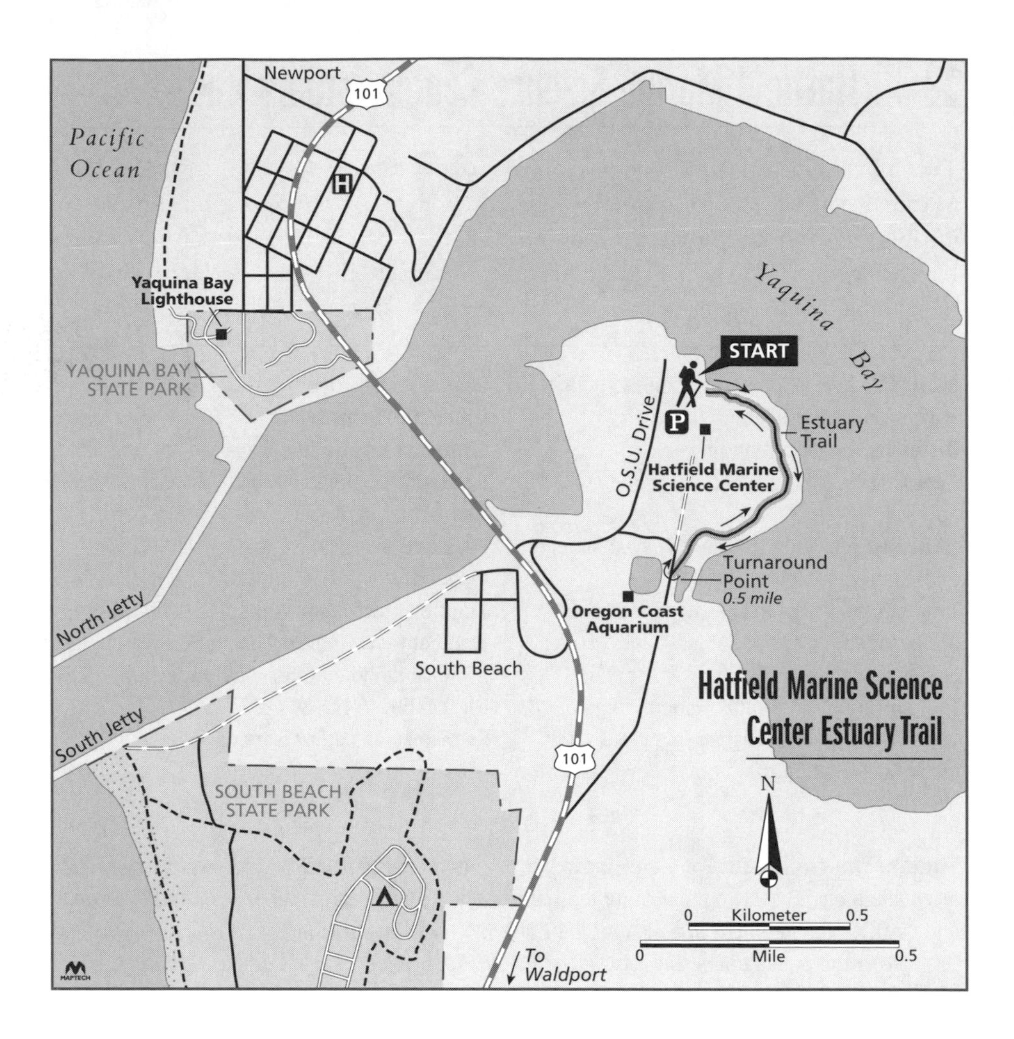

until early spring. They often congregate on sandbars, where they dine on small amounts of sand to help them digest their eelgrass meal. Other birds often spotted here include double-breasted cormorants, buffleheads, common loons, red-breasted mergansers, horned grebes, pigeon guillemots, and surf and white-winged scoters.

At 0.4 mile you'll arrive at a wood ramp that takes you across a marshy area filled with the fluffy brown plumes of cattails, arrow grass, pickleweed, seaside plantain, beach pea, and cow parsnip. After 0.5 mile you'll arrive at the end of the trail and your turnaround point.

Miles and Directions

0.0 Start walking on the signed trailhead that begins on the left side of a chain-link fence on the far side of the parking area.

0.2 Pass a covered picnic shelter on the left.

View of a productive marsh on the Estuary Trail

0.4 Begin walking on a wood ramp that takes you through a marshy area.

0.5 Arrive at the end of the trail and your turnaround point. Retrace the same route back to your starting point.

1.0 Arrive at the trailhead.

Hike Information

Local Information

Greater Newport Chamber of Commerce, 555 SW Coast Highway, Newport, OR 97439; (800) 262-7844; www.newportchamber.org.

Local Events/Attractions

Newport Seafood and Wine Festival, in February, Newport, (800) 262-7844.

Newport Microbrew Festival, in October, Newport, (800) 262-7844.

Newport Visual Arts Center, 777 NW Beach Drive, Newport; (541) 265-6540; www.coastarts.org/vac.

Oregon Coast Aquarium, 2820 SE Ferry Slip Road, Newport; (541) 867-3474; www.aquarium.org.

Local Outdoor Retailers

B-B Sport Center, 355 SW Coast Highway, Newport; (541) 265-7192.

22 Mike Miller Educational Trail

This short interpretive trail explores a unique coastal forest ecosystem in the Mike Miller Educational Area. You'll hike past old-growth Sitka spruce trees and huge rhododendrons and over a small creek where you may see blue herons, ducks, and geese feeding.

Start: This hike is located 2.8 miles south of Newport off U.S. Highway 101.
Distance: 1-mile loop.
Approximate hiking time: 30 minutes to 1 hour.
Difficulty: Easy.
Trail surface: Forest path.
Total climbing: 130 feet. Elevation profiles are not provided for hikes with less than 250 feet of elevation gain.
Lay of the land: This trail passes through old-growth Sitka spruce forest and a small creek estuary.
Seasons: Year-round.
Other trail users: None.
Canine compatibility: Dogs permitted.
Land status: County park.
Nearest town: Newport.
Fees and permits: No fees or permits required.
Map: Maptech map: Newport South, Oregon.
Trail contact: Lincoln County Public Works, 880 NE Seventh Street, Newport, OR 97365; (541) 265-5747; www.co.lincoln.or.us/lcparks.

Finding the trailhead: From the junction of U.S. Highways 101 and 20, travel 2.8 miles south on US 101 and turn left (east) at the Mike Miller Educational Area sign. Continue on a gravel road for 0.2 mile to the signed trailhead on the left side of the road. *Delorme: Oregon Atlas & Gazetteer:* Page 32, Inset 1, C1.

The Hike

This interpretive trail winds through a coastal forest made up of shore pine, Sitka spruce, Douglas fir, grand fir, and western hemlock. The route follows an old railroad grade that was used to transport lumber (and later, passengers and mail) from Yachats to Yaquina Bay. Before you start the hike, be sure to pick up a trail brochure, which points out the trail's highlights.

The gravel trail is lined with Pacific rhododendrons that grow to more than 30 feet tall. This native plant has large, pink bell-shaped flowers that bloom in March and April. Although this is Washington's state flower, it does have a strong presence in Oregon.

After 0.2 mile the trail begins climbing and the landscape changes from shore pine trees and rhododendron to large Sitka spruce trees. This noticeable difference is in part caused by the difference in soil types. The first section of the trail passes through a stabilized sand dune that once made up the shoreline of the Yaquina River. The sandy soil acts as a filter and does not retain water well. Hardy shore pine and rhododendron can tolerate this type of soil but Sitka spruce trees require richer

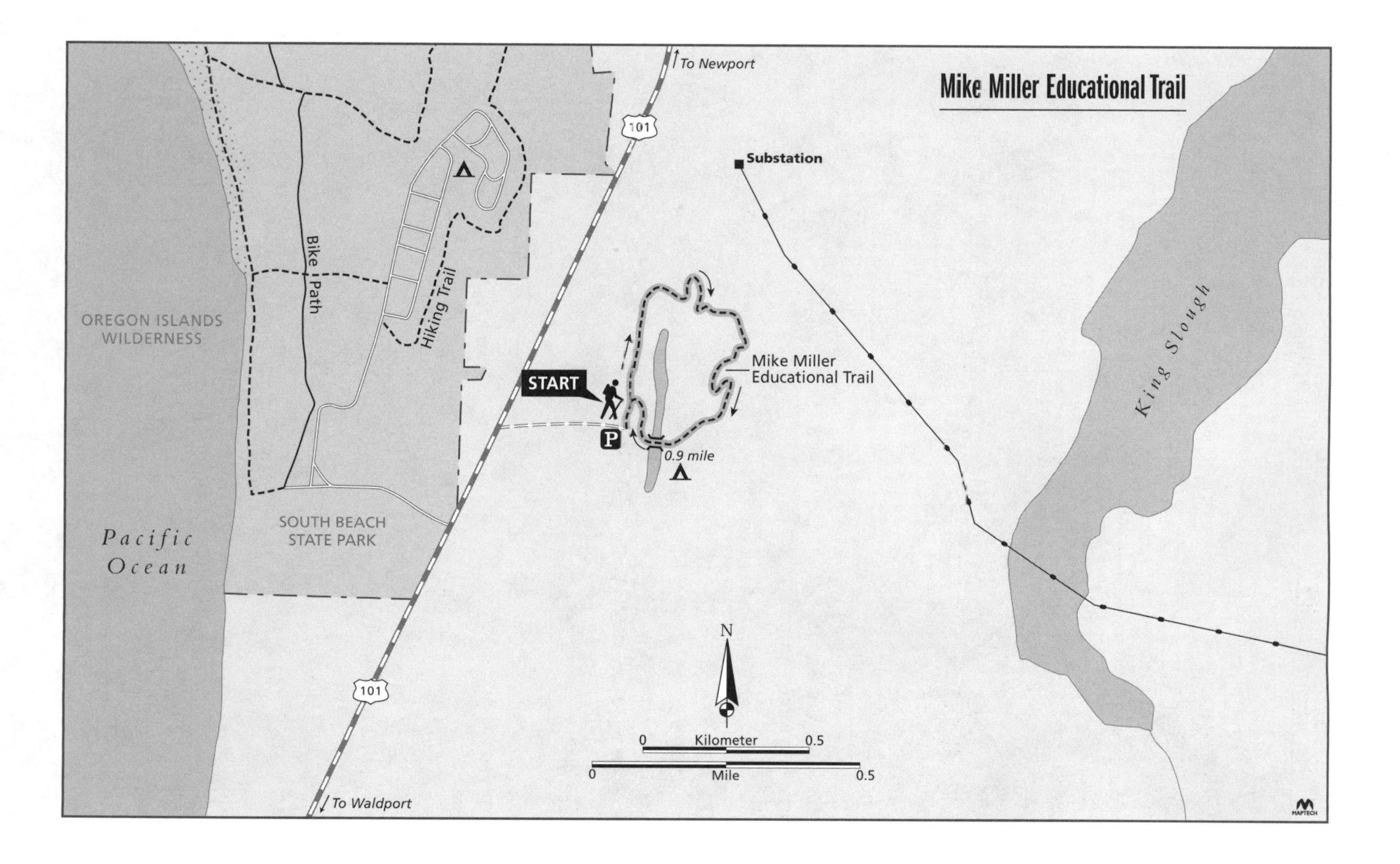
Mike Miller Educational Trail
To Newport
101
Substation
OREGON ISLANDS WILDERNESS
Bike Path
Hiking Trail
START
Mike Miller Educational Trail
0.9 mile
Pacific Ocean
SOUTH BEACH STATE PARK
King Slough
N
0 Kilometer 0.5
0 Mile 0.5
101
To Waldport
MAPTECH

topsoil that retains more water. As you hike through this large grove of trees, look for great horned owls roosting in the trees and listen for the owl's call, which is a series of hoots that can be three to eight notes long.

At 0.9 mile you'll cross a footbridge over a creek and wetland area. After crossing the bridge you have the option of turning left and walking down a short side trail to a viewing platform. Look for ducks, geese, and blue herons feeding in the creek and listen for different melodies of resident frogs.

Miles and Directions

0.0 Pick up a trail brochure at the start of the hike. Walk 10 yards to a trail junction. Turn left and look for numbered signs that correspond to descriptions in the brochure.

0.9 Cross a footbridge over a creek. **Option:** After crossing the bridge, turn left and walk to a small viewing platform of the creek and marsh.

1.0 Arrive at a trail junction, ending the loop portion of the hike. Go left and walk 10 yards to the trailhead.

Hike Information

Local Information

Greater Newport Chamber of Commerce, 555 SW Coast Highway, Newport OR 97439; (800) 262-7844; wwww.newportchamber.org.

Local Events/Attractions

Newport Seafood and Wine Festival, in February, Newport; (800) 262-7844.

Newport Microbrew Festival, in October, Newport; (800) 262-7844.

Newport Visual Arts Center, 777 NW Beach Drive, Newport; (541) 265-6540; www.coastarts.org/vac.

Oregon Coast Aquarium, 2820 SE Ferry Slip Road, Newport; (541) 867-3474; www.aquarium.org.

Local Outdoor Retailers

B-B Sport Center, 355 SW Coast Highway, Newport; (541) 265-7192.

A picturesque creek on the Mike Miller Educational Trail

23 South Beach State Park

This route offers plenty of opportunities to view wildlife and enjoy beach activities in South Beach State Park. You'll walk on the beach to the south jetty, where you can watch for wildlife and soak in the views of Yaquina Bay, Yaquina Bay Bridge, and the Yaquina Lighthouse.

Start: Day-Use Parking Area at South Beach State Park located 3 miles south of Newport off U.S. Highway 101.
Distance: 2 miles out and back (with longer options).
Approximate hiking time: 1 hour.
Difficulty: Easy.
Total climbing: None. Elevation profiles are not provided for hikes with less than 250 feet of elevation gain.
Trail surface: Sandy beach and paved path.
Lay of the land: This route travels along a long, sandy beach in South Beach State Park, located on the south side of Yaquina Bay.
Seasons: Year-round.
Other trail users: Cyclists, equestrians.
Canine compatibility: Leashed dogs permitted.
Land status: State park.
Nearest town: Newport.
Fees and permits: No fees or permits required.
Map: Maptech map: Newport South, Oregon.
Trail contact: Oregon State Parks and Recreation, Suite 1, 1115 Commercial Street NE, Salem, OR 97301; (800) 551-6949; www.oregonstateparks.org/park_209.php.

Finding the trailhead: From the junction of U.S. Highways 101 and 20 in Newport, travel 4 miles south on US 101 to the South Beach State Park turnoff. Turn right (west) and go 0.3 mile to a road junction. Turn left toward the Day-Use Picnic Area. Go 0.1 mile and turn left into a large parking area on the left. *Delorme: Oregon Atlas & Gazetteer:* Page 32, Inset 1, D1.

The Hike

This beach hike is located in 434-acre South Beach State Park and features a large campground and many trails that wind through dunes, marsh, and the beach. You'll start this hike from the day-use area on a sandy trail that begins next to the rest rooms. The trail ascends a short sand dune and then descends to a long, flat sandy beach. Once you reach the beach, turn right (north) and enjoy the sounds of the crashing surf and salty coastal wind. As you walk north look offshore for brown pelicans flying above the waves, sandpipers running back and forth with the incoming tide, and gulls resting in large groups on the beach. After a mile of fun beach walking, you'll arrive at the south jetty and the entrance to Yaquina Bay. From the south jetty you may glimpse sea lions swimming in the channel and a variety of ducks and other bird life. You'll also have good views of the Yaquina Bay Lighthouse, boats traveling to and from Newport Harbor, and the graceful arch of the historic Yaquina Bay Bridge, which was completed in 1936. From here you have the option of completing a loop back to your starting point. To complete the loop, turn right (east) on a

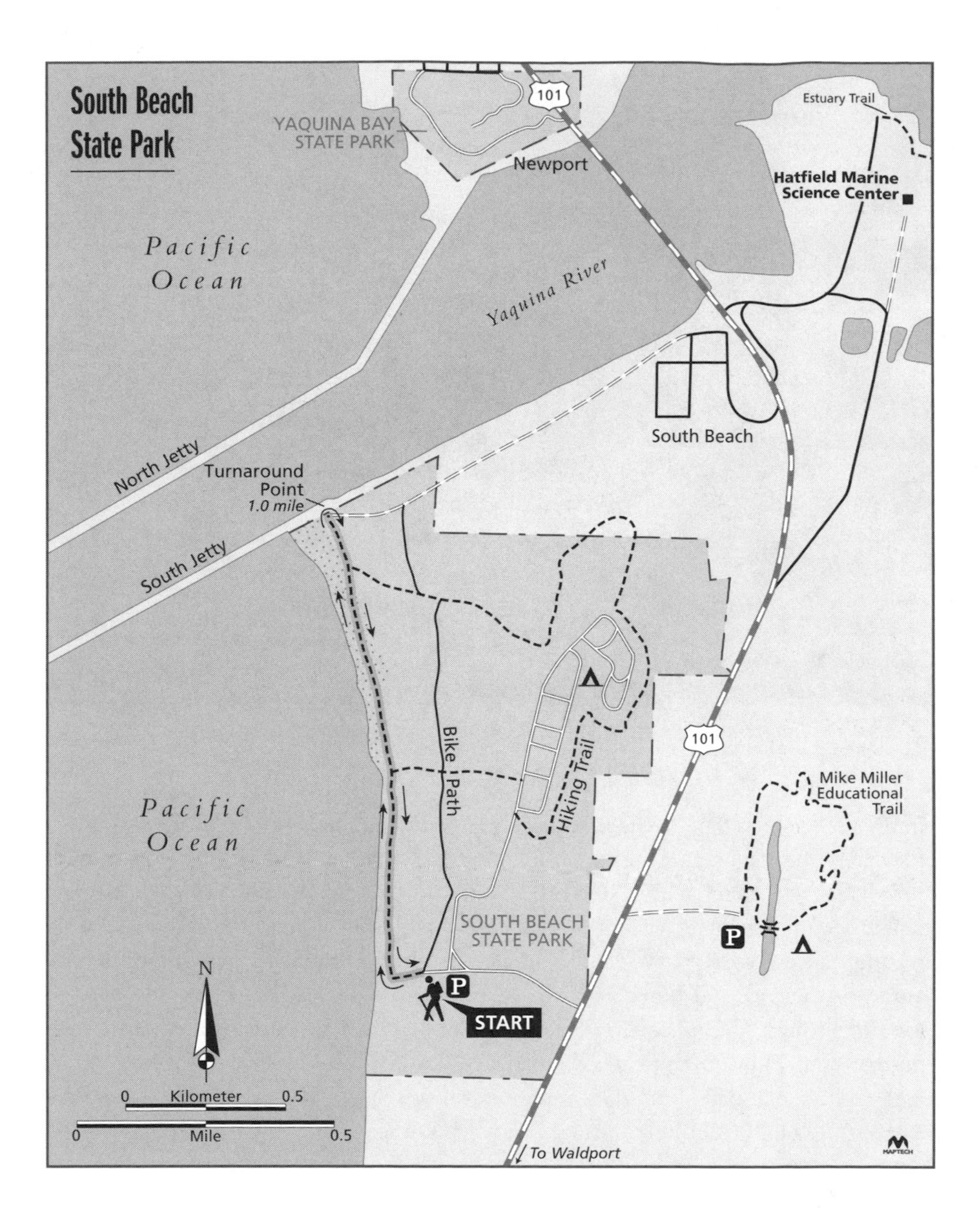

doubletrack road and continue to the junction with a paved bike path. Turn right and follow the paved bike path for 1.2 miles back to your starting point.

While you are in this area, be sure to visit the Oregon Coast Aquarium (see the Hike Information section for contact information). The aquarium contains several indoor and outdoor displays about Northwest plant and animal marine life. One of the most popular displays is the jellyfish tank—dozens of beautiful jellyfish swim

A winter rainstorm at South Beach State Park

freely in a circular tank in the middle of a large room filled with huge aquarium displays. Another favorite is the touch tank, where you can touch tidal-pool creatures such as sea anemones, starfish, and other mollusks. The outside displays are just as fascinating. You can view California sea otters, harbor seals, and sea lions and walk through an outdoor aviary where you can watch tufted puffins, pigeon guillemots, common murres, and other seabirds swimming and feeding in a natural environment. Trails outside the aquarium lead through gardens of native plants with interpretive signs. The aquarium, which also has a bookstore and cafe, is open from 10:00 A.M. to 5:00 P.M. daily from mid-September through the end of May and from 9:00 A.M. to 6:00 P.M. from June through mid-September.

Miles and Directions

0.0 Start hiking on the sandy trail that starts next to the rest rooms. Arrive at the beach and turn right (north).

1.0 Arrive at the end of the beach at the south jetty (your turnaround point). **Option:** You have the option of completing a loop. To complete the loop, turn right and continue on a doubletrack road to the junction with a paved bicycle path. Turn right onto the paved bicycle path and follow it for 1.2 miles back to your starting point.

2.0 Arrive at the trailhead.

Hike Information

Local Information

Greater Newport Chamber of Commerce, 555 SW Coast Highway, Newport, OR 97439; (800) 262-7844; www.newportchamber.org.

Local Events/Attractions

Newport Seafood and Wine Festival, in February, Newport; (800) 262-7844.

Newport Microbrew Festival, in October, Newport; (800) 262-7844.

Newport Visual Arts Center, 777 NW Beach Drive, Newport; (541) 265-6540; www.coastarts.org/vac.

Oregon Coast Aquarium, 2820 SE Ferry Slip Road Newport; (541) 867-3474; www.aquarium.org.

Local Outdoor Retailers

B-B Sport Center, 355 SW Coast Highway, Newport; (541) 265-7192.

In Addition

The Oregon Coast Trail

The Oregon Coast Trail stretches for over 360 miles along the entire Oregon Coast beginning at the South Jetty in Fort Stevens State Park at the mouth of the Columbia River and traveling south to its ending point at the California border south of Brookings. This unique long-distance trail wanders on long sandy beaches, traverses dramatic headlands, passes through rare groves of old-growth trees, meanders past scenic lighthouses, and gives you many opportunities to view amazing wildlife.

In 1959 Samuel N. Dicken, a geography professor at the University of Oregon, pioneered the idea of building this extended hiking trail. The Oregon Recreation Trails Advisory Council, an organization that promotes long-distance trails in Oregon, worked with the Oregon Parks and Recreation Department to make Dicken's north to south trail concept a reality. With the help of a feasibility study completed by the Oregon Parks and Recreation Department and trail research performed by Dicken and his wife, trail construction finally began in 1972. Today the Oregon Coast Trail is over 65 percent complete and is made up of a combination of trails that pass through state parks and federal, county, city, and private lands. Sections of the trail that are not yet complete sometimes require you to walk next to paved roads through coastal communities as well as on stretches of U.S. Highway 101.

Many sections of this trail can be completed as day hikes. Ambitious backpackers may want to complete the entire route. Many of the hikes in this guidebook travel along sections of this trail. If you are planning on completing the entire route, you can camp in hiker-biker camps that are available at most state park campgrounds on the route for only $4.00 per night. Be prepared for all types of weather (see *The Art of Hiking* for a backpacking checklist and other useful information) and be sure to check weather conditions before you leave. It is also important to carry a set of tide tables with you. Some stretches of the trail are only passable at low tide. For more information about the Oregon Coast Trail, contact the Trails Coordinator, Oregon Parks and Recreation Department, 1115 NE Commercial Street, Suite 1, Salem, OR 97301; (503) 378–1002, ext. 246; www.oregonstateparks.org.

This information was provided courtesy of the Oregon State Parks and Recreation Department.

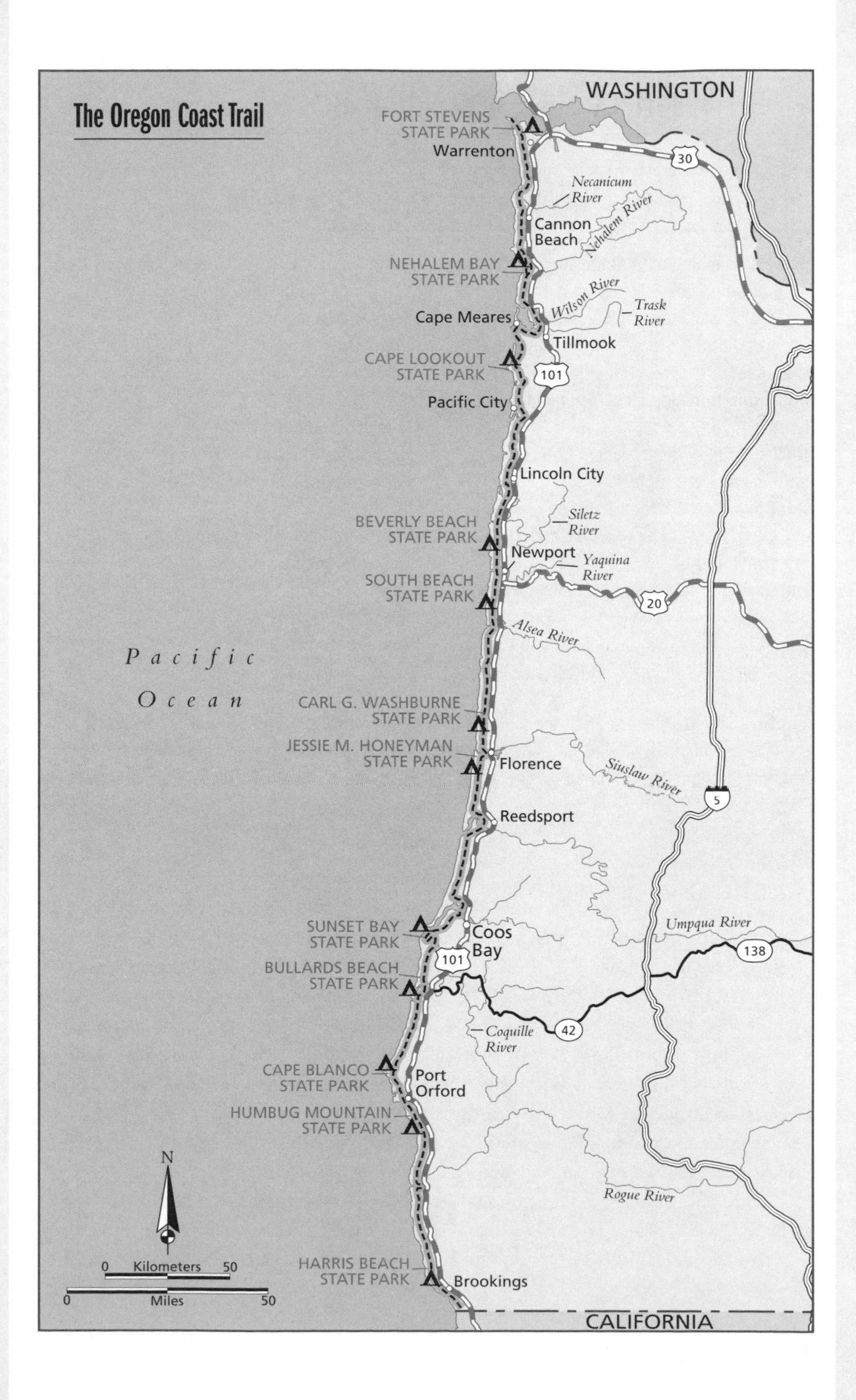

The Oregon Coast Trail
WASHINGTON
FORT STEVENS STATE PARK
Warrenton
30
Necanicum River
Nehalem River
Cannon Beach
NEHALEM BAY STATE PARK
Wilson River
Trask River
Cape Meares
Tillmook
CAPE LOOKOUT STATE PARK
101
Pacific City
Lincoln City
BEVERLY BEACH STATE PARK
Siletz River
Newport
Yaquina River
SOUTH BEACH STATE PARK
20
Alsea River
Pacific Ocean
CARL G. WASHBURNE STATE PARK
JESSIE M. HONEYMAN STATE PARK
Florence
Siuslaw River
5
Reedsport
SUNSET BAY STATE PARK
Coos Bay
Umpqua River
138
101
BULLARDS BEACH STATE PARK
42
Coquille River
CAPE BLANCO STATE PARK
Port Orford
HUMBUG MOUNTAIN STATE PARK
N
Rogue River
0 Kilometers 50
0 Miles 50
HARRIS BEACH STATE PARK
Brookings
CALIFORNIA

24 Seal Rock State Recreation Area

This route takes you on a short tour of rocky coastline and beach where you can explore tide pools and watch for abundant bird and marine life.

Start: This route starts at the Day-Use Parking Area at Seal Rock State Recreation Area, located 5 miles north of Waldport (or 14.4 miles south of Newport) off U.S. Highway 101.
Distance: 0.4 mile out and back.
Approximate hiking time: 30 minutes to 1 hour.
Difficulty: Easy due to smooth trail surface and minimal elevation gain.
Total climbing: 50 feet. Elevation profiles are not provided for hikes with less than 250 feet of elevation gain.
Trail surface: Paved path, sandy beach, and tide pools.
Lay of the land: This route takes you to a dramatic viewpoint of Elephant Rock and then travels on a scenic sandy beach to a series of tide pools you can explore at low tide.
Seasons: Year-round.
Other trail users: None.
Canine compatibility: Leashed dogs permitted.
Land status: State park.
Nearest town: Seal Rock.
Fees and permits: No fees or permits required.
Map: Maptech map: Waldport, Oregon.
Trail contact: Oregon State Parks and Recreation, Suite 1, 1115 Commercial Street NE, Salem, OR 97301; (800) 551-6949; www.oregonstateparks.org/park_207.php.

Finding the trailhead: From the junction of U.S. Highways 101 and 20 in Newport, travel 14.4 miles south (or 5 miles north of Waldport) on US 101 to the Seal Rock State Recreation Area turnoff. Turn west and park in the Day-Use Parking Area. *Delorme: Oregon Atlas & Gazetteer:* Page 32, Inset 2, A1.

The Hike

Seal Rock State Recreation Area covers five acres and features a beautiful coastal landscape made up of tide pools and rocky coastline. The basalt rocks and sea stacks present here are remnants of the Columbia River basalt flows that covered this area more than seventeen million years ago. The most dramatic rock formation in this area is Elephant Rock, which is part of the Oregon Islands National Wildlife Refuge. This important refuge is made up of more than 1,400 islands, offshore reefs, and rocks that are located along the entire Oregon Coast and provides critical nesting grounds for more than 1.2 million birds as well as sea lions and seals. Birds you may see here include pigeon guillimots, tufted puffins, common murres, pelagic cormorants, and western and glaucous-winged gulls.

Begin this hike by walking on the paved path on the left side of the rest rooms. Follow the path as it descends a pine-covered bluff to a wooden viewing platform with interpretive signs. After enjoying the gorgeous view of the rocky coastline,

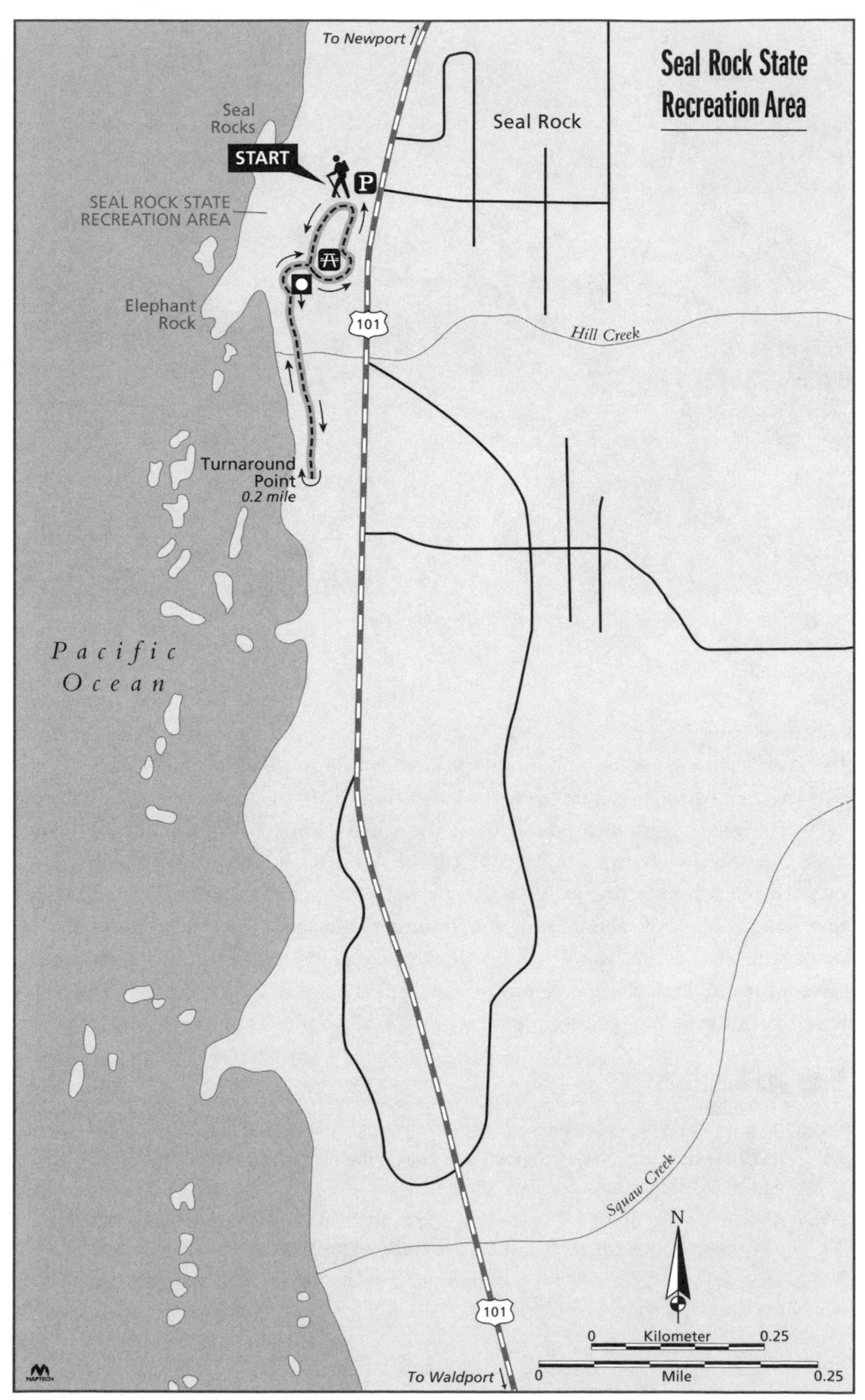
Seal Rock State
Recreation Area
To Newport
Seal Rock
Seal
Rocks
START
SEAL ROCK STATE
RECREATION AREA
Elephant
Rock
101
Hill Creek
Turnaround
Point
0.2 mile
Pacific
Ocean
Squaw Creek
N
101
0
Kilometer
0.25
0
Mile
0.25
To Waldport

Rocky coastline at the Seal Rock State Recreation Area

continue your descent on the paved path to the beach. Continue walking south on the beach and be sure to explore the numerous tide pools at low tide.

The Alsea Indians hunted sea lions and their pups at this location. In addition they harvested clams and mussels from the rocky shore. These industrious people lived in about twenty small villages along the Alsea River and Alsea Bay. They lived in cedar plank houses that would house up to four families. A large part of the tribe's diet was made up of salmon, sturgeon, flounder, and small game animals.

At the end of the beach, you'll reach your turnaround point. You'll retrace the same route back to the viewing platform, and then you'll turn right and follow a paved path through a woodsy picnic area back to your starting point.

Miles and Directions

0.0 Start hiking on the paved path located on the left side of the rest rooms. Follow the path as it descends to a viewing platform with interpretive signs. After reading about the history and geology of the area, continue your descent.

0.1 Arrive at the end of the path and a long sandy beach. Walk south along the beach and be sure to explore the tide pools that are accessible at low tide.

0.2 Arrive at the end of the beach (your turnaround point). Retrace the same route back to the viewing platform.

0.3 At the viewing platform turn right at the trail junction and follow the paved path through a picnic area back to the parking area.

0.4 Arrive at the parking area.

Hike Information

Local Information

Greater Newport Chamber of Commerce, 555 SW Coast Highway, Newport, OR 97439; (800) 262-7844; www.newportchamber.org.

Local Events/Attractions

Newport Seafood and Wine Festival, in February, Newport; (800) 262-7844.

Newport Microbrew Festival, in October, Newport; (800) 262-7844.

Newport Visual Arts Center, 777 NW Beach Drive, Newport; (541) 265-6540; www.coastarts.org/vac.

Oregon Coast Aquarium, 2820 SE Ferry Slip Road, Newport; (541) 867-3474; www.aquarium.org.

Local Outdoor Retailers

B-B Sport Center, 355 SW Coast Highway, Newport; (541) 265-7192.

25 Yachats 804 Trail

This short route is part of the Oregon Coast Trail system. It takes you along a scenic section of rocky coastline in Yachats and then hits the beach, where you can enjoy the crashing surf and view abundant wildlife.

Start: This route starts at the Smelt Sands State Wayside, 1.1 miles north of Yachats.

Distance: 3 miles out and back (with longer options).

Approximate hiking time: 30 minutes to 1 hour.

Difficulty: Easy due to well-graded paved path, flat sandy beach, and minimal elevation gain.

Total climbing: 50 feet. Elevation profiles are not provided for hikes with less than 250 feet of elevation gain.

Trail surface: Paved path.

Lay of the land: This paved path travels along rocky shoreline and continues on a long sandy beach to Vingie Creek.

Seasons: Year-round.

Other trail users: None.

Canine compatibility: Leashed dogs permitted.

Land status: State park.

Nearest town: Yachats.

Fees and permits: No fees or permits required.

Map: Maptech map: Yachats, Oregon.

Trail contact: Oregon State Parks and Recreation, Suite 1, 1115 Commercial Street NE, Salem, OR 97301; (800) 551-6949; www.oregonstateparks.org/park_207.php.

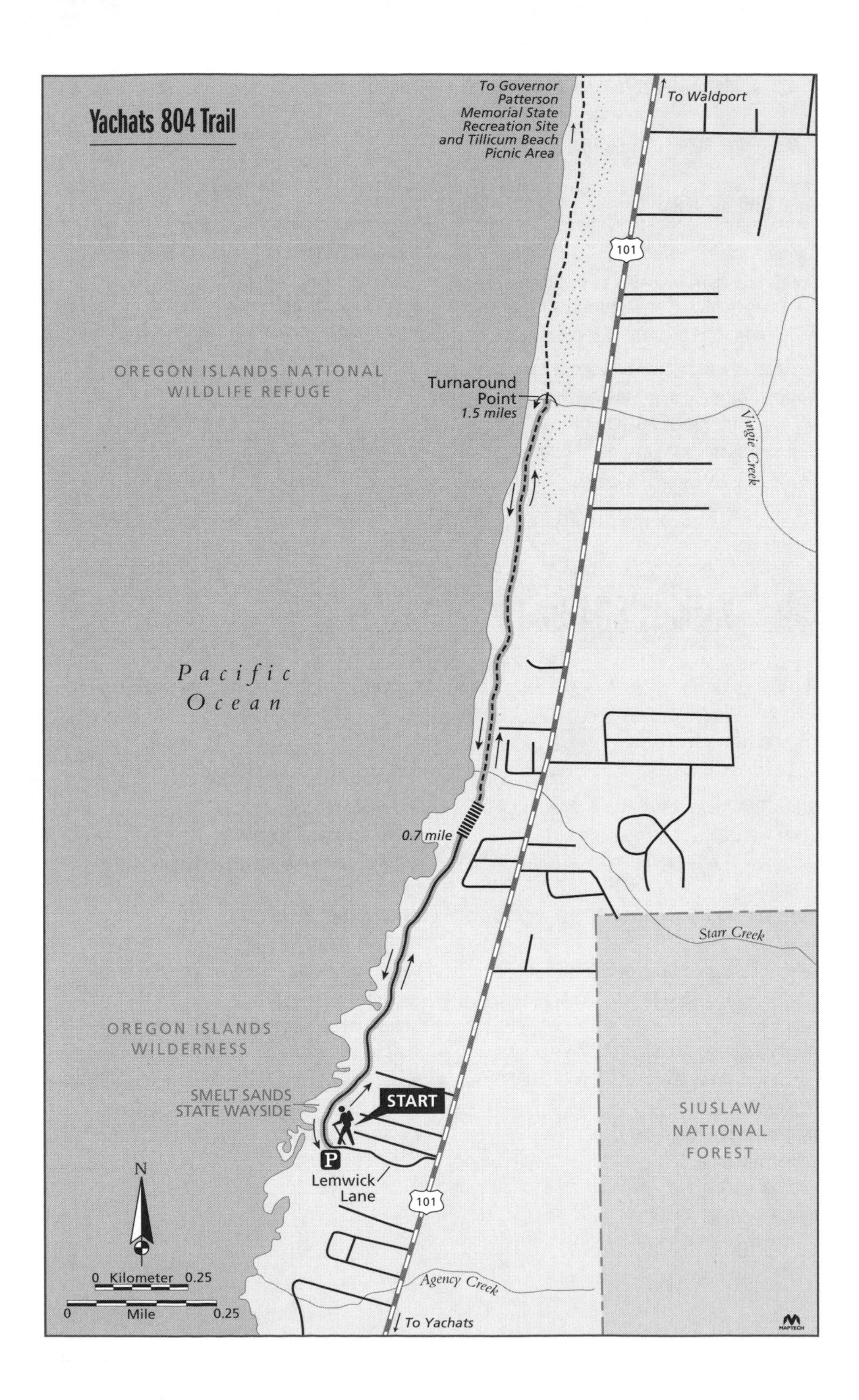
Yachats 804 Trail
To Governor Patterson Memorial State Recreation Site and Tillicum Beach Picnic Area
To Waldport
101
OREGON ISLANDS NATIONAL WILDLIFE REFUGE
Turnaround Point
1.5 miles
Vingie Creek
Pacific Ocean
0.7 mile
Starr Creek
OREGON ISLANDS WILDERNESS
SMELT SANDS STATE WAYSIDE
START
P
Lemwick Lane
101
SIUSLAW NATIONAL FOREST
N
0 Kilometer 0.25
0 Mile 0.25
Agency Creek
To Yachats

Finding the trailhead: From the bridge crossing the Yachats River in downtown Yachats, travel 1.1 miles north on U.S. Highway 101 and turn left (west) onto Lemwick Lane toward the Smelt Sands State Wayside. Continue 0.2 mile to the road's end and a parking area. *Delorme: Oregon Atlas & Gazetteer:* Page 32, Inset 2, B1.

The Hike

You'll enjoy the crashing waves and fresh sea breeze on this short, scenic trail located in the 3.9-acre Smelt Sands State Recreation Area, just north of the cozy community of Yachats (pronounced Yah-hots). The paved path parallels a stretch of rocky coastline that is made up of basalt, siltstone, and sandstone. This windblown trail is lined with salal, thimbleberry, and small Sitka spruce trees as well as less common ladies' tresses, golden-eyed grass, and leather grape-fern. Scattered hotels are also located just off the trail but do not cause too much of a distraction. This small section of coast was the center of a court battle for public ownership and right-of-way that started in the Lincoln County Circuit Court in 1984 and went all the way to the Oregon Supreme Court. Luckily the Oregon Supreme Court ruled in favor of

This rocky coastline is the remnant of an ancient lava flow.

allowing public access to this area in 1986. As you hike on this route, you'll pass two spouting horns (areas where the ocean has pushed through cracks in the lava rock and sends sprays of water into the air) and small tide pools. After 0.7 mile you'll reach the end of the paved path. Continue by walking down a set of stairs to the beach and continuing 0.8 mile north to your turnaround point at Vingie Creek. From here you have the option of continuing 1.2 miles north to the Tillicum Beach picnic area. If you are looking for an all-day adventure, continue 4.8 miles north to the Governor Patterson Memorial State Recreation Site.

Miles and Directions

0.0 Start walking on the paved path as it parallels the edge of a rocky shoreline.

0.7 Arrive at steps leading to the beach. Walk down the stairs and continue north on the long sandy beach.

1.5 Arrive at Vingie Creek and a set of small sand dunes (your turnaround point). Retrace the same route back to your starting point. **Option:** Continue 1.2 miles north to the Tillicum Beach picnic area or 4.8 miles north to the Governor Patterson Memorial State Recreation Site.

3.0 Arrive at the trailhead.

Hike Information

Local Information

Yachats Chamber of Commerce, 241 Highway 101, Yachats, OR 97498; (800) 929-0477; www.yachats.org.

Local Events/Attractions

Yachats Smelt Fry, held in July, Yachats; (800) 929-0477; www.yachats.org.

26 Alsea Falls and Green Peak Falls

Waterfall lovers will enjoy this tour of Alsea Falls and Green Peak Falls in the Alsea Falls Recreation Area. The route travels next to the South Fork Alsea River and Alsea Falls and leads you through a cool forest corridor along the banks of smooth-flowing Peak Creek to Green Peak Falls. There is a picnic area at the trailhead, and the campground is just down the road if you want to stay overnight.

Start: The trailhead is located about 49 miles east of Waldport off Oregon Highway 34 and 30 miles west of Corvallis.
Distance: 5 miles out and back.
Approximate hiking time: 2 to 3 hours.
Difficulty: Easy due to smooth trail surface and small amount of elevation gain.
Total climbing: 240 feet. Elevation profiles are not provided for hikes with less than 250 feet of elevation gain.
Trail surface: Forest path, bridges.
Lay of the land: This route travels next to the South Fork of the Alsea River to Alsea Falls and then takes you along Peak Creek to a viewpoint of Green Peak Falls.
Seasons: Year-round.
Other trail users: None.
Canine compatibility: Leashed dogs permitted.
Land status: Bureau of Land Management (BLM).
Nearest town: Alsea.
Fees and permits: No fees or permits required.
Map: Maptech map: Glenbrook, Oregon. Alsea Falls Recreation Site brochure and map published by the BLM, Salem District, 1717 Fabry Road SE, Salem, OR 97306; (503) 375-5646; www.or.blm.gov/salem.
Trail contact: Bureau of Land Management, Salem District, 1717 Fabry Road SE, Salem, OR 97306; (503) 375-5646; www.or.blm.gov/salem.

Finding the trailhead: From U.S. Highway 101 in Waldport, turn east onto OR 34, travel 39.5 miles, and enter the small town of Alsea. At an unsigned road, turn right where a sign states LOBSTER VALLEY and cross the North Fork of the Alsea River. Continue to the junction with South Fork Road and turn left where a sign reads ALSEA FALLS 9/MONROE. Go 8.7 miles (the pavement ends after 1.8 miles) and turn left at a sign for the Alsea Falls Recreation Area. Continue 0.2 mile and park in a large parking area adjacent to the trailhead.

From Corvallis travel 16 miles south on OR 99W to Monroe. In Monroe turn right at a sign for Alpine and follow signs for Alsea Falls, 13.2 miles. Turn right into the Alsea Falls Recreation Area and continue 0.2 mile and park in a large parking area adjacent to the trailhead. *DeLorme: Oregon Atlas & Gazetteer:* Page 47, B5.

The Hike

Begin this hike by walking through the shadowy canopy of a second-growth Douglas fir forest and big-leaf maple along the South Fork Alsea River. You'll take a short stroll next to the river's edge and quickly arrive at a viewpoint of Alsea Falls. This impressive cascade tumbles down a set of blocky basalt rocks into a deep pool below. Swimming is a nice trailside distraction during the summer months.

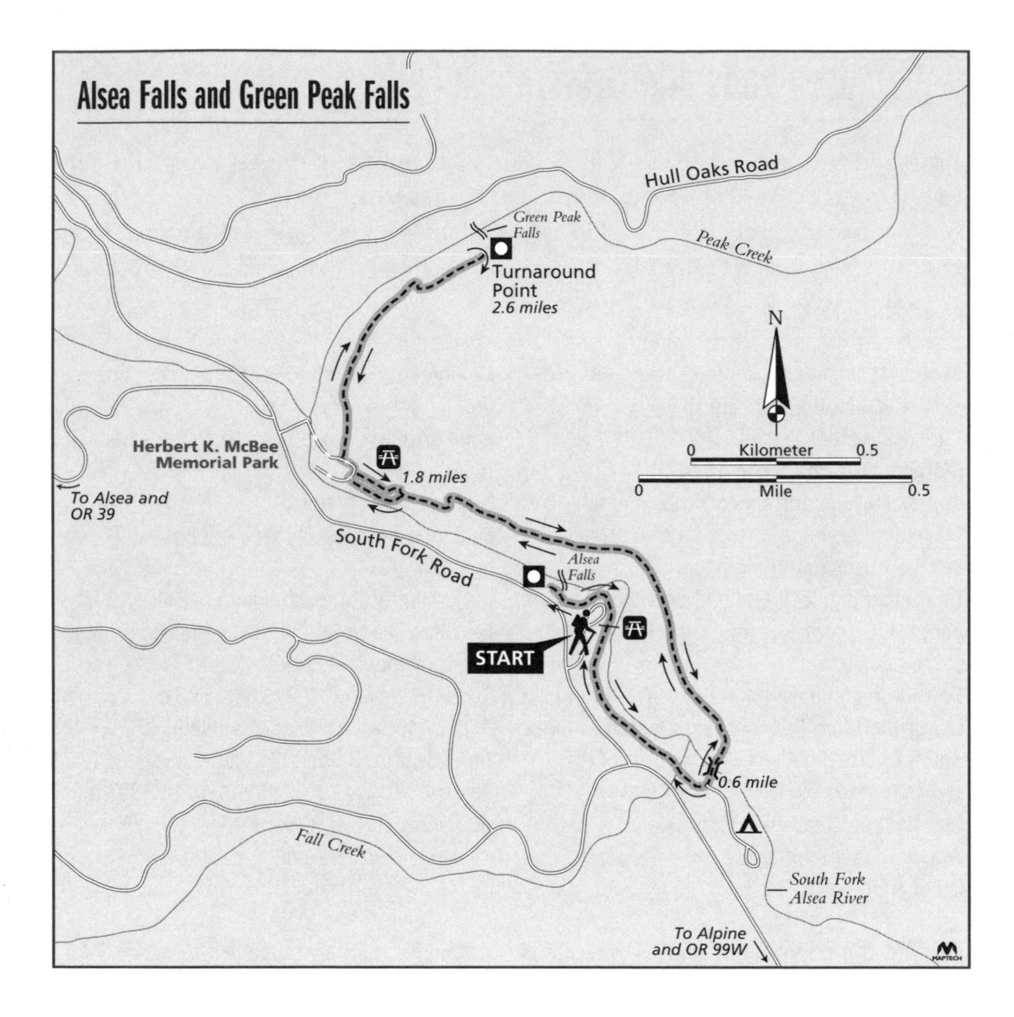

The river and falls were named after the Alsi (Alsea) Indians, who were the original inhabitants of this area. The name has many variations. Lewis and Clark called the tribe Ulseah and a U.S. Coast Survey completed by William P. McArthur in 1851 lists the tribe as Alseya. These self-sufficient people fished for salmon and steelhead from large red cedar canoes. Fish were caught with a net that was dropped between two canoes. They also made larger, 60-foot canoes for ocean travel. The tribe also hunted deer, elk, and sea lions. They harvested the leaves of skunk cabbage and cooked them in an earth oven, and wine was made out of salmonberries and blackberries.

You'll continue upstream as the trail parallels contours of the river. Notice the massive red cedar stumps that are the remains of giant old-growth trees that once stood here. These gentle giants were logged starting in the 1850s when the first white settlers arrived. If you look closely at the stumps, you can see evidence of notches in the tree where spring boards were placed. Loggers stood on the spring boards while they were sawing down the tree. After 0.6 mile you'll cross the river and continue through a maze of green decorated with the bright purple stocks of foxglove, honeysuckle, oxalis, the white triangular flowers of trillium, and small bogs filled with the thick green leaves of skunk cabbage. This area is also haven to Oregon grape—the state flower of Oregon. This plant has a close resemblance to holly. The plant has pinnate leaves with sharp spines and has clusters of small yellow flowers that develop into small, reddish-purple berries that grow in clusters like grapes. The sour berries are high in vitamin C and can be eaten raw or cooked. The leaves, stems, and roots of the plant contain a large amount of a bright yellow alkaloid substance called berberine. This substance is very effective against a variety of infections as well as liver and digestive disorders.

After 1.8 miles you'll turn onto a trail that travels next to Peak Creek for 0.8 mile, leading to a viewpoint of impressive 50-foot Green Peak Falls. From here you'll retrace the same route back to the trailhead.

Alsea Falls. Photo: Ken Skeen

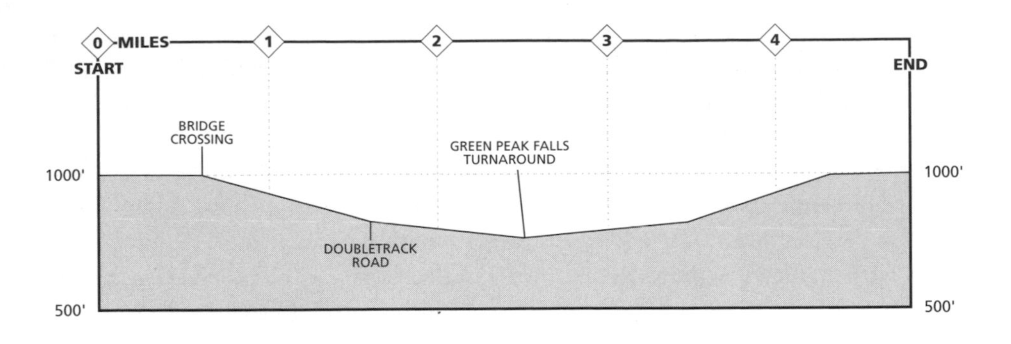

Miles and Directions

0.0 From the parking area walk down to the riverside path and turn left. Continue following the path downstream on a set of switchbacks.

0.1 Arrive at a viewpoint of the terraced cascade of Alsea Falls. After admiring the falls head back to the main riverside trail and head upstream.

0.2 Arrive back at the parking area. Go right on the riverside trail (heading upstream).

0.6 Cross a bridge over the river and then turn left and follow the path downstream.

1.8 The trail turns into a doubletrack road. Follow the road for about 75 yards and look for a brown hiker symbol on the right. Turn right and continue on the forest path as it travels next to Peak Creek.

2.5 Arrive at a viewpoint of 50-foot Green Peak Falls. Retrace the same route back to the trailhead.

5.0 Arrive at the trailhead.

Hike Information

Local Information

Waldport Chamber of Commerce, P.O. Box 669, Waldport, OR 97394; (541) 563-2133; www.casco.net/~waldport.

Local Events/Attractions

Alsea Bay Bridge Interpretive Center, 620 NW Spring Street, Waldport; (541) 563-2002.

27 Cape Perpetua Trails

Take your pick of ten trails that wind through the 2,700-acre Cape Perpetua Scenic Area. Depending on the trail you select, you can experience a botanical wonderland of coastal forest, rocky tide pools, and other ocean spectacles, such as the geyserlike Spouting Horn and the narrow rock channel of Devil's Churn. While you're here, plan on spending a few hours at the Cape Perpetua Interpretive Center. The center provides a good introduction to the plants and animals that live here as well as a look into the area's rich history.

Start: Cape Perpetua is located 3 miles south of Yachats and 22.5 miles north of Florence on U.S. Highway 101.
Distance: Trails vary in length from 0.2 mile to 10 miles.
Approximate hiking time: 30 minutes to 3 hours depending on the trail selected.
Difficulty: Easy to difficult depending on the trail selected.
Total climbing: Varies depending on trail selected.
Trail surface: The trails in the Cape Perpetua Area are a combination of forest paths and paved paths. On the Restless Waters Trail, the stairs that lead down to Devil's Churn can be wet and slippery. Sneaker waves can also catch you off guard at Devil's Churn, and dogs and children should be supervised at all times!
Lay of the land: The trails at Cape Perpetua take you through a variety of landscapes, including old-growth coastal forest, rocky tide pools, and sandy beach.
Seasons: Year-round.
Other trail users: None.
Canine compatibility: Leashed dogs permitted.
Land status: National forest.
Nearest town: Yachats.
Fees and permits: $3.00 day-use permit. A permit can be purchased from the self-pay machine in the parking area or at the visitor center.
Map: Maptech map: Yachats, Oregon.
Trail contact: Cape Perpetua Interpretive Center, 2400 Highway 101, Yachats, OR 97498; (541) 547-3289; www.newportnet.com/capeperpetua.

Finding the trailhead: From Yachats, drive 3 miles south on US 101 to the Cape Perpetua Interpretive Center, located on the left (east) side of the highway.

From Florence, drive 22.5 miles north on US 101 to the Cape Perpetua Interpretive Center, located on the right (east) side of the highway. *DeLorme: Oregon Atlas & Gazetteer:* Page 32, Inset 2, B2.

The Hike

If you're looking to explore the diversity of the Oregon Coast, you'll want to stop by the Cape Perpetua Scenic Area, located 3 miles south of Yachats and approximately 22.5 miles north of Florence off U.S. Highway 101. This 2,700-acre area preserves large stands of coastal forest and rocky tide pools.

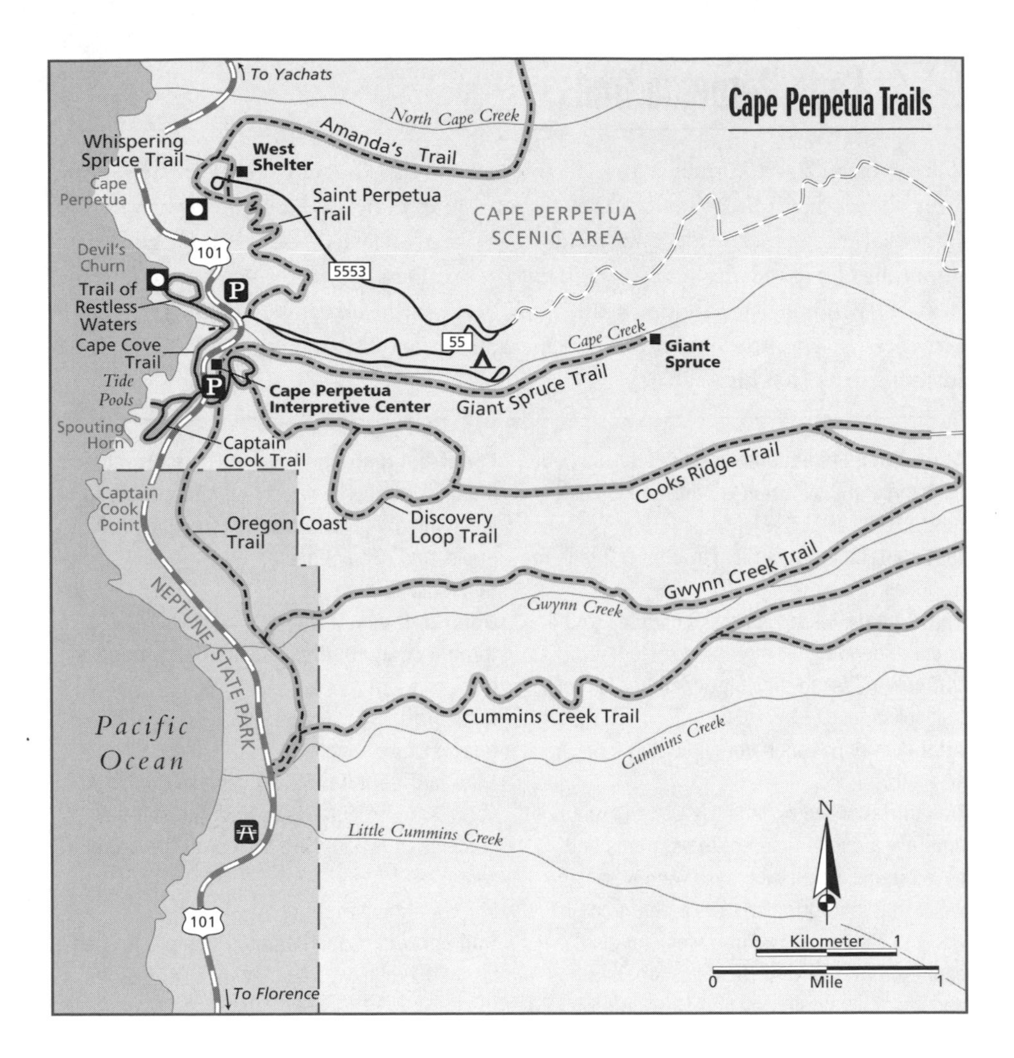

First, stop in and explore the interpretive center, where you'll receive a comprehensive overview of coastal ecology, tides and weather, whale migration, and the history of the Alsea Indian tribe. You'll find interpretive exhibits, films, naturalist lectures, and a good selection of books about coastal ecology.

Each of the ten trails in the Cape Perpetua Scenic Area has something different to offer. For craggy tide pools, sealife, and a bit of Native American culture, hit the 0.6-mile Captain Cook Trail. The trail takes you past the historic Cape Creek Camp building, used by the Civilian Conservation Corp (CCC) from 1933 to 1942 to house the workers who built many of the park's trails and structures. The trail then dips under US 101 past an Indian-shell middens site—where Native Americans discarded shells from the mussels they collected for food. The trail ultimately leads you to rocky tide pools where you'll be able to view sea stars, mussels, hermit crabs, sea anemones, and purple sea urchins. Once you've finished exploring the tide pools, continue on to a viewpoint where you can watch for the geyserlike spray of Spouting Horn, an old sea cave with a small opening in its roof. Waves surge into this cave and shoot out of the small opening, creating a spectacular sea spray.

If you want to see a 500-year-old spruce tree, take the easy 2-mile (round-trip) walk on the Giant Spruce Trail. The trail parallels Cape Creek and leads you through an old-growth forest filled with ferns, salal, thimbleberry, and skunk cabbage. At the turnaround point is the trail's prize feature, an ancient Sitka spruce tree that's about 15 feet in diameter. Another shorter trail that also gives you a feel for the diversity of the coastal forest is the 1-mile Discovery Loop Trail. If you love sweeping views, you'll want to hike on the 2.6-mile round-trip Saint Perpetua Trail, which ascends the south side of Cape Perpetua on a series of fairly steep switchbacks and rewards you with excellent views (on a clear day) of Cape Foulweather to the north and Cape Blanco to the south. For great views without the long hike, walk the easy, 0.25-mile Whispering Spruce Trail. This trail promises spectacular ocean views (on a clear day) and an opportunity to explore the West Shelter, a stone building built by the CCC. If you're in for a longer hike, try the combination Cooks Ridge/Gwynn Creek Loop Trail. This 6.4-mile loop departs from the interpretive center and winds through old-growth forests, offering up several sneak peaks at the

Devil's Churn

ocean. If you're interested in similar scenery but a lengthier hike, pack a lunch and strike out on the 10-mile Cummins Creek Loop Trail. From the interpretive center, the hike heads up the Cooks Ridge Trail and eventually hooks up with the Cummins Creek Trail for a return back to the Oregon Coast Trail. Then it's straight back to the interpretive center.

If you love to watch the churning ocean, head down the 0.4-mile Trail of Restless Waters loop to the rocky tide pool known as Devil's Churn. The rough, porous texture of the shoreline rock here is evidence of its volcanic past. Roughly forty million years ago, offshore volcanoes deposited lava along the shoreline. As the molten rock cooled, hot gases within forced their way to the surface, giving us the porous texture. The pounding surf carved into the rock to form a sea cave. At some point the roof of the cave collapsed, leaving behind the long, wide rock channel that forms Devil's Churn. The force of the waves crashing in the channel sends spectacular sprays of water dozens of feet into the air. If you're hiking with children or dogs, keep a close eye on them. The slippery surface of the rocks and sneaker waves can catch you off balance if you get too close to the edge of the channel.

Miles and Directions

The Whispering Spruce Trail is accessed 2.25 miles from the interpretive center via Forest Road 55 and then FR 5553. The Saint Perpetua Trail, Cape Cove Trail, Giant Spruce Trail, Captain Cook Trail, Oregon Coast Trail, Discovery Loop Trail, Cooks Ridge/Gwynn Creek Loop Trail, and the Cummins Creek Loop Trail can be accessed from the interpretive center. The Trail of Restless Waters starts from the Devil's Churn parking area, 0.7 mile north of the interpretive center off US 101.

A. Whispering Spruce Trail–0.25-mile loop
B. Saint Perpetua Trail–2.6 miles out and back
C. Trail of Restless Waters–0.4-mile loop
D. Cape Cove Trail–0.3 mile
E. Giant Spruce Trail–2-miles out and back
F. Captain Cook Trail–0.6-mile loop
G. Oregon Coast Trail–2.6 miles out and back
H. Discovery Loop Trail–1-mile loop
I. Cooks Ridge/Gwynn Creek Loop Trail–6.4-mile loop
J. Cummins Creek Loop Trail–10-mile loop

Hike Information

Local Information

Florence Chamber of Commerce, 270 Highway 101, Florence, OR 97439; (800) 524-4864; www.florencechamber.com.
Yachats Chamber of Commerce, 441 Highway 101, Yachats, OR 97439; (800) 929-0477; www.yachats.org.

Local Events/Attractions

Sea Lion Caves, 91560 Highway 101 North, Florence; (541) 547-3111; www.sealioncaves.com.

28 Heceta Head Lighthouse

Take a picturesque walk to one of Oregon's most photographed lighthouses. Nestled on the edge of the coastal protrusion Heceta Head, the 205-foot-tall Heceta Head Lighthouse is a welcoming beacon to ships and hikers alike.

Start: The trailhead is located 12 miles north of Florence and 14 miles south of Yachats on U.S. Highway 101.
Distance: 1 mile out and back.
Approximate hiking time: 30 minutes to 1 hour.
Difficulty: Easy due to well-maintained gravel path and minimal elevation gain.
Total climbing: 200 feet. Elevation profiles are not provided for hikes with less than 250 feet of elevation gain.
Trail surface: Gravel path.
Lay of the land: This trail takes you through a thick coastal forest, past a historic bed-and-breakfast, and to the picturesque Heceta Head Lighthouse, which is perched high on a cliff above a scenic cove.
Seasons: Year-round.
Other trail users: None.
Canine compatibility: Leashed dogs permitted.
Land status: State park.
Nearest town: Florence.
Fees and permits: $3.00 day-use fee.
Map: Maptech map: Heceta Head, Oregon.
Trail contact: Oregon State Parks and Recreation, Suite 1, 1115 Commercial Street NE, Salem, OR 97301; (800) 551-6949; www.oregonstateparks.org/park_124.php.

Finding the trailhead: From Florence, drive 12 miles north on US 101 to the Heceta Head Lighthouse State Scenic Viewpoint (also known as Devil's Elbow State Park) sign. Turn left (west) and proceed 0.3 mile to the parking area. The hike begins on the north end of the parking lot.

From Yachats, drive 14 miles south on US 101 to the Heceta Head Lighthouse State Scenic Viewpoint (also known as Devil's Elbow State Park) sign. Turn right (west) and proceed 0.3 mile to the parking area. The hike begins on the north end of the parking lot. *DeLorme: Oregon Atlas & Gazetteer:* Page 32 Inset 2, C2.

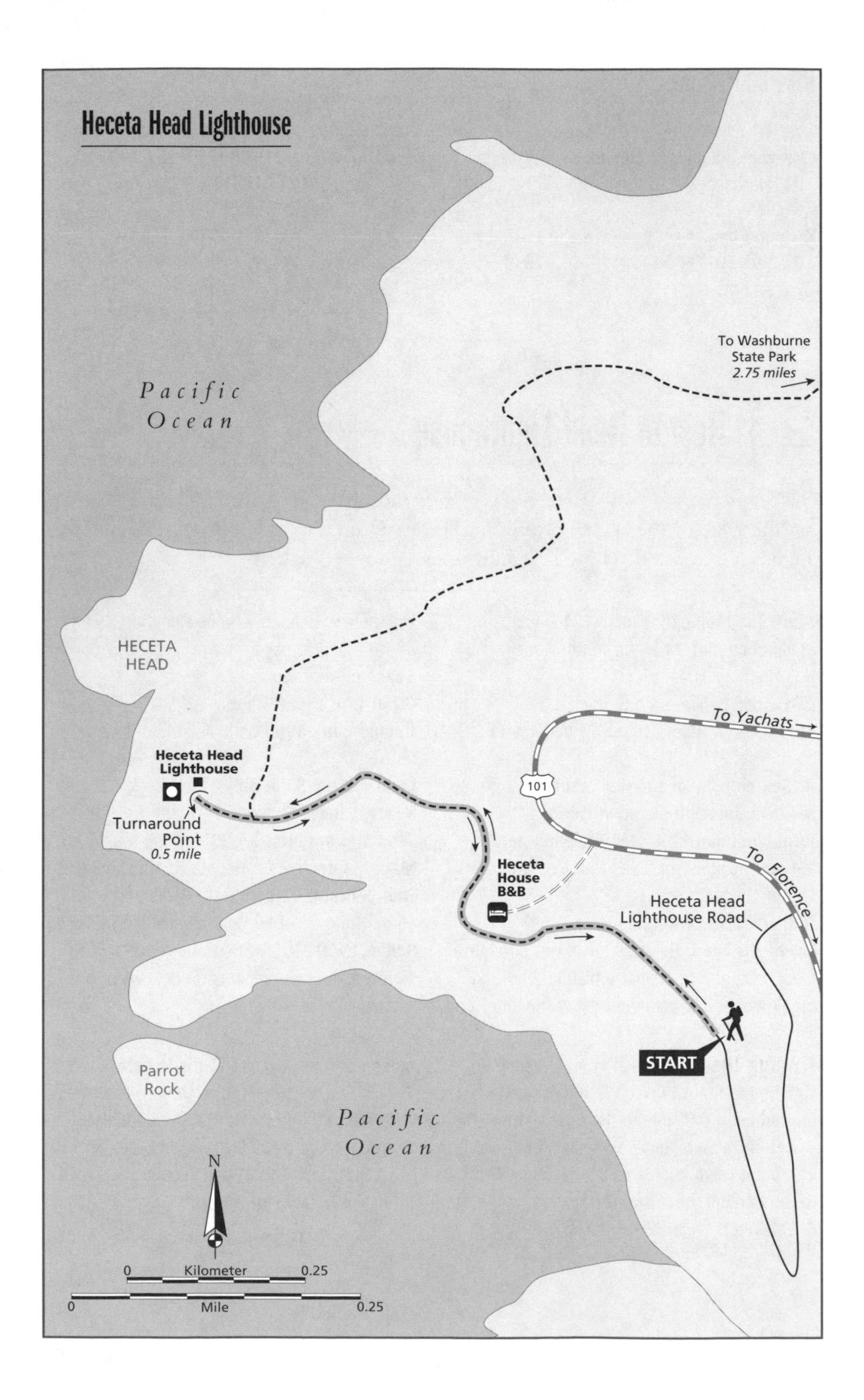
Heceta Head Lighthouse
Pacific
Ocean
HECETA
HEAD
To Washburne
State Park
2.75 miles
Heceta Head
Lighthouse
Turnaround
Point
0.5 mile
To Yachats
101
To Florence
Heceta
House
B&B
Heceta Head
Lighthouse Road
START
Parrot
Rock
Pacific
Ocean
N
0
Kilometer
0.25
0
Mile
0.25

The Hike

The Heceta Head Lighthouse (that's "huh-SEE-tuh") stands as a quiet sentinel on the Central Oregon Coast shining its beacon 21 miles out to sea. This magnificent structure was built in 1894 over a period of two years and at a cost of $80,000. The stone was shipped to the site from Oregon City, and the bricks and cement were brought in from San Francisco. Local sawmills supplied the wood, and the two-ton Fresnel lens was handcrafted and brought in by boat. The lighthouse and the scenic headland on which it sits owe their name to Captain Bruno Heceta, a Spanish captain who sailed his ship *Corvette* from Mexico to this part of the Oregon Coast. George Davidson, of the Coastal Survey, officially named the point in 1862.

The whitewashed lighthouse is accessed by a 1-mile out-and-back trail that starts at the north end of the Heceta Head Lighthouse State Scenic Viewpoint parking lot. The wide gravel path begins by climbing through a thick coastal cedar and fir forest dotted with sword fern, wild iris, and salal. Picnic tables have been set up so visitors can enjoy the sweeping view of the rocky shore and rugged cape, as well as the 220-foot crowning arch of the Cape Creek Bridge. This bridge is just one of 162 bridges designed and built by Conde McCullough, head of the bridge division for the Oregon Department of Transportation from 1920 to 1935. In fact, McCullough designed virtually all of the bridges on the Oregon Coast Highway, using innovative

This Queen Anne–style house is the former light keeper's house. It is now a bed-and-breakfast.

techniques to overcome the many challenges of building coastal bridges. One of the biggest challenges he faced was how to design bridges that used materials other than steel, which doesn't hold up well in the stormy, salty air of the Oregon coast. He also needed a material that was strong enough to span the region's wide estuaries. His solution was to use the Freyssinet method, developed in France, to build bridges that used arches made of prestressed concrete. Construction on this scenic highway began in 1927, and by 1936 the final bridges were finished.

At mile 0.2 you pass the immaculately maintained light keeper's house. Built in 1893, this lovely Queen Anne–style house is now being used by the U.S. Forest Service as an interpretive center and B&B. In the spring you may spot the teardrop-shaped petals of white lilies scattered along this section of trail. A white picket fence surrounds the house, which has three upper-story rooms. Picture windows offer a grand view of the rocky coast and lighthouse, and everything is topped off with a bright red roof.

Continue another 0.3 mile to reach the lighthouse and your turnaround point. Just before you reach the lighthouse you have the option to turn right and hike 3.0 miles north to Washburne State Park. After you've soaked in the views of the lighthouse, glance to the offshore promontory called Parrot Rock, which is an important nesting area for the Brandt's cormorants. Tours of the lighthouse are offered daily and include climbs to the top, where the intricate Fresnel lens is on display.

Miles and Directions

0.0 Start at the north end of the parking area. (FYI: Before you begin, check out the interpretive signs that give you an in-depth view of the history of the lighthouse and light keeper's house.)

0.2 Pass the light keeper's house on your right. Just before the lighthouse you'll arrive at a trail junction. Continue straight. **Option:** You can turn right and hike north. You'll arrive at Washburne State Park in 3.0 miles.

0.5 Reach 205-foot Heceta Head Lighthouse, your turnaround point.

1.0 Arrive back at the parking area.

Hike Information

Local Information

Florence Chamber of Commerce, 270 Highway 101, Florence, OR 97439; (800) 524-4864; www.florencechamber.com.

Yachats Chamber of Commerce, 441 Highway 101, Yachats, OR 97498; (800) 929-0477; www.yachats.org.

Local Events/Attractions

Sea Lion Caves, 91560 Highway 101 North, Florence; (541) 547-3111; www.sealioncaves.com.

29 Sutton Creek Recreation Area

The Sutton Creek Recreation Area has more than 6 miles of trails to explore, giving you a close-up view of a diverse coastal ecosystem made up of sand dunes, coastal forest, freshwater lakes, a coastal stream, and sandy beach. The Sutton Creek Campground has a short walk through a wet bog where you can view the interesting insect-eating plant the cobra lily.

Start: From the trailhead located approximately 5 miles north of Florence off U.S. Highway 101.
Distance: Varies depending on the trails selected.
Approximate hiking time: 1 to 4 hours.
Difficulty: Easy to moderate. The trail through the sand dunes is moderately hard. The hike to Sutton Beach requires that you ford Sutton Creek.
Total climbing: None. Elevation profiles are not provided for hikes with less than 250 feet of elevation gain.
Trail surface: Sand, dirt path, wooden walkway, and beach walking.
Lay of the land: You can hike through a coastal forest along Sutton Creek, walk through loose sand through the Sutton Creek Sand Dunes, or look at rare and interesting plants on a wooden walkway on the Bog Trail.
Seasons: Year-round.
Other trail users: None.
Canine compatibility: Leashed dogs permitted. Dogs are not allowed in certain areas from March 15 to September 30 because they may disturb the nesting of rare birds. Restricted areas are posted.
Land status: National forest.
Nearest town: Florence.
Fees and permits: $5.00 day-use fee, payable at the self-pay station at the Holman Vista Parking Area.
Map: Maptech map: Mercer Lake, Oregon.
Trail contact: Oregon Dunes National Recreation Area, 855 Highway Avenue, Reedsport, OR 97467; (541) 271-3611; www.fs.fed.us/r6/siuslaw.

Finding the trailhead: To the Sutton Creek Campground Trailhead: Drive 4.2 miles north of Florence on US 101 to Sutton Beach Road and turn left (west) at the SUTTON RECREATION sign. Proceed 0.7 mile and turn right into the Sutton Creek Campground. At the T intersection, turn left (toward the A loop of campsites) and drive approximately 0.2 mile to the Sutton Group Camp parking area, located between campsites A18 and A19. The trailhead is located on the right side of the Sutton Group Camp parking area.

To the Holman Vista Day-Use Parking Area: Drive 4.2 miles north of Florence on US 101 to Sutton Beach Road and turn left (west) at the SUTTON RECREATION sign. Drive 2 miles west to the day-use parking area. There's a $5.00 day-use fee. You can obtain a day-use permit at the self-service pay station in the parking area. *DeLorme: Oregon Atlas & Gazetteer:* Page 32, Inset 2, D2.

The Hike

The roughly 2,700-acre Sutton Creek Recreation Area preserves a unique coastal environment within Oregon's Siuslaw National Forest. Protected within the recreation

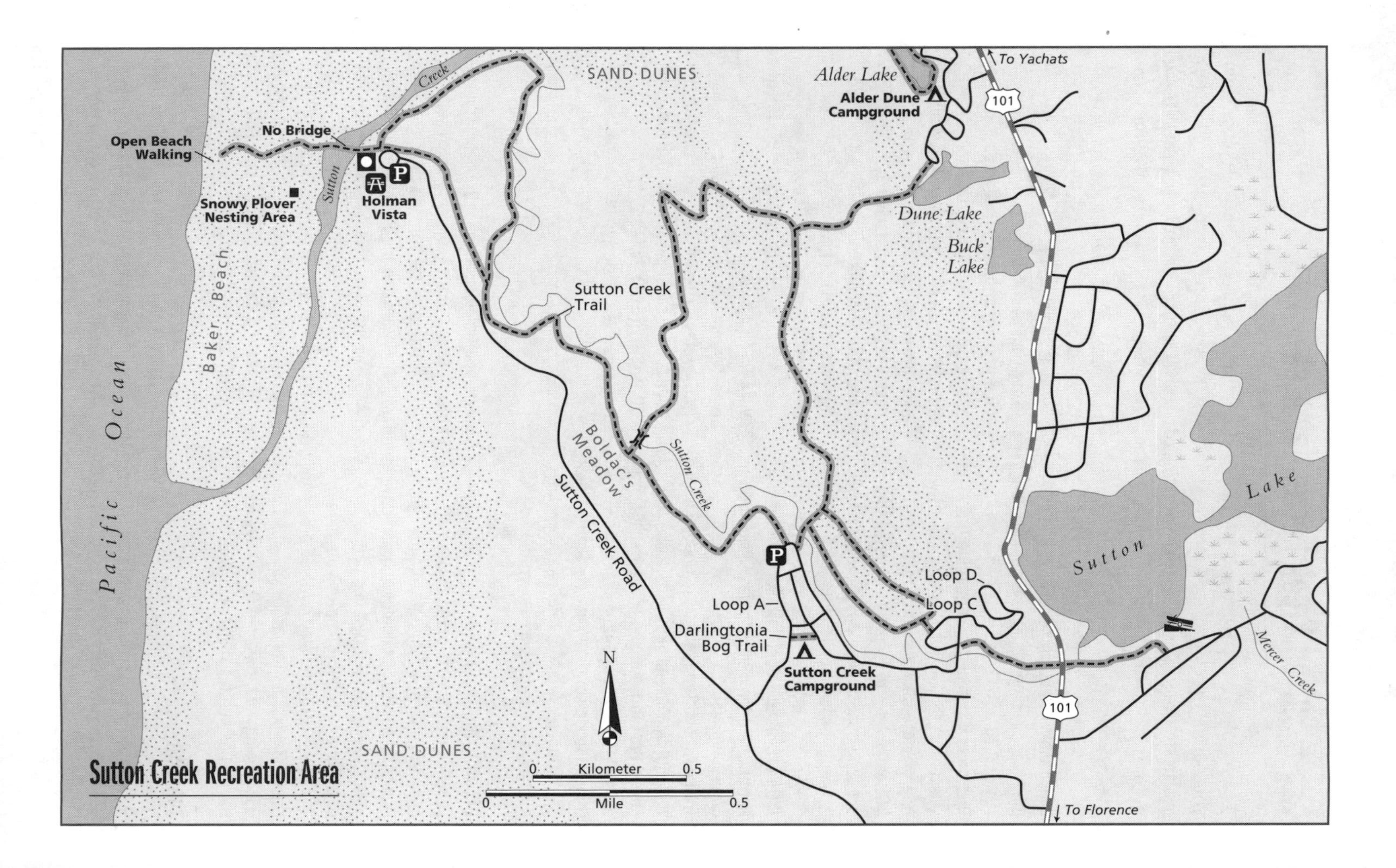
Sutton Creek Recreation Area
SAND DUNES
Alder Lake
Alder Dune Campground
To Yachats
101
Open Beach Walking
No Bridge
Creek
Sutton
Snowy Plover Nesting Area
Holman Vista
Dune Lake
Buck Lake
Baker Beach
Pacific Ocean
Sutton Creek Trail
Boldac's Meadow
Sutton Creek
Sutton Creek Road
Loop D
Loop C
Loop A
Darlingtonia Bog Trail
Sutton Creek Campground
Sutton Lake
Mercer Creek
101
To Florence
N
SAND DUNES
0 Kilometer 0.5
0 Mile 0.5

Spectacular sand dunes at Sutton Creek Recreation Area

area are fragile coastal forests and freshwater lakes, not to mention the region's trademark dunes. If you're of the mind that a sand dune is a sand dune is a sand dune, you're missing out on some interesting distinctions. The Sutton Creek area contains a variety of sand dunes, including foredunes, traverse dunes, oblique dunes, and parabola dunes.

You begin with the foredune, and as you move inland, you find hummocks, a deflation plain, transverse dunes, tree islands, oblique dunes, parabola dunes, and transition forest. Foredunes parallel the ocean and can form 20 to 30 feet high. Nowadays you'll find these dunes covered with European beach grass, a non-native plant species introduced by settlers in the early 1900s to stabilize the soil. Since being sown, the European beach grass has spread rapidly, interrupting the natural movement of sand—the mark of an active dune—and altering the landscape.

Following the foredunes are hummocks, which form when sand collects around vegetation. In winter you may notice these as small sand islands, the result of the water table rising to fill the depressions around the hummocks. Farther inland from the hummocks is the deflation plain. You can recognize a deflation plain by its fairly flat landscape. As the foredunes block new sand from moving inland, the wind carries off the remaining dry sand, leaving only wet sand behind—thus deflating the area. The wet sand is a great environment for plants such as bush lupine, Scotch broom, yarrow, and a variety of scented grasses such as the large-headed sage, salt rush, and the invasive European beach grass. Farther inland are traverse dunes, created when the northwesterly winds of summer sculpt wavy crests into 5- to 20-foot sand hills. Traverse dunes are perpendicular to the wind direction, and during the winter months the southwesterly winds tend to flatten out the crests. The next transition zone is the tree island. These small stands of trees are remnants of a prior coastal forest that was buried by the moving sand. Tree islands have steep, unstable slopes, which are highly susceptible to erosion. Even farther inland are oblique dunes. These sloped dunes can reach a height of 180 feet and can be up to a mile long. The west face of an oblique dune is long and gentle, and the east side is steep—this is due to the winds hitting the dunes from the northwest and southwest. The constant pushing of the sand from the west side creates a longer, gentler west face. Due to the winds that are constantly shaping this type of dune and its instability, plants do not grow on oblique dunes.

The transition forest zone is where the sand-dune environment meets up with the land environment. This type of forest is filled with a variety of plants that thrive in the windy, sandy environment, such as shore pines, rhododendrons, salal, and thimbleberry. The large, sandy, U-shaped ridge in the middle of the coastal forest is the parabola dune. Constant wind erodes the soil so that plants can live here.

The Sutton Creek Recreation Area is filled with a variety of trail options to explore this diverse community. From Sutton Creek Campground you can hike the 2.25-mile trail to scenic Baker Beach, the breeding ground for the endangered western snowy plover. Along the way you get a taste of ever-changing sand dunes and lush coastal forests of shore pine, rhododendrons, thimbleberry, salal, and spruce trees. You might even see otter swimming in Sutton Creek or osprey fishing along its banks. Other trail options from Sutton Creek Campground include hiking 1.75 miles to Alder Dune Campground, where you can hike to Dune Lake and Alder Lake.

If you want to see the rare insect-eating cobra lily plant, hike the wheelchair-accessible Darlingtonia Bog Trail, located just to the right of the Sutton Creek Campground entrance. These one-of-a-kind plants lure insects into their slow-but-sure traps and digest them slowly. The insects provide the much-needed nutrients that are lacking in the nutrient-poor coastal soil.

If you park at the Holman Vista day-use parking area, walk up the wheelchair-accessible walkway to Holman Vista, where you have far-reaching views of the rolling sand dunes, the scenic beach, and the rambling Sutton Creek. Notice the bent and twisted shore-pine trees. These rugged trees are called krumholzes, and their irregular shape is due to the constant wind and salt air that batter them on the windward side.

Miles and Directions

You can access the trails in the Sutton Creek Area from the Sutton Creek Campground and the Holman Vista day-use parking area trailhead. Refer to the map for individual trails.

Hike Information

Local Information

Florence Chamber of Commerce, 270 Highway 101, Florence, OR 97439; (800) 524-4864; www.florencechamber.com.

Local Events/Attractions

Oregon Dune Mushers Mail Run, held in March, Florence; (800) 255-5959.

Rhododendron Festival, held in May, Florence; (800) 524-4864; www.florencechamber.com.

WESTERN SNOWY PLOVERS The Pacific Coast breeding colonies of western snowy plovers can be found from southern Washington to Baja California. Snowy plovers are sparrow-size birds with a dusty, sand-colored back and a white underside with a black chest band. They like to nest in open sandy areas next to the water. The plover's nesting season is from mid-March through mid-September. They usually lay two to three greenish brown eggs in a sandy depression above the beach. In 2001, 110 nesting adults were counted along the southern Oregon coast. Out of 110 nests, only 34 were successful, producing 94 hatchlings. Study areas include Necanicum Spit, Bayocean Spit, Sutton Beach, Siltcoos, Dunes Overlook, Tahkenitch, Tenmile, Coos Bay North Spit, Bandon State Natural Area, New River, and Floras Lake.

The snowy plover's rapid decline is due to several different factors. The encroachment of European beach grass has caused a large amount of habitat loss. The grass stabilizes dunes and reduces the amount of unvegetated area above the tide line, making the sandy beach narrower and steeper, and ultimately making the nesting area less suitable for the birds. Predators are one of the main reasons for the decline in snowy plover populations. Major predators include gulls, crows, ravens, skunks, dogs, coyotes, foxes, cats, opossums, raccoons, hawks, and owls. The most preventable factor is human impact on nesting habitat. Off-road vehicle use, loose dogs, walking and running on the beach, and beach raking have all taken their toll.

Unfortunately, the nesting season for the snowy plover coincides with the highest traffic season of beachgoers. Measures have been introduced to help protect the snowy plover. Nesting sites are now fenced off, thereby minimizing human impact, and nest enclosures have been introduced to protect the birds from predators. After you reach the beach, keep a lookout for these quick birds as they run up and down the beach feeding on crabs, marine worms, beetles, sand hoppers, shore flies, and other insects.

30 Siltcoos Lake

This loop hike winds through a shady Sitka spruce forest, taking you to the edge of 3,500-acre Siltcoos Lake—the largest freshwater lake on the Oregon Coast. Here you'll have a good chance of seeing blue herons and a variety of other waterfowl.

Start: Siltcoos Lake Trailhead, located 7 miles south of Florence (or 13 miles north of Reedsport) on the east side of U.S. Highway 101.
Distance: 4.4-mile loop.
Approximate hiking time: 2 to 3 hours.
Difficulty: Easy.
Total climbing: 440 feet.
Trail surface: Forest path.
Lay of the land: This hike travels through a coastal forest to the shores of Siltcoos Lake.
Seasons: Year-round.
Other trail users: Mountain bikers.
Canine compatibility: Dogs permitted.
Land status: National forest.
Nearest town: Florence.
Fees and permits: Requires a Northwest Forest $5.00 day pass, or you can purchase a $30.00 annual pass. You can purchase a pass on-line at www.fs.fed.us/r6/feedemo, or by calling (800) 270-7504.
Map: Maptech maps: Florence, Goose Pasture, Fivemile Creek, Tahkenitch Creek, Oregon.
Trail contact: Siuslaw National Forest, Mapleton Ranger District, 4480 Highway 101, Building G, Florence, OR 97439; (541) 902-8526; www.fs.fed.us/r6/siuslaw.

Finding the trailhead: From Florence, travel 7 miles south on US 101. Turn left (east) at the Siltcoos Lake Trail sign.

From Reedsport, travel about 13 miles north on US 101. Turn right (east) into the Siltcoos Lake Trail parking lot. *DeLorme: Oregon Atlas & Gazetteer:* Page 32, Inset 3, A4.

The Hike

The Oregon Dunes National Recreation Area, established in 1972, is a 50-square-mile area of sand dunes that are present along a narrow band of coastline between Florence and North Bend on the southern Oregon coast. These minimountains of sand are constantly being sculpted and resculpted by the Pacific winds and, at times, can reach heights of more than 300 feet.

Millions of years ago this part of Oregon was completely under water. Comprised mostly of sand, the seafloor was eventually raised out of the ocean during the continental uplift to form the sedimentary rock that makes up Oregon's present-day coastal range. Throughout millions of years, wind and rain eroded the sandstone of the coastal mountains. The resulting sand was carried back to the ocean by rivers, where it was deposited, once again, on the ocean floor. Strong ocean currents moving northward in the winter and southward in the summer keep this sand just offshore. Tides, currents, and waves then deposit this sand on the gently sloping Oregon shores. Once the sand dries, strong prevailing coastal winds blow the smaller, lighter grains of sand inland to eventually form the giant dunes you see today.

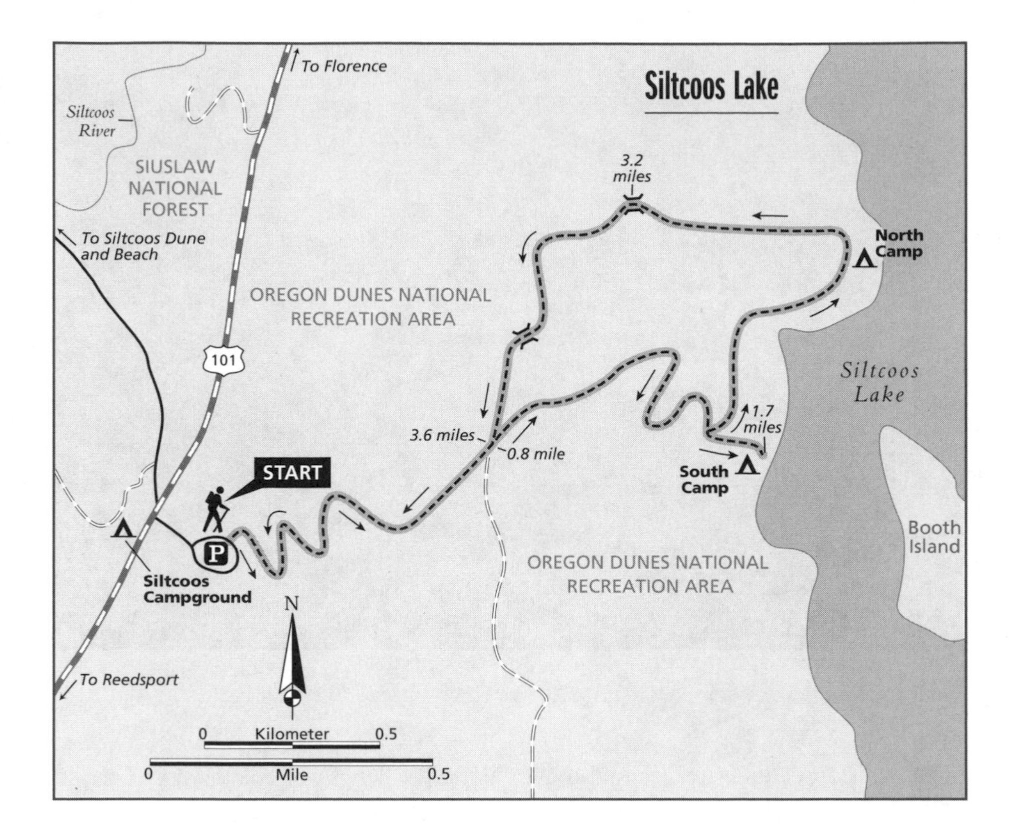

These dunes can stretch inland for up to 3 miles and intermingle with coastal forests and freshwater lakes, creating an interesting patchwork of coastal ecosystems. One unique ecosystem worth visiting is the Darlingtonia Botanical Wayside, located 5 miles north of Florence off U.S. Highway 101. A short hike into a small wetland conveys you to the park's main attraction—the insect-eating cobra lily (Darlingtonia Californica). These unique plants have resorted to their meat-eating ways because of the lack of nutrients in the coastal soil. They lure insects into their slow-but-sure traps and digest these victims for their much-needed nutrients.

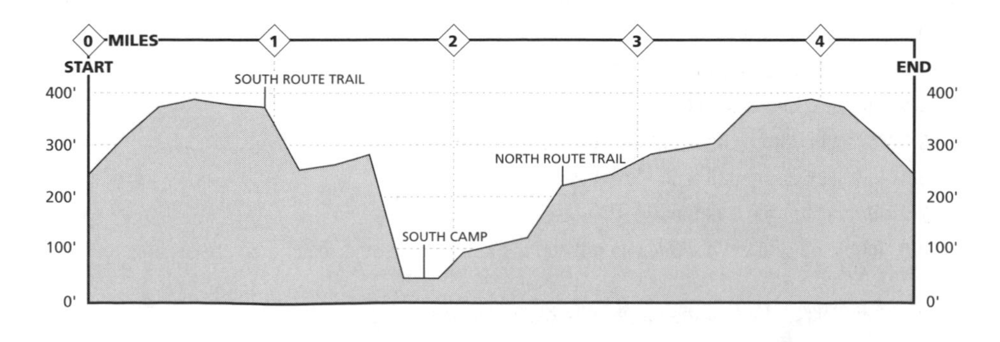

Siltcoos Lake

A variety of freshwater lakes also exist along this length of coastland as a result of sand dunes blocking small streams that once extended to the ocean. Woahink, Siltcoos, Tahkenitch, and Threemile Lakes, located between Florence and Reedsport, all have something unique to offer.

This 4.4-mile hike winds through a beautiful coastal forest and takes you to the shores of Siltcoos Lake, where you may see blue herons and a variety of ducks. This lake was named after a local Indian chief and his family and is the largest freshwater lake on the Oregon Coast, encompassing a total of 3,500 acres. It supports a number of islands and freshwater marshes and is brimming with a variety of fish, such as steelhead, cutthroat trout, bass, perch, blue gill, and catfish.

Miles and Directions

0.0 Start hiking at the signed trailhead.

0.8 Turn right and take the South Route Trail.

1.5 Turn right and descend steeply toward South Camp.

1.7 At South Camp, check out the lake, then turn around and hike back up the hill.

2.0 Turn right at the trail fork.

2.3 Turn right at the trail fork.

2.5 Turn left at the trail fork. You'll continue a short distance and reach a campsite. Stay to the left.

2.6 Turn right and follow the north route back to your starting point.

3.6 Turn right at the trail fork.

4.4 Arrive at the trailhead.

Hike Information

Local Information

Florence Chamber of Commerce, 270 Highway 101, Florence, OR 97439; (800) 524-4864; www.florencechamber.com.

Local Events/Attractions

Oregon Dune Mushers Mail Run, held in March, Florence; (800) 255-5959.

Rhododendron Festival, held in May, Florence; (800) 524-4864; www.florencechamber.com.

31 Siltcoos River Estuary Trails

Plan on spending the day exploring river, beach, and estuary environments that are teeming with wildlife.

Start: These trails can be accessed from the Stagecoach trailhead and the Lagoon trailhead, about 8 miles south of Florence (or 13 miles north of Reedsport) off U.S. Highway 101.

Distance: Varies depending on the trail selected.

Lagoon Trail—1-mile loop

Waxmyrtle Trail—2.4 miles out and back

Chief Tsiltcoos Trail—1.2-mile loop

Approximate hiking time: 30 minutes to 1 hour depending on the trail selected.

Difficulty: Easy.

Total climbing: None. Elevation profiles are not provided for hikes with less than 250 feet of elevation gain.

Trail surface: Forest path, beach, wooden ramps.

Lay of the land: These trails pass through coastal forest, river, estuary, and beach environments in the Oregon Dunes National Recreation Area.

Seasons: Year-round. The Waxmyrtle Trail may be flooded during the winter months.

Other trail users: None.

Canine compatibility: Leashed dogs permitted.

Land status: National recreation area.

Nearest town: Florence.

Fees and permits: Requires a Northwest Forest $5.00 day pass, or you can purchase a $30.00 annual pass. You can purchase a pass on-line at www.fs.fed.us/r6/feedemo, or by calling (800) 270-7504.

Map: Maptech maps: Goose Pasture, Oregon.

Trail contact: Oregon Dunes National Recreation Area, 855 Highway Avenue, Reedsport, OR 97467; (541) 271-3611; www.fs.fed.us/r6/siuslaw.

Finding the trailhead: To reach the Lagoon Trailhead: travel 8 miles south of Florence on US 101 (or 13 miles north of Reedsport), turn west on Siltcoos Beach Road, and travel 0.75 mile to the Lagoon Trailhead, located on the right side of the road at the entrance to Lagoon Campground. To reach the Stagecoach Trailhead (which gives you access to the Chief Tsiltcoos and

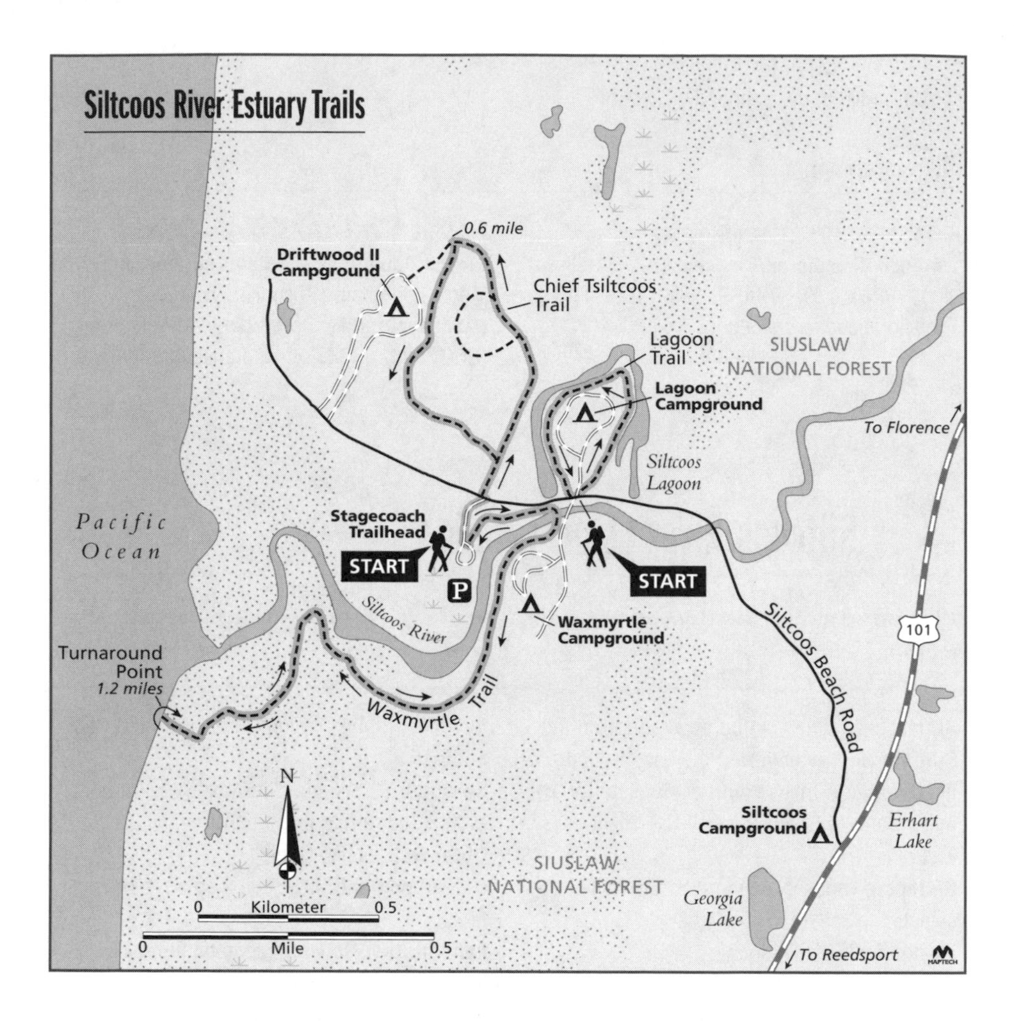

Waxmyrtle Trails), continue west on Siltcoos Beach Road 0.25 mile to a parking area located on the left side of the road. *DeLorme: Oregon Atlas & Gazetteer:* Page 32, Inset 3, A4.

The Hike

Take your pick of three different trails that explore the Siltcoos River Estuary. You can hike along the shores of the smooth-flowing Siltcoos River on the Waxmyrtle Trail, walk around a lush lagoon on the Lagoon Trail, or stroll through a woodsy setting on the Chief Tsiltcoos Trail.

The Waxmyrtle Trail gives you opportunities to view abundant bird life along the Siltcoos River. If you're lucky you may spot osprey soaring overhead searching for the next fish meal. The trail travels through coastal woodlands along the south bank of the river. After 0.9 mile you'll turn right and continue following a sandy roadbed to where it ends at the beach after 1.2 miles. This area is an important snowy plover nesting site. Watch for posted signs that identify protected areas. After exploring the beach return on the same trail. If you are still feeling adventurous, you can explore the Chief Tsiltcoos Trail, which can be accessed opposite the Stagecoach trailhead. This 1.2-mile loop trail travels through a lush coastal forest made up of shore pine, salal, huckleberries, and wild rhododendrons (that start blooming in March). This trail also has a shorter loop option that circles a small, forested bluff.

Another hiking option is the 1-mile Lagoon Loop Trail. This trail is made up of dirt paths and boardwalks that circle a small lagoon that was once a tributary of the Siltcoos River. The tributary was cut off when Siltcoos Beach Road was built. From this trail you may see nutria, beaver, blue herons, snowy egrets, or bitterns. If you want to stay overnight, you have your choice of three campgrounds: Driftwood Campground II, Lagoon Campground, and Waxmyrtle Campground.

Miles and Directions

Lagoon Trail

0.0 Start walking on the trail located on the right side of the Lagoon Campground Entrance Road. Follow the loop trail as it circles a small lagoon and Lagoon Campground.

1.5 Arrive at the trailhead.

Siltcoos River

Waxmyrtle Trail

0.0 From the Stagecoach trailhead parking lot, start walking on the signed trail that travels east and parallels Siltcoos Beach Road.

0.2 Turn right and cross a bridge over the Siltcoos River. After crossing the bridge turn right onto the forest path that travels along the south bank of the river.

0.9 Turn right and follow a sandy roadbed to the beach.

1.2 Arrive at the beach and your turnaround point. Retrace the same route back to the trailhead.

2.4 Arrive at the trailhead.

Chief Tsiltcoos Trail

0.0 From the Stagecoach trailhead cross Siltcoos Beach Road and start walking on the signed forest path. Go about 30 yards to a trail junction. Go right to start the loop portion of the hike.

0.1 Continue straight (right) at the trail junction.

0.6 Turn left at the trail junction. (FYI: The trail that heads right goes to Driftwood II Campground.)

1.2 Turn right at the trail junction to end the loop portion of the hike. Go 30 yards to the junction with Siltcoos Beach Road. Cross the road and arrive at the trailhead.

Hike Information

Local Information

Florence Chamber of Commerce, 270 Highway 101, Florence, OR 97439; (800) 524-4864; www.florencechamber.com.

Local Events/Attractions

Oregon Dune Mushers Mail Run, held in March, Florence; (800) 255-5959.

Rhododendron Festival, held in May, Florence; (800) 524-4864; www.florencechamber.com.

32 Tahkenitch Creek

This pleasant loop route takes you through a coastal dune environment along picturesque Tahkenitch Creek in the Oregon Dunes National Recreation Area.

Start: The trailhead is located 9.2 miles north of Reedsport (or 12 miles south of Florence) off U.S. Highway 101.
Distance: 1.5-mile loop (with longer options).
Approximate hiking time: 45 minutes to 1 hour.
Difficulty: Easy due to smooth trail surface and minimal elevation gain.
Total climbing: 50 feet. Elevation profiles are not provided for hikes with less than 250 feet of elevation gain.
Trail surface: Forest path and sandy trail.
Lay of the land: This route travels through coastal forest and dunes along the shores of charming Tahkenitch Creek in the Oregon Dunes National Recreation Area.
Seasons: Year-round.
Other trail users: None.
Canine compatibility: Leashed dogs permitted.
Land status: National Recreation Area.
Nearest town: Reedsport.
Fees and permits: Requires a Northwest Forest $5.00 day pass, or you can purchase a $30.00 annual pass. You can purchase a pass on-line at www.fs.fed.us/r6/feedemo, or by calling (800) 270-7504.
Map: Maptech map: Tahkenitch Creek, Oregon.
Trail contact: Oregon Dunes National Recreation Area, 855 Highway Avenue, Reedsport, OR 97467; (541) 271-3611; www.fs.fed.us/r6/siuslaw.

Finding the trailhead: From the junction of Oregon Highway 38 and US 101 in Reedsport, travel 9.2 miles north (or 12 miles south of Florence) on US 101 to the Tahkenitch Creek trailhead, located on the west side of the highway.

The Hike

This short loop hike is one of three loop hikes that you can try from the Tahkenitch trailhead. This route covers 1.5 miles, and the other optional routes are 2.5 and 4 miles long. You can also hike to the beach and hook up with the Tahkenitch Dunes Trail.

You'll start this route by walking through thick coastal woodland dotted with pink-flowered rhododendrons and blue-berried salal. Soon you'll arrive at a nice viewpoint of smooth-flowing Tahkenitch Creek when you reach a footbridge spanning the creek. Look for mink, otters, ducks, and geese. After 0.4 mile you'll begin the loop portion of the hike. Here the landscape changes to a dune environment characterized by small, transitional islands dotted with shore pine trees, grassy meadows, and small sand dunes covered with European beach grass, yellow-flowered Scotch broom, and yarrow. As you continue you can hear the distant roar of waves crashing on the beach. Western snowy plovers nest in the sandy areas at the mouth of Tahkenitch Creek as well as on the beach. The nesting season is from March 15

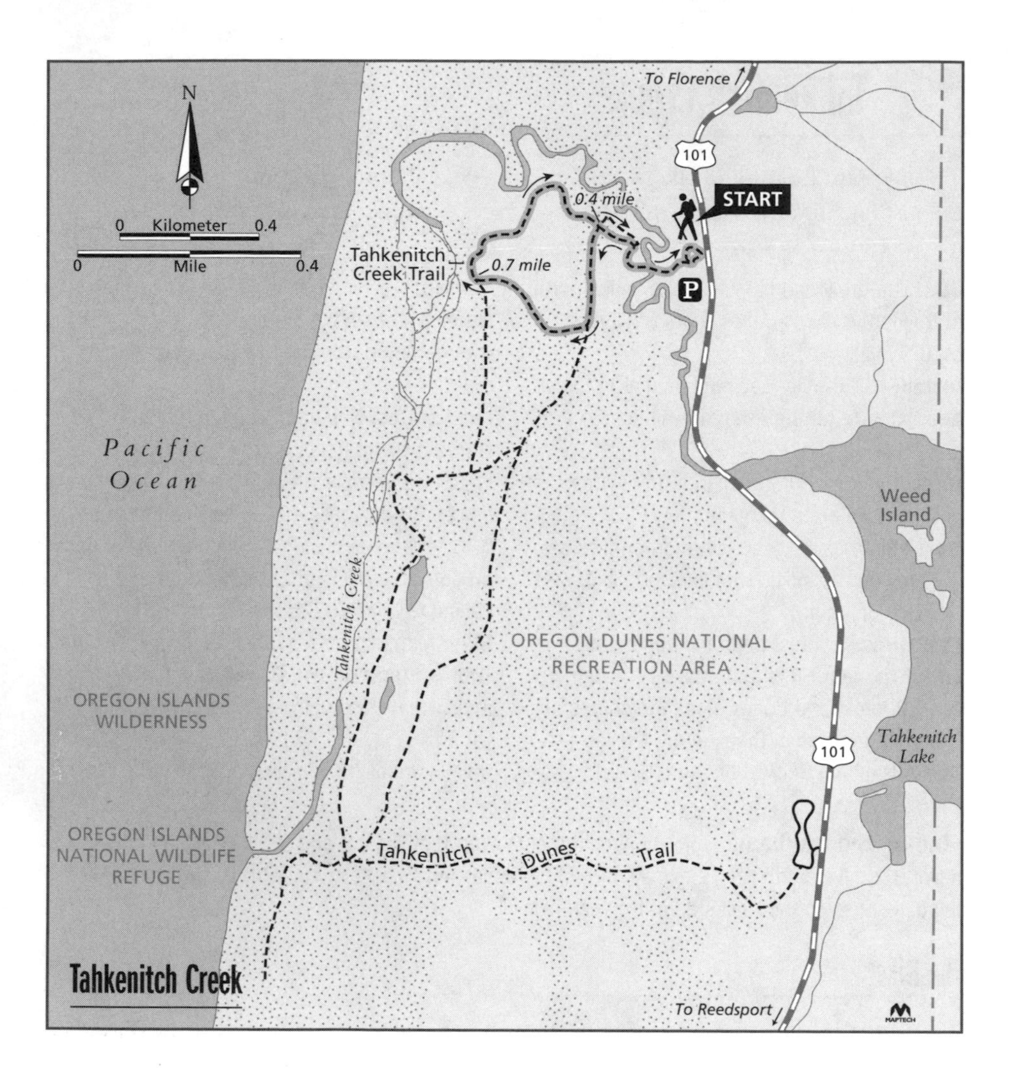

to September 15. If you decide to head to the beach, watch for signs marking protected areas. If you have a canine hiking partner with you, be sure to keep him on a leash so he doesn't disturb these rare, endangered birds.

Near the end of the loop portion of the hike, you'll be able to view the lazy curves of the creek and have another good opportunity to watch for wildlife.

Miles and Directions

0.0 Start walking on the signed path as it descends to a nice viewpoint of picturesque Tahkenitch Creek.

0.1 Cross the creek over a wooden footbridge.

Picturesque Tahkenitch Creek ▶

0.2 Turn left at the trail fork.

0.4 Turn right at the trail junction. At the next trail junction and trail sign, go left and start the loop portion of the hike.

0.6 Turn right at the signed trail junction.

0.7 Turn right at the trail junction. **Side trip:** Turn left to complete an optional 2.5-mile loop or a 4-mile loop.

0.8 The trail parallels the edge of the creek.

1.1 Turn left at the trail junction (you've now completed the loop portion of the hike).

1.5 Arrive at the trailhead.

Hike Information

Local Information

Oregon Dunes National Recreation Area, 855 Highway Avenue, Reedsport, OR 97467; (541) 271-3611; www.fs.fed.us/r6/siuslaw.

Local Events/Attractions

Umpqua Discovery Center, 409 Riverfront Way, Reedsport; (541) 271-4816.

Local Outdoor Retailers

Reedsport Outdoor Store, 2049 Winchester Avenue, Reedsport; (541) 271-2956.

33 Lake Marie

This tour takes you on an easy stroll around charming Lake Marie in Umpqua Lighthouse State Park. Additional highlights include the option to hike across sand dunes to the beach, watch for migrating gray whales, and view the Umpqua River Lighthouse.

Start: The trailhead is located 5.7 miles southwest of Reedsport off U.S. Highway 101 in Umpqua Lighthouse State Park.
Distance: 1.4 miles.
Approximate hiking time: 1 hour.
Difficulty: Easy due to smooth trail surface and minimal elevation gain.
Total climbing: 25 feet. Elevation profiles are not provided for hikes with less than 250 feet of elevation gain.
Trail surface: Paved path and forest path.
Lay of the land: This easy route circles Lake Marie in Umpqua Lighthouse State Park.
Seasons: Year-round.
Other trail users: None.
Canine compatibility: Leashed dogs permitted.
Land status: State park.
Nearest town: Reedsport.
Fees and permits: No fees or permits required.
Map: Maptech map: Winchester Bay, Oregon.
Trail contact: Oregon State Parks and Recreation, 1115 Commercial Street NE, Suite 1, Salem, OR 97301; (800) 551-6949; www.oregonstateparks.org/park_121.php.

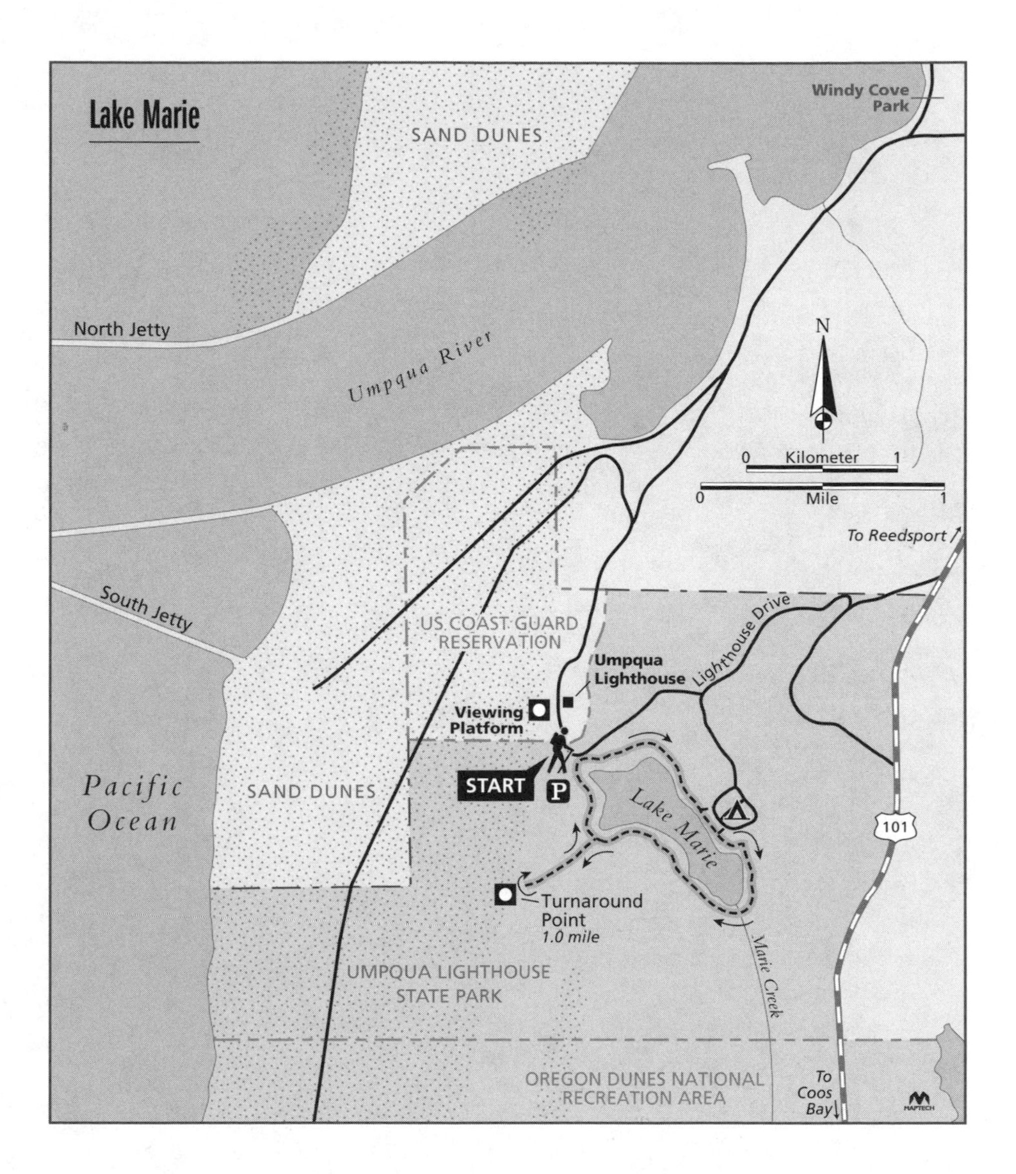

Finding the trailhead: From the junction of Oregon Highway 38 and US 101 in Reedsport, travel 5 miles (or 22 miles north of Coos Bay) south to the junction with Lighthouse Drive. Turn west and go 0.1 mile to a road junction. Turn right and go 0.6 mile to a day-use picnic area at Lake Marie in Umpqua Lighthouse State Park. *DeLorme: Oregon Atlas & Gazetteer:* Page 32, Inset 3, C1.

The Hike

Umpqua Lighthouse State Park covers 450 acres and has a diversity of natural features including sand dunes and coastal forest. One of the highlights of the park is

picturesque five-acre Lake Marie. This nonmotorized lake is ringed with a Sitka spruce forest and a scenic campground. This route begins in the day-use picnic area located at the north end of the lake. You'll start hiking in a clockwise direction on a paved path lined with a thick understory of pink-flowered rhododendrons (that bloom starting in March), blue-berried salal, and huckleberries. After 0.8 mile you'll turn left at the trail junction and continue 0.2 mile to the edge of the forest, where you'll enter the Umpqua Scenic Dunes. You have the option of walking 0.5 mile through the hilly dunes to the beach. After viewing the dunes return to the lake trail. Back on the lake loop, you'll complete this route in another 0.2 mile.

To view the Umpqua River Lighthouse, head west on Lighthouse Drive another 0.1 mile to a parking area and whale-watching platform (with interpretive signs) located on the left side of the highway. The lighthouse is located across from the parking area. The 65-foot lighthouse was completed in 1894, replacing a former lighthouse that was destroyed when the Umpqua River flooded in 1861. This lighthouse is equipped with a 5-foot by 10-foot Fresnel lens that weighs two tons, is made of 800 hand-cut prisms, and has a visibility of 19 miles. If you are in this area anytime from December through June, watch for the far-off spouts of gray whales.

If you want to stay overnight, plan on staying at the park's campground, which features rental cabins with views of Lake Marie.

Miles and Directions

0.0 Start hiking in a clockwise direction on the paved path that starts adjacent to the parking area. Ignore side trails that head left.

0.8 Turn left at the trail junction.

1.0 Arrive at the edge of a large area of sand dunes. After checking out the dunes, turn around and head back to the lake trail.

1.2 Turn left on the lake trail.

1.4 Arrive at the trailhead.

Hike Information

Local Information

Oregon Dunes National Recreation Area, 855 Highway Avenue, Reedsport, OR 97467; (541) 271-3611; www.fs.fed.us/r6/siuslaw.

Local Events/Attractions

Umpqua Discovery Center, 409 Riverfront Way, Reedsport; (541) 271-4816.

Local Outdoor Retailers

Reedsport Outdoor Store, 2049 Winchester Avenue, Reedsport; (541) 271-2956.

Enjoying an early morning swim in Lake Marie

Central Coast Honorable Mentions

N Lost Creek State Recreation Site

You'll enjoy beachcombing and whale watching on the long flat sandy beach where Lost Creek joins the ocean. The Oregon Coast Trail passes down the wild stretch of beach where brown pelicans and gulls fly offshore and the crashing waves and salty wind beckon you to explore. After your beach adventure you can eat your lunch and enjoy ocean views from the picnic area. This recreation site is located 7 miles south of Newport off U.S. Highway 101. For more information contact Oregon State Parks and Recreation, 1115 Commercial Street NE, Suite 1, Salem, OR 97301; (800) 551–6949; www.oregonstateparks.org/park_205.php. *DeLorme: Oregon Atlas & Gazetteer:* Page 32, Inset 1, D1.

O Ona Beach State Park

Covering 237 acres, Ona Beach State Park offers a wide sandy beach and recreational opportunities on Beaver Creek, which empties into the ocean at Ona Beach. The word "Ona" is a Native American word that translates to "razor clam." At one point in time these tasty clams were abundant at this beach. Picnic sites are located along the creek in a large grassy area. This recreation site is located 8 miles south of Newport off U.S. Highway 101. For more information, contact Oregon State Parks and Recreation, 1115 Commercial Street NE, Suite 1, Salem, OR 97301; (800) 551–6949; www.oregonstateparks.org/park_206.php. *DeLorme: Oregon Atlas & Gazetteer:* Page 32, Inset 1, D1.

P Horse Creek–Harris Ranch

This difficult 9.2-mile out-and-back trek features pristine, old-growth Douglas fir, western red cedar, and Sitka spruce forest. Start hiking on the Horse Creek Trail located next to a small registration booth. The trail starts off level for the first few miles and then descends rapidly on a series of switchbacks for about 1,400 feet until it intersects pretty Drift Creek after 3.6 miles. To continue hiking along the creek, head right onto Harris Ranch Trail, which follows the creek for about another mile. The turnaround point is where this trail fords Drift Creek. To get there from Waldport, head 7 miles north on U.S. Highway 101. Turn right onto North Beaver Creek Road and go 1 mile to a road junction. Turn left at the junction and drive 2.7 miles to another road junction. Turn right onto North Elkhorn Road and proceed another 5.8 miles to the junction with Forest Road 50. Turn left on FR 50 and go 1.4 miles to the junction with Forest Road 5087. Turn right onto FR 5087 and continue another 3.4 miles to the trailhead. For more information contact Siuslaw National Forest, Waldport Ranger District, 1094 SW Pacific Highway, Waldport, OR 97394; (541) 563–3211; www.fs.fed.us/r6/siuslaw. *DeLorme: Oregon Atlas & Gazetteer:* Page 46, A1.

Q Beachside State Park

This 16.7-acre state park is located right next to a wide expanse of sandy beach and is one of the few state parks on the Oregon Coast that has campsites with an ocean view. A bubbling creek is the dividing line between the campground and the day-use area. Beach activities are the highlight here. You can access miles of sandy beach from the day-use area or the campground. To get there from Waldport, travel 4 miles south on U.S. Highway 101. For more information contact Oregon State Parks and Recreation, 1115 Commercial Street NE, Suite 1, Salem, OR 97301; (800) 551–6949; www.oregonstateparks.org/park_122.php. *DeLorme: Oregon Atlas & Gazetteer:* Page 32, Inset 2, A1.

R Carl G. Washburne Memorial State Park

This large state park and campground covers 1,089 acres and features a variety of habitat ranging from sandy beach to forested sand dunes. One of the highlights of the park is a 6-mile out-and-back hike to Heceta Head Lighthouse from the campground. You'll begin this hike on the Valley Trail, which is located before the pay station to the campground. The trail follows China Creek and leads you to an open grassy meadow where you may get to see some Roosevelt elk. The trail leads you through a boggy area, and then to U.S. Highway 101. Cross the highway and continue your adventure by turning onto Hobbit Trail, which winds through a coastal landscape filled with shore pine, Sitka spruce, and thick borders of salal. You'll hike for a short ways on this trail and then come to a trail junction. Turn left onto the Heceta Head Trail, which will take you to the Heceta Head Lighthouse. Once you reach the lighthouse, you can watch for seabirds nesting in the high cliffs surrounding it. If you aren't up for such a long hiking adventure, you can hike 0.5 mile to the beach and enjoy beach activities on a 5-mile-long stretch of beach. The Beach Trail can be accessed between campsites 40 and 42. This state park is located 14 miles north of Florence on US 101. For more information contact Oregon State Parks and Recreation, 1115 Commercial Street NE, Suite 1, Salem, OR 97301; (800) 551–6949; www.oregonstateparks.org/park_123.php. *DeLorme: Oregon Atlas & Gazetteer:* Page 32, Inset 2, C2.

S Pawn Old Growth Trail

This easy 0.8-mile trail takes you on a journey through magnificent old-growth Douglas fir and western red cedar forest. A brochure at the trailhead will provide you with detailed information about this amazing forest. To get there from Florence, head east on Oregon Highway 126. Go 1 mile and turn left onto North Fork Road. Continue 11 miles on North Fork Road to the junction with Upper North Fork Road. Continue straight on Upper North Fork Road for 5.4 miles. Turn right onto Elk Tie Road and go a short distance to the trailhead. For more information contact Siuslaw National Forest, Mapleton Ranger District, 4480 Highway 101, Building G, Florence, OR 97439; (541) 902–8526; www.fs.fed.us/r6/siuslaw. *DeLorme: Oregon Atlas & Gazetteer:* Page 46, D1.

T Sweet Creek Falls

This easy 2.2-mile out-and-back route takes you on a tour along the banks of bouldery Sweet Creek. From the Homestead trailhead, start walking upstream. You'll pass small waterfalls and, after 1.1 miles, you'll reach 20-foot Sweet Creek Falls (your turnaround point). Head up a short side trail to a fantastic viewpoint of the upper falls. To get there from Florence, head 15 miles east (or 46 miles west of Eugene) on Oregon Highway 126 to Mapleton, to the junction with Sweet Creek Road. Turn south onto Sweet Creek Road and travel 10.2 miles to the Homestead trailhead on the right. This trail requires a $5.00 Northwest Forest Pass. For more information contact Siuslaw National Forest, Mapleton Ranger District, 4480 Highway 101, Building G, Florence, OR 97439; (541) 902–8526; www.fs.fed.us/r6/siuslaw. *DeLorme: Oregon Atlas & Gazetteer:* Page 40, A1.

U Taylor Dunes Trail

This 3.2-mile moderate out-and-back loop takes you through a beautiful coastal forest and dune environment. Start by hiking north from the parking area and crossing the Carter Campground Entrance Road. Follow the forest path as it parallels quiet Taylor Lake on the right. At 0.3 mile you'll arrive at a trail junction. Go left and continue 0.2 mile to a viewing platform surrounded by big Sitka spruce trees. After enjoying views of the dunes and far-off beach, head back to the trail junction and turn left. Follow the blue-banded posts for 0.5 mile to the junction with the Carter Dunes Trail. Turn right and continue 0.5 mile to a beautiful beach (your turnaround point). Retrace the same route back to the trailhead. To get there from Reedsport, travel 12 miles north (or 9 miles south of Florence) on U.S. Highway 101 to the Taylor Lake trailhead, located on the west side of the highway. Turn west and then take an immediate left into the trailhead parking area. This hike requires a $5.00 Northwest Forest Pass. For more information contact Oregon Dunes National Recreation Area, 855 Highway Avenue, Reedsport, OR 97467; (541) 271–3611; www.fs.fed.us/r6/siuslaw. *DeLorme: Oregon Atlas & Gazetteer:* Page 32, Inset 3, B1.

V Dunes Overlook

This easy 2-mile hike takes you to a scenic viewpoint overlooking expansive dunes in the Oregon Dunes National Recreation Area. From the parking area walk out to a viewing platform and then walk on a paved sidewalk and long wooden ramp to the start of the sandy hiking trail. Use the guideposts to find your way across the dunes to a secluded beach (your turnaround point). To get there from Reedsport, travel 11 miles north (or 10 miles south of Florence) on U.S. Highway 101 to the Dunes Overlook trailhead, located on the west side of the highway. This hike requires a $5.00 Northwest Forest Pass. For more information contact Oregon Dunes National Recreation Area, 855 Highway Avenue, Reedsport, OR 97467; (541) 271–3611; www.fs.fed.us/r6/siuslaw. *DeLorme: Oregon Atlas & Gazetteer:* Page 32, Inset 3, B1.

W Tahkenitch Dunes–Three Mile Lake

This difficult 6.5-mile-loop route explores a unique dune environment in the Oregon Dunes National Recreation Area. Begin the hike at the signed trailhead (both the Tahkenitch Dunes and Three Mile Lake Trails begin as the same trail). After hiking 0.25 mile, the trail forks. Go left and continue hiking on the Three Mile Lake Trail through a second-growth conifer forest. After about 2.7 miles, the trail skirts the edge of Three Mile Lake before reaching the beach at 3 miles. Turn right and walk north along the beach about 1.5 miles. Hook up with the Tahkenitch Dunes Trail on your right and walk 2 miles through dunes and forest back to your starting point. To get there from Florence, travel 12.5 miles south on U.S. Highway 101 (or 8 miles north of Reedsport) to Tahkenitch Campground and the trailhead. This hike requires a $5.00 Northwest Forest Pass. For more information contact Oregon Dunes National Recreation Area, 855 Highway Avenue, Reedsport, OR 97467; (541) 271–3611; www.fs.fed.us/r6/siuslaw. *DeLorme: Oregon Atlas & Gazetteer:* Page 32, Inset 3, B1.

X Kentucky Falls

This moderate 4-mile out-and-back trail descends 760 feet through a mossy forest of western hemlock and Douglas fir dotted with trillium, sword fern, and oxalis.

After about 0.5 mile you'll arrive at the shimmering double cascade of Upper Kentucky Falls. Continue about another 1.5 miles to a viewpoint of Lower Kentucky Falls and North Fork Falls (your turnaround point). To get there from Reedsport, head north on U.S. Highway 101, cross a bridge over the Umpqua River, and turn right (northeast) onto Smith River Road (Forest Road 48). Go approximately 14.5 miles on Smith River Road and turn left (north) onto North Fork Road. Go about 10 miles on North Fork Road to the intersection with FR 23. Turn right onto FR 23 and follow signs to Kentucky Falls. After another 9.8 miles you'll arrive at a T intersection. Turn left onto FR 919 and continue 2.6 miles to the trailhead. For more information contact the Mapleton Ranger District, 10692 Highway 126, Mapleton, OR 97453; (503) 268–4473; www.fs.fed.us/r6/siuslaw/mapleton. *DeLorme: Oregon Atlas & Gazetteer:* Page 40, A2.

Y North Fork Smith River

This difficult 17.4-mile out-and-back route travels along the banks of the North Fork Smith River, which is filled with many great swimming spots. You'll hike through a jungly coastal forest where you can admire huge old-growth Douglas firs. You are treated at the trail's turnaround point with a great view of Kentucky Falls. To get there from Reedsport, head north on U.S. Highway 101, cross a bridge over the Umpqua River, and turn right (northeast) onto Smith River Road (Forest Road 48). After about 15 miles turn left (north) onto North Fork Road 48A. Continue about 9.5 miles to a road junction and go right toward Mapleton. Go 0.5 mile to another road junction and turn right on FR 23. Continue 4 miles to the trailhead parking area on the left side of the road. For more information contact the Mapleton Ranger District, 10692 Highway 126, Mapleton, OR 97453; (503) 268–4473; www.fs.fed.us/r6/siuslaw/mapleton. *DeLorme: Oregon Atlas & Gazetteer:* Page 40, A2.

Z Jessie M. Honeyman State Park

This popular state park boasts a large campground located next to sand dunes and provides access to 82-acre Cleawox Lake and 350-acre Woahink Lake. Hikes you may like to try include a 0.5-mile trail that takes you from the Cleawox Lake picnic areas to Lily Lake, which is bordered by colorful rhododendrons. A second nature trail connects the Cleawox day-use area with the group camp on Woahink Lake. If you want to check out the beach, you can take a 2-mile hike over a series of sand dunes to the beach. This state park is located 3 miles south of Florence on U.S. Highway 101. Swimming, fishing, canoeing, and kayaking are also popular activities here. This park requires a $3.00 day-use fee. For more information contact Oregon State Parks and Recreation, 1115 Commercial Street NE, Suite 1, Salem, OR 97301;

(800) 551–6949; www.oregonstateparks.org/park_134.php. *DeLorme: Oregon Atlas & Gazetteer:* Page 32, Inset 3, A1.

AA Umpqua Dunes

This 1-mile interpretive loop takes you through a madrone and manzanita forest, wetlands, and magnificent coastal dunes. If you are feeling like a longer hiking adventure, continue through the dunes 2.5 miles to the beach. Look for posts with blue bands to guide your way. To get to this hike travel 10.5 miles south of Reedsport on U.S. Highway 101 (or 12 miles north of North Bend) to the signed Umpqua Dunes trailhead located on the west side of US 101. A $5.00 Northwest Forest Pass is required. For more information contact Oregon Dunes National Recreation Area, 855 Highway Avenue, Reedsport, OR 97467; (541) 271–3611; www.fs.fed.us/r6/siuslaw. *DeLorme: Oregon Atlas & Gazetteer:* Page 32, Inset 3, C3.

BB Blue Bill Lake

This easy 1.2-mile hike circles 60-acre Blue Bill Lake and takes you through a unique coastal ecosystem. To get there from Reedsport, travel 23 miles south (or 2 miles north of North Bend) on U.S. Highway 101. Turn west onto Horsfall Road and continue to the signed trailhead. A $5.00 Northwest Forest Pass is required. For more information contact Oregon Dunes National Recreation Area, 855 Highway Avenue, Reedsport, OR 97467; (541) 271–3611; www.fs.fed.us/r6/siuslaw. *DeLorme: Oregon Atlas & Gazetteer:* Page 33, A6.

South Coast

You can expect fewer people and more undeveloped coastline on the South Coast. Visit Sunset Bay State Park to view the Cape Arago Lighthouse, admire golden sandstone cliffs and tour a botanical garden at Shore Acres State Park, and observe sea lions at Cape Arago State Park. These state parks are located southwest of Coos Bay on the Cape Arago Highway. While you are in this area, be sure to visit the South Slough Marine Estuarine Preserve and Interpretive Center. You can explore this 4,700-acre preserve on a variety of nature trails. The interpretive center has exhibits explaining estuarine ecology and displays describing the plants and animals that live here.

As you continue south, be sure to stop and explore the small town of Bandon, which features many unique shops, art galleries, restaurants, and dozens of cozy bed-and-breakfasts. Destinations you should check out in the Bandon area include the Coquille River Lighthouse and the Bandon State Natural Area.

To truly get away from it all, visit Cape Blanco State Park, located 9 miles northwest of Port Orford. This wild and rugged park features many scenic and uncrowded trails and the 59-foot Cape Blanco Lighthouse, which is the oldest lighthouse in Oregon. Another historical structure here is the Hughes House Museum, built in 1898.

If you want to visit two rare tree species, visit Alfred A. Loeb State Park, located 7.5 miles southwest of Brookings. This state park features two nature trails that take you on a journey through groves of rare Oregon myrtle and coastal redwoods. The park has a campground that serves as a good base camp for exploring the immediate area, as well as other hiking opportunities in the Kalmiopsis Wilderness.

Moving farther east, the wild and rugged Kalmiopsis Wilderness and the Siskiyou National Forest dominate, each offering a unique array of plants and animals that call the Illinois River home. Take a tour along the Illinois River Trail to get a closer look at the deep canyon that it has carved over the millennia. To view two picturesque lakes, visit the glacier-carved basin that is home to Vulcan Lake and Babyfoot Lake, which is ringed with old-growth Brewers spruce trees.

34 Sunset Bay, Shore Acres, and Cape Arago State Parks

Get your camera ready to snap great photos of the rocky coastline along this scenic stretch of the Oregon Coast. This trail begins at Sunset Bay State Park and takes you on a journey along the cliff edges to Shore Acres State Park and Cape Arago State Park. The rocky coastline is a haven for sea lions. As you near Cape Arago State Park, you can hear their noisy raucous from almost a mile away.

Start: The Oregon Coast Trail marker adjacent to the rest rooms in the day-use picnic area in Sunset Bay State Park.
Distance: 8.8 miles out and back.
Approximate hiking time: 3 to 4 hours.
Difficulty: Moderate due to trail length.
Total climbing: 48 feet. Elevation profiles are not provided for hikes with less than 250 feet of elevation gain.
Trail surface: Dirt, gravel, and paved paths and roads.
Lay of the land: Hike through a coastal forest and along sandstone cliffs south to Cape Arago State Park.
Seasons: Year-round.
Other trail users: None.
Canine compatibility: Not dog friendly. Dogs are allowed in Sunset Bay State Park but are not allowed in Cape Arago State Park.
Land status: State park.
Nearest town: Coos Bay.
Fees and permits: No fees or permits required.
Map: Maptech maps: Charleston and Cape Arago, Oregon.
Trail contact: Oregon State Parks and Recreation, 1115 Commercial Street NE, Suite 1, Salem, OR 97301; (800) 551-6949; www.oregonstateparks.org.

Finding the trailhead: From Coos Bay, follow the signs to Charleston Harbor and Ocean Beaches. Drive southwest for about 12 miles on the Cape Arago Highway to Sunset Bay State Park. When you reach the park, turn into the day-use picnicking area, located on the west side of the highway. Look for the Oregon Coast Trail marker located on the right side of the rest rooms. *DeLorme: Oregon Atlas & Gazetteer:* Page 33, B5.

The Hike

Some of the most beautiful stretches of rocky coast and forest can be found along the Oregon Coast Trail between Sunset Bay State Park and Cape Arago State Park. Hemmed in and protected by golden sandstone cliffs, the beautiful Sunset Bay forms the focal point of Sunset Bay State Park. This secluded piece of the coast is thought to have served as a safe haven for ships waiting out the furious storms that often hit the Oregon Coast. The park was once part of the enormous estate of lumberman, shipbuilder, and founder of North Bend, Louis B. Simpson. Simpson had his home 2 miles south in what is now Shore Acres State Park. In 1913 Simpson oversaw the building of the Sunset Bay Inn, situated on the edge of Sunset Bay.

The Oregon Coast Trail takes off from the day-use picnic area and parallels the cliff's edge through a thick Sitka spruce forest. As the trail winds its way south, you'll

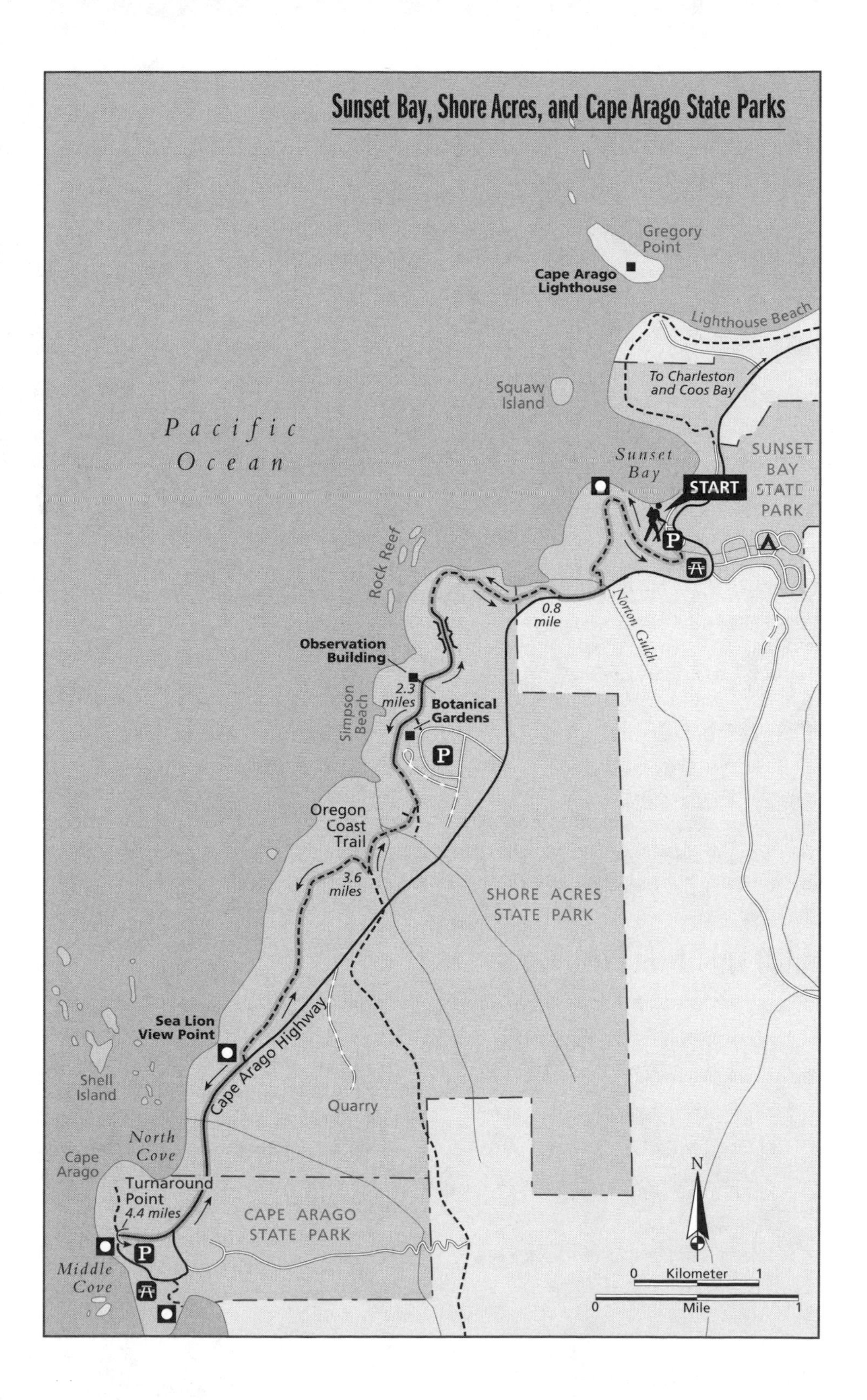

Sunset Bay, Shore Acres, and Cape Arago State Parks
Gregory Point
Cape Arago Lighthouse
Lighthouse Beach
To Charleston and Coos Bay
Squaw Island
Pacific Ocean
Sunset Bay
SUNSET BAY STATE PARK
START
Rock Reef
Norton Gulch
0.8 mile
Observation Building
2.3 miles
Botanical Gardens
Simpson Beach
Oregon Coast Trail
3.6 miles
SHORE ACRES STATE PARK
Sea Lion View Point
Cape Arago Highway
Shell Island
Quarry
North Cove
Cape Arago
Turnaround Point
4.4 miles
CAPE ARAGO STATE PARK
Middle Cove
N
0 Kilometer 1
0 Mile 1

Scenic sandstone cliffs at Shore Acres State Park

have sneak peaks at the golden, steep-walled sandstone cliffs. Many of the layers in these cliffs are curved, matching the ocean currents that formed them more than 45 million years ago when this area was under a shallow sea. After 1.4 miles you'll have a scenic view of the bay and the Cape Arago Lighthouse, one of only nine lighthouses that grace Oregon's coastline. Located on a rocky outcrop just off Gregory Point, the scenic lighthouse rises 100 feet above the ocean and stands 44 feet tall. Built in 1934, it's the third lighthouse to occupy this same site. Its predecessors were built in 1866 and 1908—both fell prey to the harsh elements along this stretch of the Oregon Coast.

At mile 2.1 you reach 743-acre Shore Acres State Park, also formerly part of the Louis J. Simpson estate. Simpson discovered this scenic part of the coast in 1905 and bought 320 acres for $4,000. He then built an elaborate estate on the grounds, with stables, a carriage house, tennis courts, and beautiful cultivated gardens. At mile 2.3 you come to a glass-enclosed observation building that stands on the site of Simpson's former estate.

GRAY WHALE FACTS

- **A gray whale mother carries her calf for thirteen months before giving birth.**
- **Calves weigh about a ton when they are born, and their mother's milk contains 53 percent butterfat.**
- **A calf can grow to be 26 feet long in twelve months.**
- **It takes a calf eight years to reach sexual maturity.**

From this vantage point the wild rocky coast stretches for miles in both directions and thundering waves create many great picture opportunities. From December through June you may spot some gray whales on their semiannual migration from Baja, Mexico, to Alaska. At mile 2.4 you come to a view of the beautiful botanical gardens, which are meticulously maintained by Oregon State Parks and Recreation. Within the botanical gardens are a Japanese garden, two rose gardens, and other formal flower gardens. From February through March daffodils are in peak bloom; from April through mid-May the azaleas and rhododendrons steal the show; and from June through September roses are in full bloom.

You'll arrive at Cape Arago State Park after 4.4 miles. The 134-acre park sits atop a 200-foot rocky cliff. Offshore is Simpson Reef, home to large colonies of seals and sea lions. You'll be able to hear their raucous calling from several wildlife viewing points in the park. This scenic cape was named after Dominique F. J. Arago, a French physicist and geographer (1786–1853). This rocky headland was also once part of the large Simpson estate. It was handed over to the state of Oregon in 1932. There are three coves you can hike to in this park—North, Middle, and South. If you enjoy exploring tide pools, be sure to take a side trip to South Cove. North Cove is closed from March to July each year to protect sea lions and seal pups.

Miles and Directions

0.0 Start at the day-use picnicking area at Sunset Bay State Park. Look for the wooden Oregon Coast Trail marker just to the right of the rest rooms, which indicates the start of the trail. As you begin walking on the trail, you'll see a sign that reads SHORE ACRES 2 MILES.

0.1 Turn right at the trail fork. (Left opens into a grassy picnic area.)

0.3 (FYI: Good views of Sunset Bay and offshore rock formations.)

0.6 Turn left at a trail junction. The trail winds up a fern-covered hillside to a paved road.

0.8 Reach the paved road and turn right. Walk along the road. Approach a set of wooden steps on your right and turn right. Take the steps over the metal road barrier.

1.3 Turn right at the trail fork.

1.4 (FYI: You'll pass a good viewpoint of the bay and the Cape Arago Lighthouse to your right.)

2.1 Reach Shore Acres State Park. The path turns from dirt to pavement when you enter the park. (Note: Dogs are not allowed in the park.)

2.2 Turn right at the trail fork. (If you go left you'll enter a parking area.) Come to another fork and stay right. The trail parallels a wooden rail fence.

2.3 Arrive at an observation building on your left.

2.4 Turn right where a sign indicates SIMPSON BEACH. **Option:** You can turn left here and view the Botanical Garden.

2.7 Arrive at Simpson Beach. The paved path ends. Turn left and cross a stream. Continue walking on the trail and cross a second stream.

2.9 Turn right at a T junction.

3.5 Turn right at the trail fork. (FYI: Listen closely for the calls from the sea lion colony in Cape Arago State Park.)

3.6 Turn right at a T junction.

3.8 Turn right at the junction with a paved road. Walk into the paved parking area of Sea Lion Viewpoint. Continue walking parallel to U.S. Highway 101 for 0.6 mile until you reach Cape Arago State Park.

4.4 Arrive at your turnaround point and return on the same route back to your vehicle.

8.8 Arrive at the trailhead.

Hike Information

Local Information

Bay Area Chamber of Commerce, 50 Central Avenue, Coos Bay, OR 97420; (800) 824-8486; www.oregonsbayareachamber.com.

Local Events/Attractions

Charleston Merchants' Annual Crab Feed, held in February, Charleston; (800) 824-8486.

Local Outdoor Retailers

Big 5 Sporting Goods, 1659 Virginia Street, Coos Bay; (541) 751-0522.

35 Coquille River Lighthouse

This route takes you on a beach trek in Bullards Beach State Park to view the historic Coquille River Lighthouse.

Start: The trailhead is located in Bullards Beach State Park about 4 miles north of Bandon off U.S. Highway 101.
Distance: 3.4 miles out and back (with longer options).
Approximate hiking time: 1.25 to 2 hours.
Difficulty: Easy due to short length of route and no elevation gain.
Total climbing: None. Elevation profiles are not provided for hikes with less than 250 feet of elevation gain.
Trail surface: Sandy beach.
Lay of the land: This route travels on a long sandy beach to the Coquille Lighthouse in Bullards Beach State Park.
Seasons: Year-round.
Other trail users: Equestrians.
Canine compatibility: Leashed dogs permitted.
Land status: State park.
Nearest town: Bandon.
Fees and permits: No fees or permits required.
Map: Maptech map: Bullards, Oregon.
Trail contact: Oregon State Parks and Recreation, 1115 Commercial Street NE, Suite 1, Salem, OR 97301; (800) 551-6949; www.oregonstateparks.org/park_71.php.

Finding the trailhead: From Bandon, travel 3 miles north (or 21 miles south of Coos Bay) on US 101 to the Bullards Beach State Park turnoff. Turn west and continue 1.3 miles to a road junction (ignore turnoffs for the campground and picnic areas). Turn right and park in a large parking area on the right side of the road.

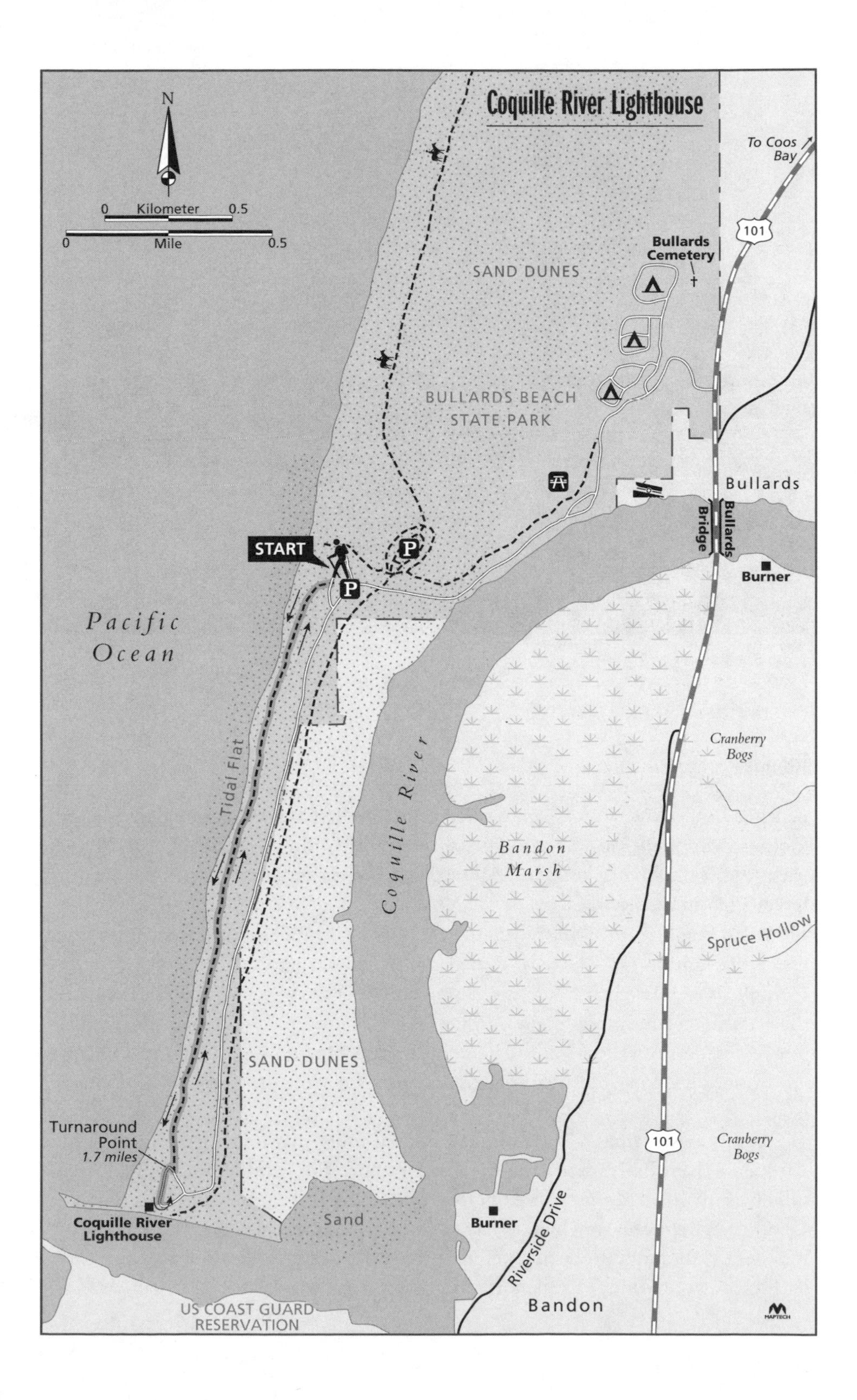
Coquille River Lighthouse
N
0 Kilometer 0.5
0 Mile 0.5
To Coos Bay
101
Bullards Cemetery
SAND DUNES
BULLARDS BEACH STATE PARK
Bullards
Bullards Bridge
START
P
P
Burner
Pacific Ocean
Tidal Flat
Coquille River
Cranberry Bogs
Bandon Marsh
Spruce Hollow
SAND DUNES
Turnaround Point
1.7 miles
101
Cranberry Bogs
Coquille River Lighthouse
Sand
Burner
Riverside Drive
US COAST GUARD RESERVATION
Bandon
MAPTECH

Coquille River Lighthouse

The Hike

Bullards Beach State Park is sandwiched between the Coquille River and the Pacific Ocean and is made up of dunes, coastal forest, wetlands, and beach. The 1,289-acre park features hiking, biking, and equestrian trails, a campground, and the Coquille River Lighthouse.

You'll begin your hiking adventure by walking south along the beach until you reach the lighthouse, which is located on the north jetty at the entrance to the Coquille River. The lighthouse was illuminated in 1896 to help steer mariners across the hazardous bar. Interestingly, this lighthouse is powered by a solar-powered system. Volunteers offer tours of the lighthouse from May through October. Once you are finished viewing the lighthouse, you can return on the same route along the beach.

You can also return via a 2.7-mile optional route that follows the shores of the Coquille River for 2.3 miles and then runs next to the paved entrance road for 0.4 mile back to your starting point. On this route you can view amazing bird life in the Coquille River Estuary, which is part of the Bandon National Wildlife Refuge. You may see cormorants, great blue herons, brown pelicans, Canada geese, scoters, mallard ducks, green-winged teal, northern pintails, and red-breasted mergansers.

If you feel like staying overnight, be sure to check out the spacious campground, which features sites with full electrical hookups as well as corrals for horses. If you don't feel like roughing it, stay in one of the campground's comfy yurts.

Miles and Directions

0.0 From the parking area go left and walk south along the beach for 1.7 miles to the lighthouse parking area. From the parking area continue a short distance to view the lighthouse.

1.7 Arrive at the lighthouse (your turnaround point). **Option:** You can continue east on a sandy road that parallels the jetty for 0.4 mile and then turn left and follow the river's shoreline north for 1.9 miles to the junction with the park's entrance road. Turn left and continue 0.4 mile along the road to your starting point.

3.4 Arrive at the trailhead.

Hike Information

Local Information

Bandon Chamber of Commerce, 300 Second Street, Old Town, Bandon, OR 97411; (541) 347-9616; www.bandon.com.

Local Events/Attractions

Bandon Wine and Food Festival, held in April, Bandon; (503) 228-8336.

36 Babyfoot Lake

This easy, 2-mile out-and-back trail takes you through part of the Babyfoot Lake Botanical Area, home to many rare plant species that are found only in the unspoiled Kalmiopsis Wilderness. After 1 mile of hiking, you reach Babyfoot Lake, which sits in a dramatic glacial cirque surrounded by timbered hillsides that contain a large population of the rare Port Orford cedar and Brewers spruce trees.

Start: The trailhead is located 15.6 miles north of Cave Junction and about 60 miles northeast of Brookings off U.S. Highway 199 (the Redwood Highway).
Distance: 2 miles out and back.
Approximate hiking time: 1 hour.
Difficulty: Easy due to smooth trail surface and minimal elevation gains.
Total climbing: 360 feet.
Trail surface: Well-maintained forest path.
Lay of the land: Hike through an old-growth forest to Babyfoot Lake in the Kalmiopsis Wilderness.
Seasons: Mid-June through October.
Other trail users: None.
Canine compatibility: Dogs permitted.
Land status: Wilderness.
Nearest town: Cave Junction.
Fees and permits: $5.00 Northwest Forest Pass. You can purchase a pass on-line at www.fs.fed.us/r6/feedemo, or by call calling (800) 270-7504. A free self-issue wilderness permit (available at the trailhead) is also required.
Map: Maptech map: Josephine Mountain, Oregon.
Trail contact: Siskiyou National Forest, Illinois Valley Ranger District, 26568 Redwood Highway, Cave Junction, OR 97523; (541) 592-4000; www.fs.fed.us/r6/siskiyou.

Finding the trailhead: From Brookings, travel 20 miles south on U.S. Highway 101 to Crescent City and turn east onto US 199 (the Redwood Highway). Travel about 45 miles northeast on US 199 to Cave Junction. From Cave Junction, travel north for 4 miles on US 199 (the Redwood Highway) and turn left (west) onto Eight Dollar Road (this turns into Forest Road 4201 after you enter the Siskiyou National Forest). Drive on FR 4201 for 11.3 miles to the intersection with FR 140. Turn left onto FR 140 and drive 0.3 mile to the trailhead on the right side of the road. *DeLorme: Oregon Atlas & Gazetteer:* Page 18, C2.

The Hike

Babyfoot Lake is located in a glacial cirque surrounded by forested hills and rocky bluffs. This high mountain lake is situated in the wild and rugged 179,655-acre Kalmiopsis Wilderness—one of five wilderness areas located in the Siskiyou National Forest. A short, easy 1-mile trail leads you to this quiet lake through an old-growth forest—part of the 352-acre Babyfoot Lake Botanical Area, which was established in 1963 to protect the Brewers spruce and other rare plant species.

Due to its gentle terrain and easy access off Forest Road 140, the Babyfoot Lake Trail can be crowded during the summer months. The trail begins by winding

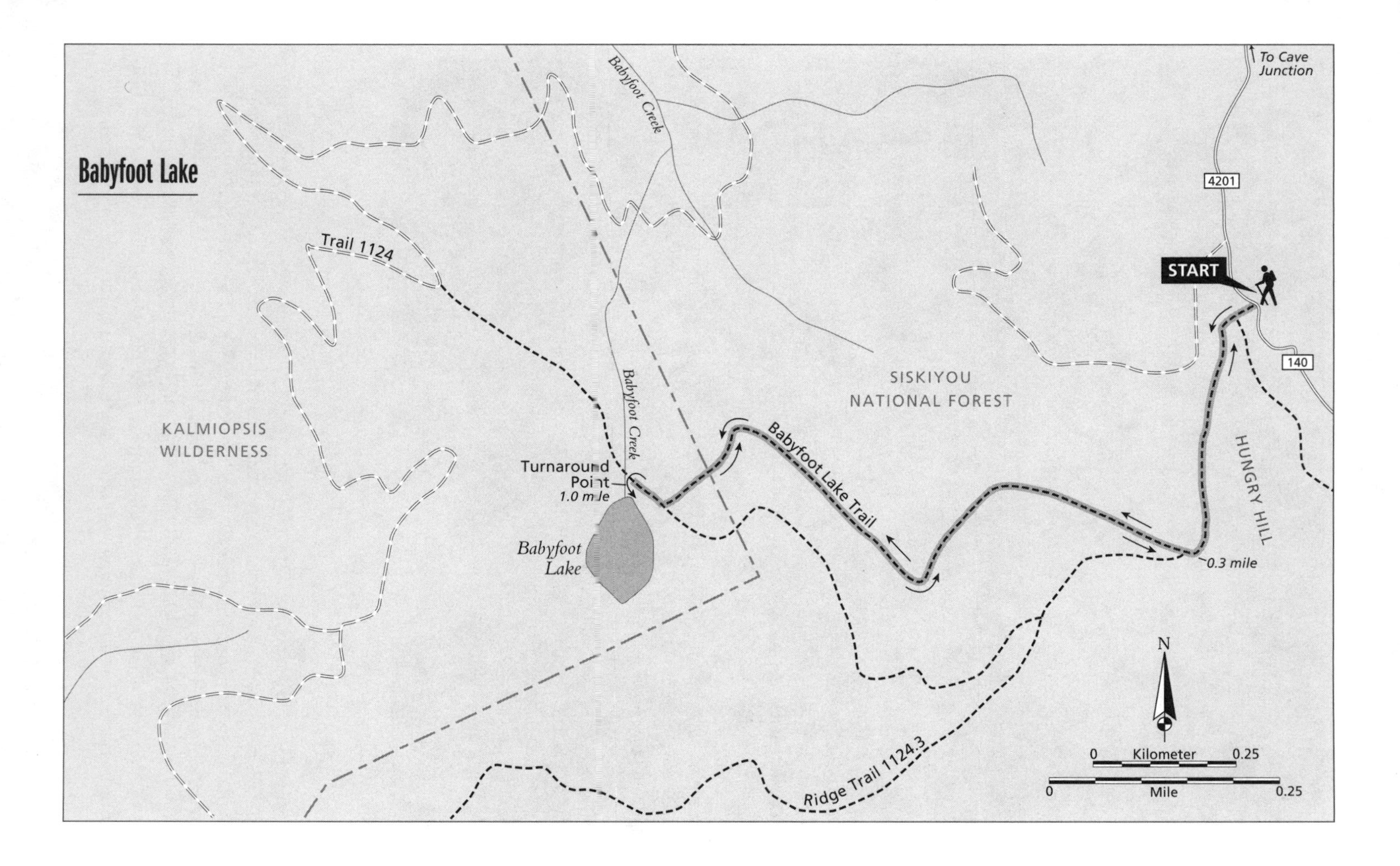
Babyfoot Lake
To Cave Junction
4201
140
START
HUNGRY HILL
0.3 mile
SISKIYOU NATIONAL FOREST
Babyfoot Lake Trail
Babyfoot Creek
Babyfoot Creek
Turnaround Point
1.0 mile
Babyfoot Lake
Trail 1124
KALMIOPSIS WILDERNESS
Ridge Trail 1124.3
N
0 Kilometer 0.25
0 Mile 0.25

Babyfoot Lake

through an old-growth forest of Brewers spruce, Douglas fir, Shasta red fir, sugar pine, Port Orford cedar, and incense cedar. Interspersed on the forest floor are vine maple, western sword fern, parsley fern, and fragile fern. In open areas you may see the bright colors of wildflowers such as bleeding hearts, rattlesnake orchid, Siskiyou iris, Newberry's penstemon, pussy paws, spreading phlox, and twinflower.

When you reach the lake, you'll want to plan on staying for a while. You may want to take a refreshing swim, search for rare endemic plants (be sure to bring your

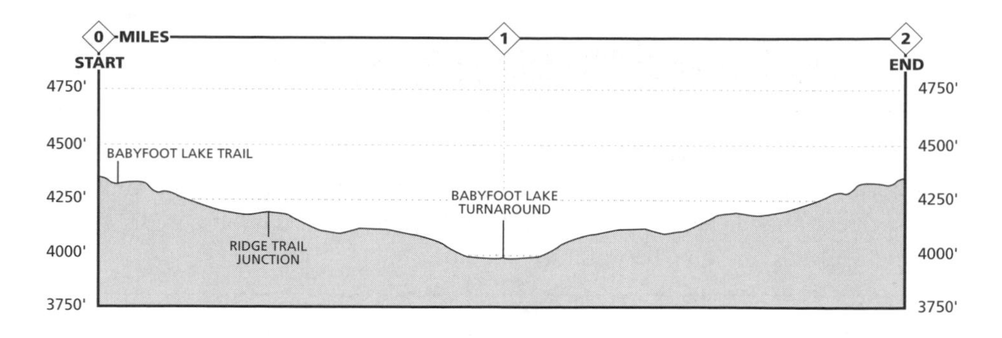

plant field guide), or have a picnic. If you love to fish, try your luck at catching some Eastern brook trout, which are present in small quantities in the lake.

While you are in the Caves Junction area, be sure to check out Oregon Caves National Monument, located 20 miles southeast of Cave Junction on Oregon Highway 46. This national monument was established in 1909 to showcase its main attraction, a large cave carved by the Styx River. You can see this magnificent cave by taking the 90-minute guided tour. You'll see almost a half mile of fascinating rock chambers filled with stalactites and intricately carved rock columns. This national monument also contains nature trails that will help you learn about the 80 species of birds, 35 species of mammals, and more than 110 species of plants present in the park. The 3.3-mile Big Tree Trail loop trail takes you on a tour of an old-growth Douglas fir forest. The 1-mile Cliff Nature Trail has interpretive signs that help you learn about the geology, plants, and animals present in the wild and rugged Siskiyou Mountains.

Miles and Directions

0.0 Start from the wooden trailhead sign. A sign indicates BABYFOOT LAKE .75/CANYON PEAK TRAIL 4. (Note that the trail is actually a mile in length.) Be sure to fill out a self-issue wilderness permit at the trailhead.

0.3 Turn right at the trail fork. (FYI: If you go left here, a sign indicates RIDGE TRAIL 1124.3.)

1.0 Reach Babyfoot Lake and your turnaround point. Retrace the same route back to your starting point.

2.0 Arrive at the trailhead.

Hike Information

Local Information

The Brookings-Harbor Chamber of Commerce, 16330 Lower Harbor Road, Brookings, OR 97415; (800) 535-9469; www.brookingsor.com.

Local Events/Attractions

Oregon Caves National Monument, 19000 Caves Highway, Cave Junction; (541) 592-2100; www.nps.gov/orca.

Azalea Festival, held Memorial Day weekend, Brookings; (800) 535-9469.

Local Outdoor Retailers

Loring's Lighthouse Sporting Goods, 554 Chetco Lane, Brookings; (541) 469-2148.

37 Cape Ferrelo to Whalehead Beach

This hike takes you on the Oregon Coast Trail through the heart of Samuel H. Boardman State Park. You'll walk through thick Sitka spruce forest, past bubbling coastal creeks, on wild and windy headlands with fantastic views of offshore sea stacks and rocky islands, and on a beautiful secluded beach.

Start: The trailhead is located 5 miles north of Brookings on U.S. Highway 101 at the Cape Ferrelo Viewpoint parking area.
Distance: 9.4 miles out and back.
Approximate hiking time: 3 to 4 hours.
Difficulty: Moderate due to the steep ascents and descents through forest and open headlands. The beach walking can be difficult due to high winds and soft sand.
Total climbing: 380 feet.
Trail surface: Well-maintained dirt path, short sections of pavement, stream crossings, and soft sandy beach hiking.
Lay of the land: Hike through a coastal forest and open, windy headlands and then descend several steep switchbacks to Whalehead Beach for a flat, sandy beach walk to your turnaround point.
Seasons: Year-round.
Other trail users: None.
Canine compatibility: Leashed dogs permitted.
Land status: State park.
Nearest town: Brookings.
Fees and permits: $3.00 day-use fee.
Map: Maptech map: Brookings and Carpenterville, Oregon.
Trail contact: Oregon State Parks and Recreation, 1115 Commercial Street NE, Suite 1, Salem, OR 97301; (800) 551-6949; www.oregonstateparks.org.

Finding the trailhead: From Brookings, travel 4.8 miles north on US 101 and turn left (west) at the Cape Ferrelo Viewpoint. Continue 0.2 mile to the parking area. The hike begins in the northwest corner of the parking area. *DeLorme: Oregon Atlas & Gazetteer:* Page 17, C13.

The Hike

The charming coastal town of Brookings lies 6 miles north of the California-Oregon border on the bay of the Chetco River and boasts uncrowded beaches, spectacular bluffs and offshore rock formations, a busy fishing harbor, prize fishing on the Chetco River, and some of the warmest weather on the Oregon Coast. Established in 1908, Brookings is the namesake of the Brookings family, who founded the Brookings Lumber and Box Company. In the past, logging was the chief industry here, but now tourism, Easter lily bulb production (Brookings is the nation's leader), and sport fishing are also major industries in this bustling seaport. Large-scale Easter lily bulb production in the Chetco Valley began during World War II when Japanese and Holland lily bulb imports were halted in the United States. Bulbs that sold for about a nickel apiece before the war were going for $1.00 during the war. This high price soon made bulb production a profitable way to make a living in Curry County. During the war the amount of lily bulb growers exploded

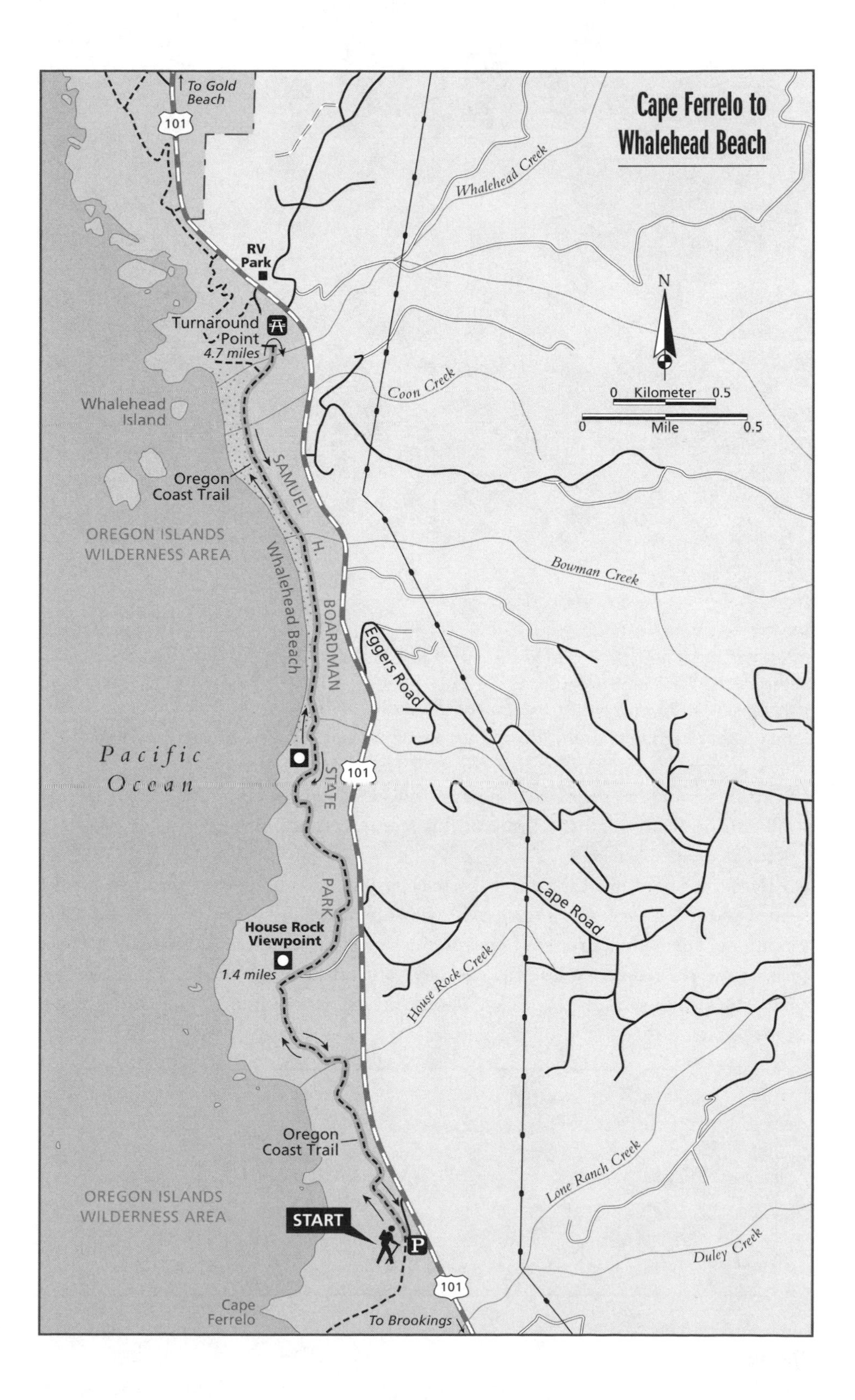

Cape Ferrelo to Whalehead Beach
To Gold Beach
101
RV Park
Whalehead Creek
Turnaround Point
4.7 miles
Coon Creek
0 Kilometer 0.5
0 Mile 0.5
Whalehead Island
Oregon Coast Trail
SAMUEL H. BOARDMAN STATE PARK
OREGON ISLANDS WILDERNESS AREA
Whalehead Beach
Bowman Creek
Eggers Road
Pacific Ocean
Cape Road
House Rock Viewpoint
1.4 miles
House Rock Creek
Oregon Coast Trail
Lone Ranch Creek
OREGON ISLANDS WILDERNESS AREA
START
P
Duley Creek
Cape Ferrelo
To Brookings

Whalehead Beach

to about 1,000. Some growers were making $10,000 to $20,000 per acre growing bulbs. Currently ten large production farms are active in the Brookings area, producing about 95 percent of the Easter lily bulbs worldwide.

Another highlight to the Brookings area is Samuel H. Boardman State Park. This 1,471-acre park stretches for more than 12 miles along the rugged coastline north of Brookings and has several access points off U.S. Highway 101. The Oregon Coast Trail runs right through the heart of this scenic area and promises you a pleasant, uncrowded coastal trek.

Begin the hike from the Cape Ferrelo parking area and wind through a Sitka spruce and red cedar forest interspersed with open meadows filled with vibrant purple lupine. There are also several viewpoints along this section that give you a sneak peak at the rugged rocky sea stacks located just off of Whalehead Beach. After 1.4 miles you come to House Rock Viewpoint, an excellent vantage point for spotting

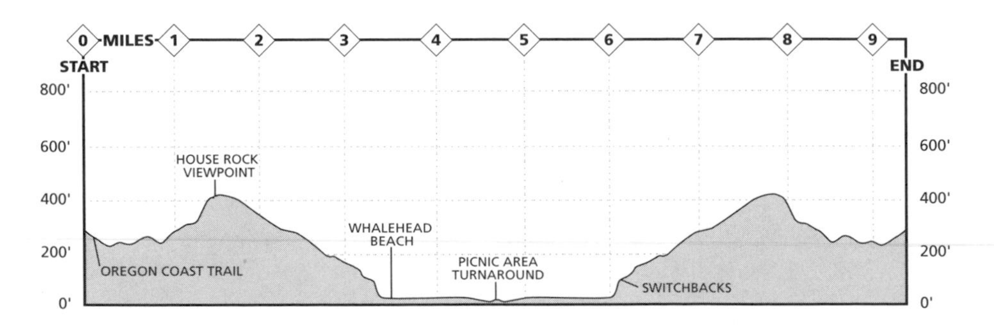

migrating gray whales. As you continue north the trail re-enters the forest and begins to descend steeply down a series of switchbacks. After 2.8 miles you emerge from the forest onto a scenic, open headland. The trail descends steeply to sandy Whalehead Beach. Continue walking north on the beach for another 1.6 miles, past large rocky outcrops, and offshore you'll see Whalehead Island—which clearly resembles the shape of a whale. At last you arrive at your turnaround point, where you'll find a scenic picnic spot and rest rooms.

Miles and Directions

0.0 Start at the north end of the viewpoint parking area at the wooden Oregon Coast Trail marker.

1.4 Reach the House Rock Viewpoint. Continue walking straight on the paved sidewalk. **Side trip:** You can take a detour here by turning left and viewing the Samuel H. Boardman monument.

2.0 Cross a wooden bridge over a creek. Notice the small, cascading waterfall to your right.

2.3 (FYI: There's a good viewpoint to your left.)

2.5 Turn left at the trail fork. Cross a wooden bridge over a creek.

2.8 The trail takes you into an open area on a scenic headland above Whalehead Beach. Descend steeply down a series of switchbacks to Whalehead Beach.

3.1 Reach Whalehead Beach. Cross a small stream and continue walking north on the sandy beach.

4.2 Cross a stream.

4.3 Near the end of the beach. Veer to the right and look for the wooden Oregon Coast Trail marker.

4.4 Reach the marker indicating the continuation of the trail north.

4.6 Pass the wooden stairs to your left. (FYI: If you take these stairs, you'll walk through a 0.25-mile tunnel to an RV Park.)

4.7 Arrive at a paved parking and picnic area with rest rooms. Turn around here and retrace the same route back to the trailhead.

9.4 Arrive at the trailhead.

Hike Information

Local Information

The Brookings-Harbor Chamber of Commerce, 16330 Lower Harbor Road, Brookings, OR 97415; (800) 535-9469; www.brookingsor.com.

Local Events/Attractions

Oregon Caves National Monument, 19000 Caves Highway, Cave Junction; (541) 592-2100; www.nps.gov/orca.

Azalea Festival, held Memorial Day weekend, Brookings; (800) 535-9469.

Local Outdoor Retailers

Loring's Lighthouse Sporting Goods, 554 Chetco Lane, Brookings; (541) 469-2148.

38 Illinois River Trail

Take a tour in a rugged gorge carved by the wild and scenic Illinois River. This remote, well-maintained trail follows the Illinois River for 27 miles and gives you a unique glimpse into the wonders of the Kalmiopsis Wilderness, a 179,655-acre wilderness filled with deep gorges and rocky ridges and home to many rare plant species. Be prepared for a long, twisty drive to the trailhead. Due to this trail's remoteness, we recommend that you plan on backpacking the trail. If you don't want to backpack, the 8-mile out-and-back section of the trail described here gives you a good introduction to this beautiful, uncrowded wilderness area. If you care to stay the night, there's a campground at the trailhead.

Start: The Briggs Creek trailhead is located about 40 miles south of Grants Pass off U.S. Highway 199 (the Redwood Highway).
Distance: 8 miles out and back.
Approximate hiking time: 3 to 4 hours.
Difficulty: Moderate.
Trail surface: Well-maintained dirt and gravel path.
Lay of the land: The hike parallels the wild and scenic Illinois River in the Kalmiopsis Wilderness.
Seasons: May through October.
Other trail users: None.
Canine compatibility: Dogs permitted.
Land status: Wilderness.
Nearest town: Selma.
Fees and permits: $5.00 Northwest Forest Pass. You can purchase a pass on-line at www.fs.fed.us/r6/feedemo, or by call calling (800) 270-7504. A free self-issue wilderness permit is also required and can be obtained at the trailhead.
Map: Maptech map: York Butte, Oregon.
Trail contact: Siskiyou National Forest, Galice Ranger District, 200 NE Greenfield Road, Grants Pass, OR 97526; (541) 471-6500; www.fs.fed.us/r6/siskiyou.

Finding the trailhead: From Grants Pass, take I-5 exit 55, indicated by the Oregon Caves and Crescent City sign. Turn south on US 199 (the Redwood Highway) and drive 21.6 miles to Selma. From US 199 in Selma, turn right (west) onto Forest Road 4103 (Illinois River Road) at the flashing yellow light. The pavement ends and turns to a rough, rocky dirt road after 11 miles. At mile 17.8 the road forks; go left. At mile 18 the road forks again; go right. There is a sign here that warns you that this road is not recommended for low-clearance vehicles. If you are driving a passenger car, it is recommended that you park here and walk the remaining mile to the trailhead.

From Brookings, travel 20 miles south on U.S. Highway 101 to Crescent City and turn east onto US 199. Travel about 55 miles northeast on US 199 to Selma. From US 199 in Selma, turn left (west) on FR 4103 (Illinois River Road) at the flashing yellow light. The pavement ends and turns to a rough, rocky dirt road after 11 miles. At mile 17.8 the road forks; go left. At mile 18 the road forks again; go right. There is a sign here that warns you that this road is not recommended for low-clearance vehicles. If you are driving a passenger car, it is recommended that you park here and walk the remaining mile to the trailhead. *Delorme: Oregon Atlas & Gazetteer:* Page 18, A2.

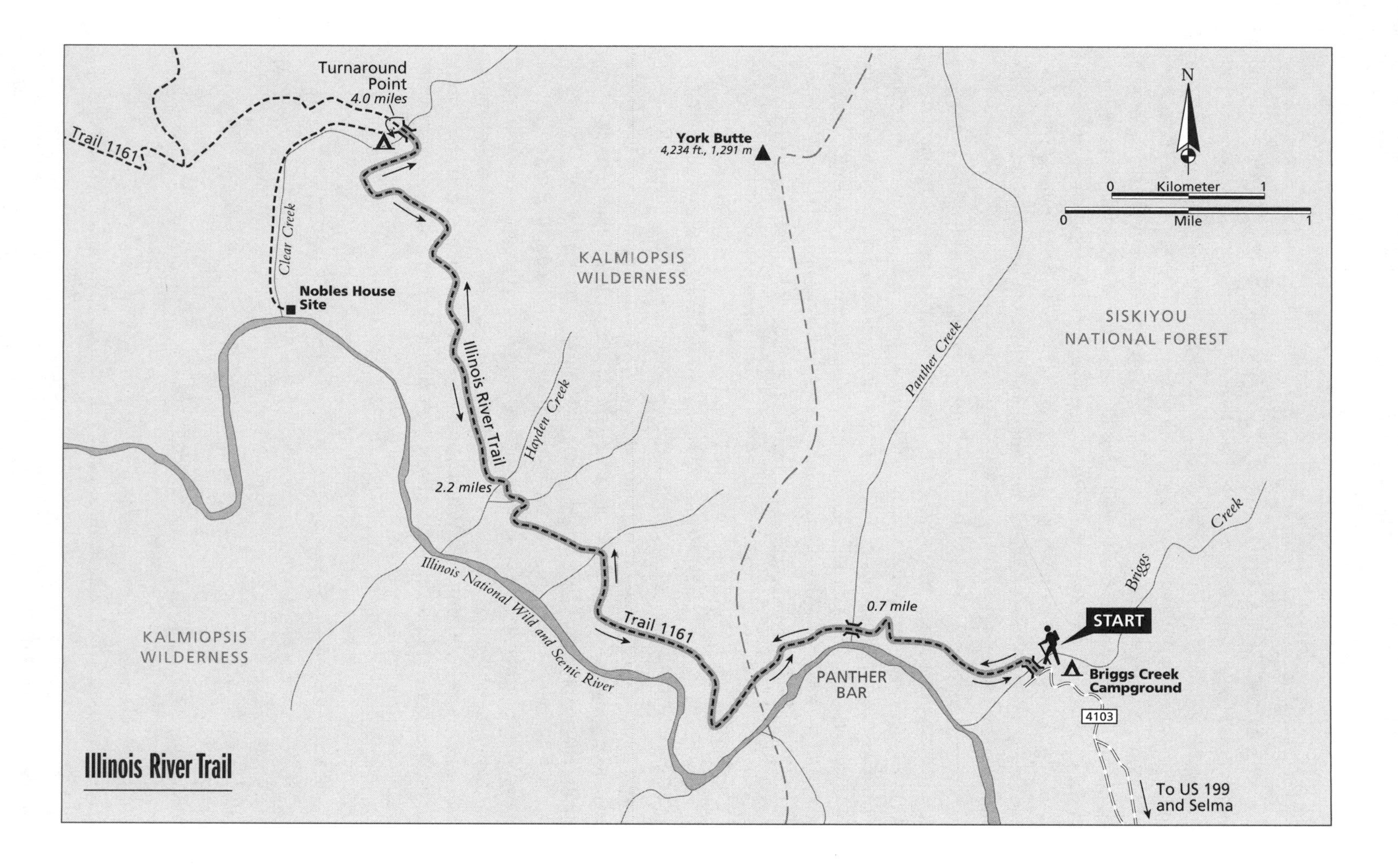
Illinois River Trail
Turnaround Point
4.0 miles
Trail 1161
York Butte
4,234 ft., 1,291 m
N
0
Kilometer
1
0
Mile
1
Clear Creek
Nobles House Site
KALMIOPSIS WILDERNESS
SISKIYOU NATIONAL FOREST
Illinois River Trail
Hayden Creek
Panther Creek
2.2 miles
Illinois National Wild and Scenic River
Trail 1161
0.7 mile
Briggs
Creek
START
KALMIOPSIS WILDERNESS
PANTHER BAR
Briggs Creek Campground
4103
To US 199 and Selma

The Hike

The Illinois River Trail is located in the 179,655-acre Kalmiopsis Wilderness—one of Oregon's biggest and least-crowded wilderness areas. Two words describe this wilderness best: rugged and remote. Characterized by deep river and creek gorges and high ridges, this part of Oregon is home to many rare plant species. The namesake of the Kalmiopsis Wilderness, the pink-flowering kalmiopsis leachiana, can be found clinging to rocky ridges and hillsides. This plant begins blooming in late April and blooms through the end of June. Plants that live in this region are tolerant of the high rainfall in the winter months—the average winter rainfall can range from 100 to 150 inches—and the dry, scorching summers, when temperatures can reach the mid- to upper 90s.

The Kalmiopsis Wilderness is part of the ancient Klamath Mountains. The mountains were formed when the North American plate pushed up against the Pacific Ocean bottom approximately 200 million years ago. This push-and-shove affair produced high mountain ridges where ocean fossils have been found. The rocks found in this wilderness area are of varied origins, from oceanic crust to ocean-floor lavas. This mountainous region is also rich in metals such as copper, cobalt, platinum, chromite, nickle, iron, manganese, and gold. Old mining operations are dotted throughout the region; the largest producing mine, Gold Peck (located north of Baby Creek), was shut down in 1952.

The Illinois River Trail takes you right through the heart of this wilderness. The trail follows the river along a high ridge, taking you over Bald Mountain on a well-graded path for 27 miles to its terminus at Oak Flat, near Agness. Before you begin hiking on the trail, be sure to fill out a wilderness permit. You begin by walking on a path that crosses over Briggs Creek and then slowly ascends through a forest of Douglas fir, canyon live oak, and orange madrone trees (identifiable by their rusty orange-colored, papery bark). Along the way you'll see the low-growing, bushy manzanita and chinkapin. Another plant to look out for, though you may not appreciate it as much, is poison oak. When you catch your first glimpse of the Illinois River, you'll notice its dark green color, which is due to the serpentinite rock that's present along the river's course.

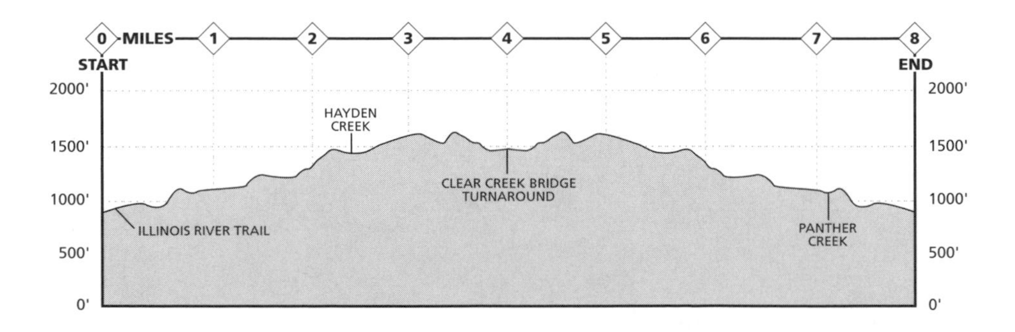

The rugged and wild Kalmiopsis River gorge

As the trail climbs you'll pass rough, rocky outcrops of lava rock that offer scenic viewpoints of the river and the river gorge. The river flows over large boulders and through narrow shoots, filling the current with huge, challenging rapids. Not surprisingly, this river is the most difficult white-water rafting river in Oregon and attracts a few brave rafters and kayakers to run its rapids. The greatest obstacle on the river is the Green Wall—a rip-roaring, Class-V, boulder-strewn rapid that tests even the most experienced rafters and kayakers. (This rapid is located several miles away from the section of trail on which you're hiking, but you'll also see many rapids along this section.)

If you plan on backpacking this trail, you'll reach a good camping spot at Clear Creek (the hike's turnaround point). You cross a bridge over the creek, and there are some level campsites to your left. There is also an unmaintained trail that leads down to bubbling Clear Creek, where you can wade or filter water if you're running low. Keep in mind that black bears live in this wilderness area, so you should hang your food if you are camping. Other critters you may see on your journey include blue-tailed skinks, chattering Douglas squirrels, western fence lizards, and (last but certainly not least) rattlesnakes.

Miles and Directions

0.0 Start at the wooden trailhead marker at the end of FR 4103. Start walking on the Illinois River Trail (Trail 1161) and cross a wooden bridge spanning Briggs Creek.

0.7 Cross a wooden bridge over Panther Creek.

2.2 Cross a wooden bridge over Hayden Creek.

4.0 Cross a bridge over Clear Creek. This is your turnaround point. (FYI: After you cross the bridge, there are some campsites to your left. There is also an unmaintained trail that leads down to the creek if you want to cool off.) Retrace the same route back to the trailhead.

8.0 Arrive at the trailhead.

Hike Information

Local Information

Grants Pass/Josephine County Chamber of Commerce, 1995 NW Vine Street, Grants Pass, OR 97528; (800) 547-5927; www.grantspasschamber.org.

Local Events/Attractions

Wild Rogue Balloon Festival, held the first weekend in June, Grants Pass; (800) 547-5927.

Local Outdoor Retailers

Big Five Sporting Goods, 310 NE Agness Avenue, Grants Pass; (541) 955-9519.

39 Vulcan Lake

Experience the raw beauty of the rugged and remote Kalmiopsis Wilderness. This scenic hike takes you over an open, windswept ridge to a viewpoint of a spectacular glacier-carved basin that cradles Vulcan Lake. Once you reach this scenic lake, and descend down the ridge, you'll want to spend hours sitting atop the boulder-strewn lakeshore staring at the crystal-clear water of this high-alpine lake.

Start: The trailhead is located about 30 miles east of Brookings on Forest Road 260.
Distance: 2.2 miles out and back.
Approximate hiking time: 1 to 2 hours.
Difficulty: Moderate due to a fairly steep ascent up a ridge.
Total climbing: 270 feet.
Trail surface: Graded dirt path with some rocky sections.
Lay of the land: Hike up an open, prominent ridge and then descend into a scenic rock basin to the shore of Vulcan Lake.
Seasons: Mid-June through October.
Other trail users: None.
Canine compatibility: Dogs permitted.
Land status: Wilderness.
Nearest town: Brookings.
Fees and permits: $5.00 Northwest Forest Pass. You can purchase a pass on-line at www.fs.fed.us/r6/feedemo, or by call calling (800) 270-7504. A self-issue wilderness permit (available at the trailhead) is also required.
Map: Maptech map: Chetco Peak, Oregon.
Trail contact: Siskiyou National Forest, Chetco Ranger District, 555 Fifth Street, Brookings, OR 97415; (541) 469-2196; www.fs.fed.us/r6/siskiyou.

Finding the trailhead: From Brookings, turn onto North Bank Chetco River Road from U.S. Highway 101 and drive 15.8 miles to Forest Road 1909 and turn right. At mile 18.4 come to a fork and go right. Follow the signs indicating VULCAN PEAK AND THE KALMIOPSIS WILDERNESS. At mile 23.6 the road comes to a T intersection. Turn right where a sign indicates VULCAN LAKE. The road becomes very rough and rocky. At mile 25.6 come to a fork and turn left. At mile 28.4 pass Red Mountain Prairie Campground on your left. At mile 29.1 come to a fork and turn left onto FR 260, where the sign indicates VULCAN LAKE. The road becomes rougher and rockier and narrow, making it difficult to turn around. At mile 30.8 reach the trailhead at the road's end. *DeLorme: Oregon Atlas & Gazetteer:* Page 18, C1.

The Hike

Established in 1907 the 1,163,484-acre Siskiyou National Forest contains within its boundaries the Klamath, Coast, and Siskiyou Mountain ranges. The wild and rugged Siskiyou National Forest boasts five wilderness areas: Grassy Knob, Red Buttes, Siskiyou, Wild Rogue, and the Kalmiopsis. Of these five, the 179,655-acre Kalmiopsis Wilderness is the largest.

The Kalmiopsis Wilderness is the namesake of a pre–ice age shrub named kalmiopsis leachiana—one of the oldest members of the heath family. More than 153 miles of trails wander through this rugged area of steep ridges and rugged river

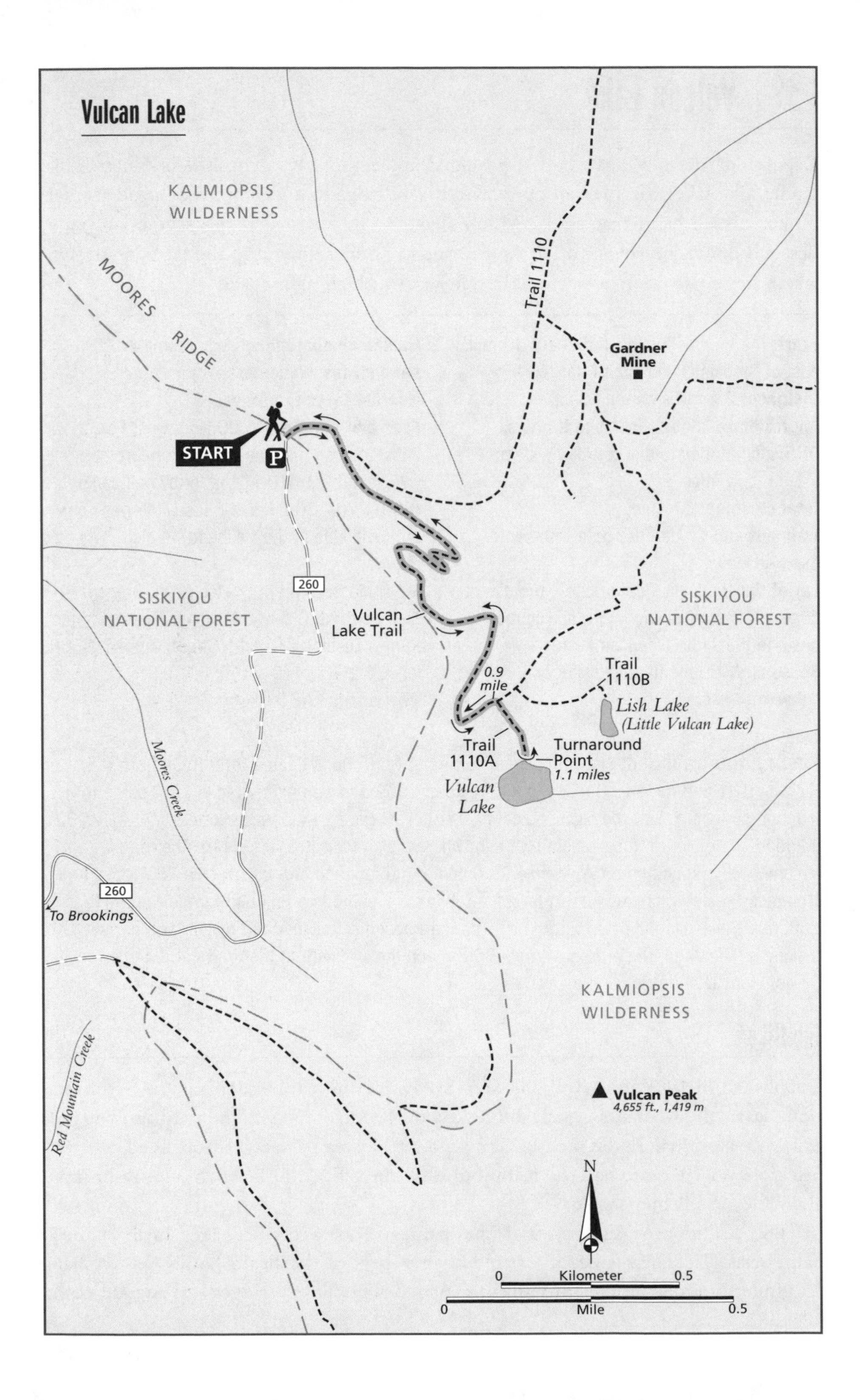
Vulcan Lake
KALMIOPSIS WILDERNESS
MOORES RIDGE
START
P
Trail 1110
Gardner Mine
260
SISKIYOU NATIONAL FOREST
Vulcan Lake Trail
SISKIYOU NATIONAL FOREST
0.9 mile
Trail 1110B
Lish Lake
(Little Vulcan Lake)
Trail 1110A
Turnaround Point
1.1 miles
Vulcan Lake
Moores Creek
260
To Brookings
KALMIOPSIS WILDERNESS
Vulcan Peak
4,655 ft., 1,419 m
Red Mountain Creek
N
0 Kilometer 0.5
0 Mile 0.5

Early season hiking on the Vulcan Lake Trail

gorges. This diverse wilderness area is also known for its rare and unique plants, many of which have adapted to the harsh soils derived from peridotite and serpentinite rocks. Weather, climate, and geological forces have also played a role in the type of plants that live in this remote corner of southern Oregon. Some of the hardwood tree species you'll find here include golden chinkapen, Pacific madrone, Oregon

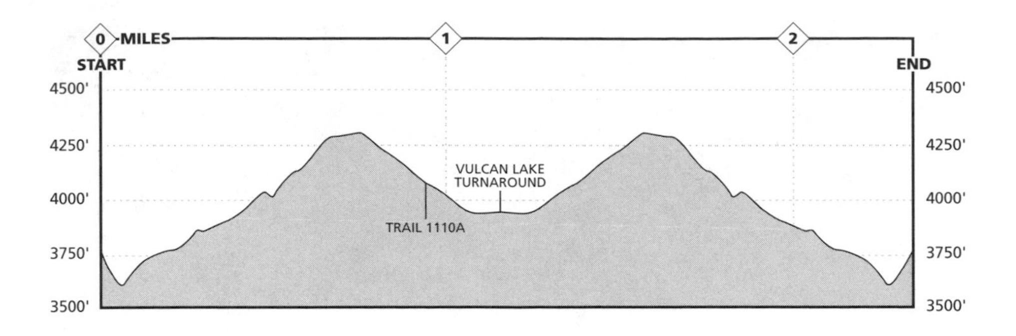

myrtlewood, California black oak, tan oak, canyon live oak, and Oregon white oak. Woody shrubs found here that are considered rare and sensitive include Howell's manzanita, kalmiopsis plant, Sierra-laurel, Del Norte willow, and Tracy's willow. Rare and sensitive herbaceous plants include Bolander's onion, Waldo rockcress, Siskiyou sedge, purple toothwort, short-lobed paintbrush, clustered lady's slipper, rigid willow herb, deer fleabane, Siskiyou fritillaria, and Siskiyou monardella, plus many more.

For millions of years, erosional forces have been shaping the Kalmiopsis Wilderness. Now-extinct glaciers carved many of the lake basins, such as Babyfoot Lake, Vulcan Lake, Rough and Ready Lakes, and Chetco Lake. The hike to Vulcan Lake gives you an inside look at the geological forces that have shaped this area. The trail begins by switchbacking steeply up an open ridge to a spectacular overlook. The trail then crosses a saddle on the ridge and descends across an open slope filled with different species of manzanita plants. There are numerous viewpoints of the lake along the way. After a mile you reach Vulcan Lake. This seven-acre lake rests at an elevation of approximately 4,000 feet in a spectacular red-rock basin at the foot of 4,655-foot Vulcan Peak. The blue-green lake is stocked with rainbow trout and is the home to the California newt (salamander). The lake's shoreline is strewn with large, oddly shaped boulders that make wonderful places to hang out, eat your lunch, and gaze at the lake before heading back to the trailhead.

Miles and Directions

0.0 Start from the trailhead sign located at the end of Forest Road 260. Be sure to fill out a self-issue wilderness permit.

0.1 Turn right at the trail fork.

0.9 Turn right where a sign indicates, TRAIL 1110A. (FYI: Trail 1110B goes left toward Little Vulcan Lake.)

1.1 Reach Vulcan Lake and your turnaround point. Retrace the same route back to the trailhead.

2.2 Arrive at the trailhead.

Hike Information

Local Information

The Brookings-Harbor Chamber of Commerce, 16330 Lower Harbor Road, Brookings, OR 97415; (800) 535-9469; www.brookingsor.com.

Local Events/Attractions

Oregon Caves National Monument, 19000 Caves Highway, Cave Junction; (541) 592-2100; www.nps.gov/orca.

Azalea Festival, held Memorial Day weekend, Brookings; (800) 535-9469.

Local Outdoor Retailers

Loring's Lighthouse Sporting Goods, 554 Chetco Lane, Brookings; (541) 469-2148.

40 Alfred A. Loeb State Park Nature Trails

This hike through Alfred A. Loeb State Park offers a rare glimpse of two hard-to-find tree species: the Oregon myrtlewood and the redwood. The Riverview Trail follows the banks of the salmon- and steelhead-rich Chetco River through an old grove of Oregon myrtle trees. The Redwood Nature Trail loops through a grove of immense coast redwood trees. Both trails include numbered markers that correspond to a detailed brochure pointing out all the highlights. The state park also has a campground and all kinds of fun things to see and do. You can swim in the Chetco River, fish, or rent a charter boat in nearby Brookings Harbor. In addition the park is the gateway to the 179,655-acre Kalmiopsis Wilderness and its hundreds of miles of trails, numerous lakes, and rugged river gorges.

Start: The trailhead is located 7.5 miles east of Brookings in Alfred A. Loeb State Park.
Distance: 4.2 miles out and back.
Approximate hiking time: 1.5 to 2 hours.
Difficulty: Easy.
Total climbing: 400 feet.
Trail surface: Well-maintained dirt path.
Lay of the land: The Riverview Trail parallels the Chetco River through an old grove of myrtlewood trees. The Redwood Nature Trail loops through an ancient redwood grove.
Seasons: Year-round.
Other trail users: None.
Canine compatibility: Leashed dogs permitted.
Land status: State park.
Nearest town: Brookings.
Fees and permits: $3.00 day-use fee.
Map: Maptech map: Mount Emily, Oregon.
Trail contact: Oregon State Parks and Recreation, 1115 Commercial Street NE, Suite 1, Salem, OR 97301; (800) 551-6949; www.oregonstateparks.org/park_72.php.

Finding the trailhead: From Brookings, head east on North Bank Chetco River Road from U.S. Highway 101. Drive 7.5 miles and turn right into Alfred A. Loeb State Park. Come to a fork in the road and go left. Proceed to the picnic area and park in a parking area on your right. *DeLorme: Oregon Atlas & Gazetteer:* Page 17, D3.

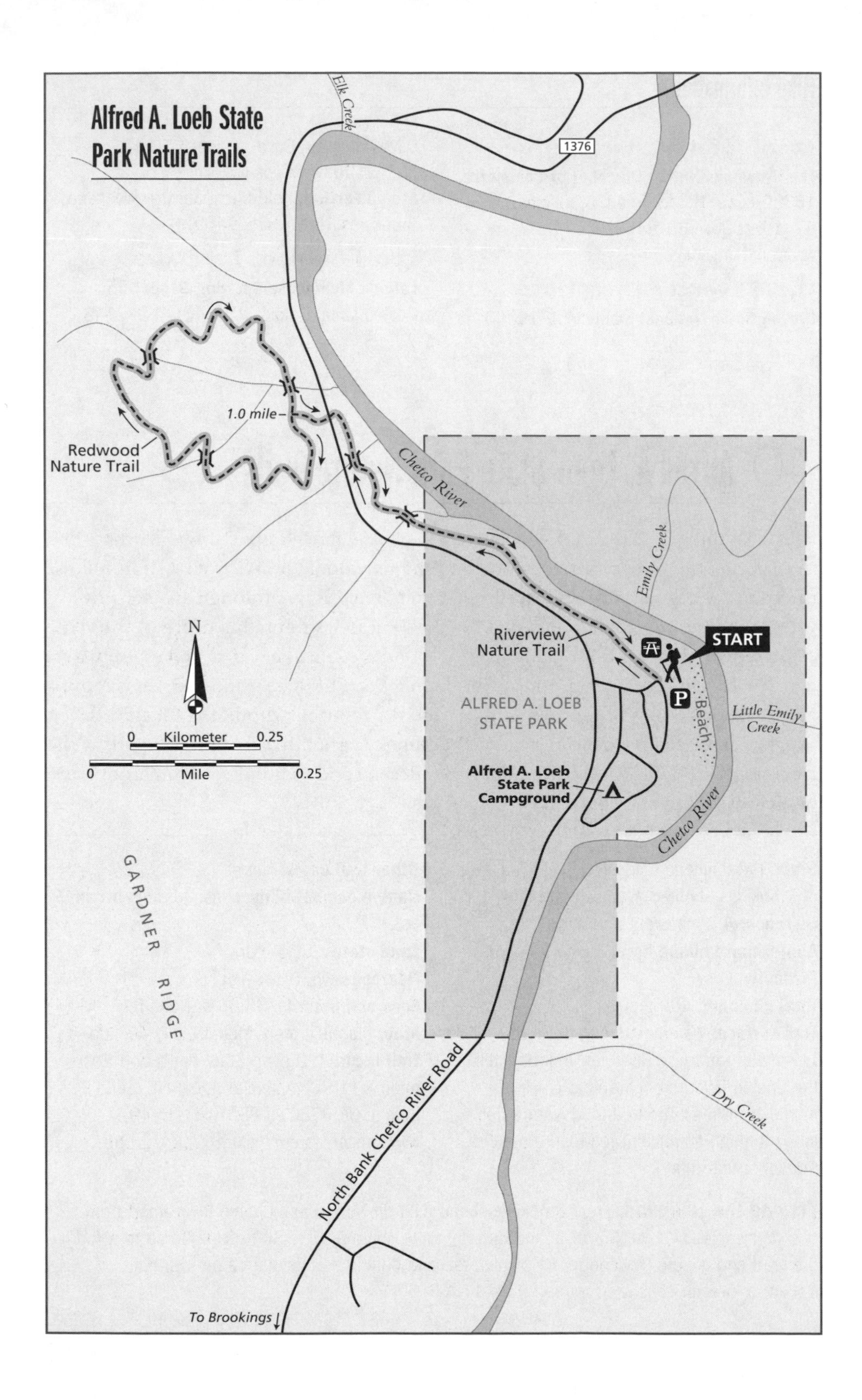

Alfred A. Loeb State Park Nature Trails
Elk Creek
1376
1.0 mile
Redwood Nature Trail
Chetco River
Emily Creek
Riverview Nature Trail
START
N
0 Kilometer 0.25
0 Mile 0.25
ALFRED A. LOEB STATE PARK
Beach
Little Emily Creek
Alfred A. Loeb State Park Campground
Chetco River
GARDNER RIDGE
North Bank Chetco River Road
Dry Creek
To Brookings

The Hike

The Riverview and Redwood Nature Trails take you on a journey through groves of two hard-to-find tree species: the Oregon myrtle (also know as Coos Bay laurel) and the giant coast redwood. Be sure to pick up the descriptive brochure at the trailhead, so you can identify these and other plant species found along the trails.

The trail begins as an easy ramble through a lush grove of Oregon myrtle, Douglas fir, western hemlock, and red alder. As you walk the path, look for the distinctive gumdrop shape of the Oregon myrtle tree. This broad-leafed evergreen grows in small groves in the wet coastal regions of Oregon and California and is a member of the laurel family—the same family as avocado, camphor, cinnamon, and sassafras. The oil from the myrtle's fragrant and spicy leaves is often used to scent candles and perfumes. The leaves are also an excellent seasoning for soups and sauces—Native Americans made a soothing tea from the leaves. The beautiful wood is used to make furniture and souvenirs.

An impressive redwood tree on the Redwood Nature Trail. Photo: Ken Skeen

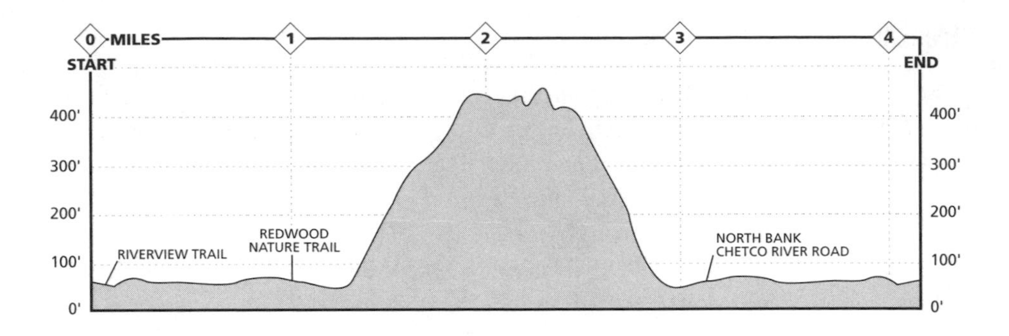

The trees provide a shady canopy that creates a perfect growing environment for the feathery maidenhair fern, the spiked sword fern, deer fern, and the edible salmonberry. You'll also notice an abundance of English ivy, a non-native plant that competes with the indigenous species for precious forest real estate. Poison oak also can be found lurking along this trail, so watch out. As you walk along, you'll catch glimpses of the wide-running Chetco River. This calm, deep river meets the Pacific Ocean at Brookings Harbor—home to one of Oregon's largest fishing fleets. The river has some of the largest steelhead and salmon runs on the coast of Oregon and is popular with sport fisherman. It's also home to several good swimming holes—keep your eyes peeled. At mile 1.1 the Riverview Trail comes to a paved road. Across the road is the beginning of the Redwood Nature Trail. From here it's a series of steep switchbacks through a tall, silent grove of 300- to 800-year-old coast redwood trees (*Sequoia sempervirens*). Redwood trees (there are three varieties) are found in only three regions of the world: The coast redwood is found along the northern California coast and at the tip of the southern Oregon coast; the Sierra redwood (*Sequoiadendron gigantia*) is found in a small section of the Sierra Nevada Mountains; and the dawn redwood (*meta Sequoia*) is found in a remote area of China.

Coast redwoods can live for more than 2,000 years, growing as high as 300 feet with a diameter of 20 feet. These hardy trees have several survival strategies that account for their longevity. Their thick bark is fire and rot resistant, and they have the ability to grow a lateral root system, which allows them to re-establish themselves after floods. If a redwood tree falls over, new trees spring up from the limbs of the parent tree to create a grove of small trees in fairly straight rows.

As you continue walking up the path, you'll see native rhododendrons and tan oak trees, which commonly grow in the company of redwoods. The bright red and pink flowers of the rhododendron can be seen blooming in early spring. The tan oak tree can be identified by its fuzzy acorns. Finally, you'll see the delicate pink flowers and cloverlike leaves of redwood sorrel. The Redwood Loop ends after 1.9 miles. Continue back to your starting point on the Riverview Trail. If you want to stay and explore the state park more, check out the campground. If you don't want to rough it, try staying in one of the park's cabins.

Miles and Directions

0.0 Start in the parking area signed for the Riverview trailhead. Walk across the paved road to the trailhead sign that indicates the start of the Riverview Trail. (Note: Be sure to pick up a trail brochure. There are trail markers that correspond to descriptions in the brochure. Be sure to take the time to read about the plants and wildlife described.)

0.5 (FYI: Walk through an area that has edible salmonberries.)

1.0 Cross North Bank Chetco River Road and arrive at the Redwood Nature trailhead. There are rest rooms and a picnic table here.

1.1 Turn left on the Redwood Nature Trail. (Note: This trail also has trail markers that are described in the brochure.)

3.1 The loop trail ends. Turn left and walk 1.1 miles on the Riverview Trail back to your car.

4.2 Arrive at the Riverview trailhead.

Hike Information

Local Information

The Brookings-Harbor Chamber of Commerce, 16330 Lower Harbor Road, Brookings, OR 97415; (800) 535-9469.

Local Events/Attractions

Oregon Caves National Monument, 19000 Caves Highway, Cave Junction; (541) 592-2100; www.nps.gov/orca.

Azalea Festival, held Memorial Day weekend, Brookings; (800) 535-9469.

Local Outdoor Retailers

Loring's Lighthouse Sporting Goods, 554 Chetco Lane, Brookings; (541) 469-2148.

South Coast Honorable Mentions

CC South Slough Estuarine Preserve

You can explore a series of trails through a wetland ecosystem at this 4,700-acre Coos Bay estuary. Paths lead through fresh- and saltwater marshes, mudflats, and floodplains. The visitor center is open from 8:30 A.M. to 4:30 P.M. Monday through Friday during winter and from 8:30 A.M. to 4:30 P.M. daily during summer. To get there from Coos Bay or North Bend, follow signs to Charleston, Shore Acres State Park, and Ocean Beaches. From Charleston, head west on Cape Arago Highway and in 0.1 mile turn left (south) onto Seven Devils Road. Follow signs to South Slough Sanctuary and Bandon. Drive 4.5 miles, turn left at the interpretive center, and continue to a parking area. The trailhead is past the interpretive center to the left of a panel entitled JOURNEY TO THE SEA. For more information contact South Slough National Estuarine Research Reserve, P.O. Box 5417, Charleston, OR 97420; (541) 888–5558; www.southsloughestuary.com. *DeLorme: Oregon Atlas & Gazetteer:* Page 33, B6.

DD Golden and Silver Falls State Natural Area

This spectacular trail takes you on a tour of the shimmering cascades of Golden Falls and Silver Falls. Start by crossing a bridge over Silver Creek. At the trail junction, head left and enjoy the shady canopy of old-growth Douglas fir trees. At 0.4 mile turn left to view the billowing 160-foot cascade of Silver Falls. After viewing the falls, head back to the main trail and turn left. Continue uphill as the trail follows the edge of a steep cliff to the viewpoint of Golden Falls at 0.9 mile (your turnaround point). For a less-precipitous view of Golden Falls, take the right fork at the beginning of the hike and walk 0.3 mile to the viewpoint. To get there from U.S. Highway 101 in Coos Bay, head east on the Coos River Highway, following signs to Allegany. Travel 13.5 miles east on the north side of the Coos River to the town of Allegany. From here follow state park signs another 9.5 miles to the Golden and Silver Falls State Natural Area. For more information contact Oregon State Parks and Recreation, Suite 1, 1115 Commercial Street NE, Salem, OR 97301; (800) 551–6949; www.oregonstateparks.org/park_96.php. *DeLorme: Oregon Atlas & Gazetteer:* Page 34, A1.

EE Bandon State Natural Area

The first access point you'll find is a viewpoint overlooking Face Rock. The face on this rock is supposed to represent Ewauna, the daughter of Chief Siskiyou. You'll also be able to see a series of sea stacks that are part of the National Wildlife Refuge System. From here a trail leads down to the beach and to a picnic area with tables.

If you continue south on U.S. Highway 101, the next access point you'll arrive at is the Devil's Kitchen area. Hiking trails lead to the beach and a picnic area next to a picturesque creek. Continuing south on US 101, you'll come to two more access points. The third and fourth access points feature beach access but do not have picnic or rest-room facilities. This park has several different access points off of US 101 from 1 to 5 miles south of Bandon. For more information contact Oregon State Parks and Recreation, Suite 1, 1115 Commercial Street NE, Salem, OR 97301; (800) 551–6949; www.oregonstateparks.org/park_64.php. *DeLorme: Oregon Atlas & Gazetteer:* Page 33, D5.

FF New River

Several different trails explore the New River area, which is haven to an abundance of wildlife, including mallard ducks, northern pintails, green-winged teal, bufflehead, hooded mergansers, and tundra swans. Raptors you may see include peregrine falcons, northern harriers, and bald eagles. Trails lead through coastal forest, open meadows, and to viewpoints of the New River, which is an outlet stream of Floras Lake. To get there from Bandon, travel 9 miles south (or 18 miles north of Port Orford) on U.S. Highway 101 to the junction with Croft Lake Road. Turn west onto Croft Lake Road and go 1.5 miles to a road fork. Turn right and continue to the first trailhead adjacent to a small group of buildings. For more information contact BLM, Coos District, 1300 Airport Lane, Coos Bay, OR 97459; (888) 809–0839; www.or.blm.gov/coosbay/. *DeLorme: Oregon Atlas & Gazetteer:* Page 25, A5.

GG Cape Blanco State Park

This uncrowded state park is a great place to enjoy the sights and sounds of the southern Oregon coast. Set up a base camp at the scenic campground and spend a few days exploring the 8 miles of hiking trails through a diverse coastal ecosystem. The Oregon Coast Trail can be accessed from the south end of the campground. Additional hiking trails lead to several viewpoints and the beach. Photographers and wildlife lovers will enjoy the natural beauty of this park, with its high chalky bluffs, black sand beach, and offshore sea stacks, which are home to herds of sea lions and prime nesting sites for seabirds. If you're a history buff, don't miss exploring the 59-foot Cape Blanco Lighthouse, which is the oldest lighthouse in Oregon. Another historical structure at this state park is the Hughes House Museum, built in 1898 by Patrick Hughes. This eleven-room, two-story, Victorian-style mansion was built out of old-growth Port Orford cedar at a cost of $3,800. It's open for tours April through September during the summer and is filled with delightful antique furniture and old photos depicting the life of the former 1,000-acre dairy ranch that the house sits on. To get to Cape Blanco State Park, drive 46 miles south of Coos Bay or 4 miles north of Port Orford on U.S. Highway 101 to the junction with Cape Blanco Road. Turn west and drive 5 miles on Cape Blanco Road to Cape Blanco State Park. For more information contact Oregon State Parks and Recreation, Suite 1, 1115 Commercial Street NE, Salem, OR 97301; (800) 551–6949; www.oregonstateparks.org/park_62.php. *DeLorme: Oregon Atlas & Gazetteer:* Page 24, B4.

HH Humbug Mountain State Park

The centerpiece of Humbug Mountain State Park is 1,761-foot Humbug Mountain, which is the highest point on the coast. A 5.5-mile strenuous loop hike takes you to the summit of this mountain from the campground. To reach the trailhead from the campground, cross a bridge over Brush Creek and proceed through the tunnel under U.S. Highway 101. The trail passes through maple and myrtle wood trees and leads you through sections of old-growth Douglas fir. You'll come to a junction in about a mile that is the start of the loop portion of the trail. If you go to the right, you'll come to a viewpoint. Looking north you'll see Redfish Rocks, Port Orford, and Cape Blanco. Keep following the trail as it loops back around to rejoin the main trail. At this junction you can hike up a short steep trail that leads to a viewpoint looking south toward Gold Beach. To get there from Port Orford, drive 6 miles south on US 101 to the park entrance on the left (east) side of the highway. If you are coming from Gold Beach, the park is located 21 miles to the north. For more information contact Oregon State Parks and Recreation, Suite 1, 1115 Commercial Street NE, Salem, OR 97301; (800) 551–6949; www.oregonstateparks.org/park_56.php. *DeLorme: Oregon Atlas & Gazetteer:* Page 25, C5.

II Port Orford Heads State Park

Port Orford Heads State Park features a wind-sheltered picnic area adjacent to the historic Port Orford Heads United States Coast Guard Lifeboat Station, which was built in 1934. It now houses a museum that you can tour. You can take your pick of several short trails that lead to scenic views from this high windblown headland. To get there from U.S. Highway 101 in Port Orford, turn west onto Ninth Street and continue for 0.2 mile to the junction with Arizona Street. Turn left onto Arizona Street and continue 0.9 mile to a parking area. For more information contact Oregon State Parks and Recreation, Suite 1, 1115 Commercial Street NE, Salem, OR 97301; (800) 551–6949; www.oregonstateparks.org/park_61.php. *DeLorme: Oregon Atlas & Gazetteer:* Page 24, C4.

The Art of Hiking

Whenever you go hiking try to follow a leave-no-trace philosophy to help protect our wild places and wild things. Here are some guidelines to follow.

Zero impact. Always leave an area just like you found it—if not better than you found it. Avoid camping in fragile, alpine meadows and along the banks of streams and lakes. Use a camp stove versus building a wood fire. Pack up all of your trash and extra food. Bury human waste at least 100 feet from water sources under 6 to 8 inches of topsoil. Don't bathe with soap in a lake or stream—use prepackaged moistened towels to wipe off sweat and dirt, or bathe in the water without soap.

Shore Acres State Park

Leave no weeds. Noxious weeds tend to out-compete (overtake) our native flora, which in turn affects animals and birds that depend on the flora for food. Noxious weeds can be harmful to wildlife. Yes, just like birds and furry critters, we humans can carry weed seeds from one place to another. Here are a couple of things hikers can do to minimize the spread of noxious weeds. First learn to identify noxious weeds and exotic species. Then regularly clean your boots, tents, packs, and hiking poles of mud and seeds. Brush your dog to remove any weed seed. Avoid camping and traveling in weed-infested areas.

Stay on the trail. Paths serve an important purpose; they limit our impact on natural areas. Straying from a designated trail may seem innocent, but it can cause damage to sensitive areas—damage that the area may take years to recover from, if it can recover at all. Even simple shortcuts can be destructive. So, please, stay on the trail.

Keep your dog under control. You can buy a flexilead, which allows your dog to go exploring along the trail and also allows you to reel him in if other hikers approach, or if he decides to chase a rabbit scurrying by. Always obey leash laws and be sure to bury your dog's waste or pack it out in resealable plastic bags.

Yield to horses. In many cases you are sharing the trail with other wilderness travelers, namely horses. When you approach these animals on the trail, always step quietly off the trail and let them pass. If you are wearing a large backpack, it's a good idea to sit down and speak in a friendly voice to let the horse know you are present. From a horse's perspective, a hiker wearing a large backpack is a scary trail monster, and these sensitive animals can be easily spooked.

Respect other trail users. Often you're not the only one on the trail. With the rise in popularity of multiuse trails, you'll have to learn a new kind of respect, beyond the nod and "hello" approach you're used to. You should first investigate whether you're on a multiuse trail, and assume the appropriate precautions. When you encounter motorized vehicles (ATVs, motorcycles, and 4WDs), be acutely aware. Though they should always yield to the hiker, often they're going too fast or are too lost in the buzz of their engine to react to your presence. If you hear activity ahead, step off the trail just to be safe. Now you're not likely to hear a mountain biker coming, so the best bet is to know whether you share the trail with them. Cyclists should always yield to hikers, but that's of little comfort to the hiker. Be aware. When you approach horses or pack animals on the trail, always step quietly off the trail, preferably on the downhill side, and let them pass. If you're wearing a large backpack, it's often a good idea to sit down. To some animals, a hiker wearing a large backpack might appear threatening.

Getting into Shape

Unless you want to be sore, and possibly have to shorten your trip or vacation, be sure to get in shape before a big hike. If you're terribly out of shape, start a walking program early, preferably eight weeks in advance. Start with a fifteen-minute walk during your lunch hour or after work and gradually increase your walking time to an hour. You should also increase your elevation gain. Walking briskly up hills really strengthens your leg muscles and gets your heart rate up. If you work in a storied office building, take the stairs instead of the elevator. If you prefer going to a gym, walk the treadmill or use a stairmaster. You can further increase your strength and endurance by walking with a loaded backpack. Stationary exercises you might consider are squats, leg lifts, sit-ups, and push-ups. Other good ways to get in shape include biking, running, aerobics, and, of course, short hikes.

Preparedness

Take the necessary time to plan your trip. Whether going on a short day hike or an extended backpack trip, always prepare for the worst. In order to remain comfortable (and to survive if you really want to push it), you need to concern yourself with the basics: water, food, and shelter. Don't go on a hike without having these bases covered.

Water. Even in frigid conditions, you need at least two quarts of water a day to function efficiently. Add heat and taxing terrain and you can bump that figure up to one gallon. That's simply a base to work from—your metabolism and your level of conditioning can raise or lower that amount. Unless you know your level, assume that you need one gallon of water a day. Now, where do you plan on getting the water? Preferably not from natural water sources. These sources can be loaded with intestinal disturbers, such as bacteria, viruses, and fertilizers. Giardia lamblia, the most common of these disturbers, is a protozoan parasite that lives part of its lifecycle as a cyst in water sources. The parasite spreads when mammals defecate in water sources. Once ingested, Giardia can induce cramping, diarrhea, vomiting, and fatigue within two days to two weeks after drinking the contaminated water. Giardia is treatable with the prescription drug Flagyl. If you believe you've contracted Giardia, see a doctor immediately.

Treating water. The best and easiest solution to avoid polluted water is to carry your water with you. A good rule is to carry a liter of water for every two hours you are planning on hiking. This is a viable solution for most day hikes, but for daylong hikes and overnight backpack trips, you'll need to look into treating your water. There are three methods to treating water: boiling, chemical treatment, and filtering. If you boil water it's recommended that you do so for ten to fifteen minutes. This is often impractical because you're forced to exhaust a great deal of your fuel supply. You can opt for chemical treatment (e.g., Potable Aqua), which will kill Giardia but will not take care of other chemical pollutants. Another drawback to chemical treatments is the unpleasant taste of the water after it's been treated. You can remedy this by adding powdered drink mix to the water. Filters are the preferred method for treating water. Filters remove Giardia and organic and inorganic contaminants, and don't leave an aftertaste. Water filters are far from perfect, as they can easily become clogged or leak if a gasket wears out. It's always a good idea to carry a backup supply of chemical-treatment tablets in case your filter decides to quit on you.

Food. If we're talking about survival, you can go days without food, as long as you have water. But we're talking about comfort here. Try to avoid foods that are high in sugar and fat, such as candy bars and potato chips. These food types are harder to digest and are low in nutritional value. Instead bring along foods that are easy to pack, nutritious, and high in energy (e.g., bagels, nutrition bars, dehydrated fruit, gorp, and jerky). Complex carbohydrates and protein are your best food friends. If you are on an overnight trip, easy-to-fix dinners include rice or pasta dinners and soup mixes. A few spices are lightweight and can really perk up a meal. Freeze-dried meals are nice for long trips, but they are expensive and bulky. If you do a lot of long backpacks, invest in a dehydrator. For a tasty breakfast, you can fix hot oatmeal with brown sugar and reconstituted milk powder topped off with banana chips. If you like a hot drink in the morning, bring along herbal tea bags or hot chocolate. If you are a coffee junkie, you can purchase coffee that is packaged like tea bags. Prepackage all of your meals in heavy-duty resealable plastic bags to keep food from spilling in your pack. These bags can be reused to pack out trash. Prepackaging also minimizes extra trash in the form of boxes and cans. Avoid bringing glass containers into the backcountry as broken glass can pose some serious problems.

Shelter. The type of shelter you choose depends less on the conditions than on your tolerance for discomfort. Shelter comes in many forms—tent, tarp, lean-to, bivy sack, cabin, and cave. Tents are the logical and most popular choice for overnight backpack trips as they're lightweight and packable, and you can rest assured that you always have shelter from the elements. Before you leave on your trip, anticipate what the weather and terrain will be like and plan for the type of shelter that will work best for your comfort level.

Finding a campsite. If there are established campsites, stick to those. If not, start looking for a campsite early—like around 3:30 or 4:00 P.M. Stop at the first decent site you see. Depending on the area, it could be a long time before you find another suitable location. Pitch your camp in an area that's level. Make sure the area is at least 200 feet from fragile areas such as lakeshores, meadows, and stream banks. Avoid camping on the beach because when the tide comes in you and your gear will be at risk. And try to avoid areas thick in underbrush, as they can harbor insects. If you are camping in stormy, rainy weather, look for a rock outcrop or a shelter in the trees to keep the wind from blowing your tent all night. Be sure that you don't camp under trees with dead limbs that might break off on top of you. Also try to find an area that has an absorbent surface, such as sandy soil or forest duff. This, in addition to camping on a surface with a slight angle, will provide better drainage. By all means, don't dig trenches to provide drainage around your tent—remember, you're practicing minimum-impact camping.

First Aid

It's always a good idea to carry a first-aid kit when you're out on the trail. Many companies produce lightweight, compact kits. Look for a kit that contains the following items.

- Band-Aids
- moleskin
- sterile gauze and dressings
- white surgical tape
- ace bandage
- antihistamine
- aspirin
- Betadine solution
- first-aid book
- Tums
- tweezers
- scissors
- antibacterial wipes
- triple-antibiotic ointment
- plastic gloves
- sterile-cotton-tip applicators
- syrup of ipecac (to induce vomiting)
- thermometer
- wire splint

Here are a few tips on dealing with and hopefully preventing certain ailments.

Sunburn. To avoid sunburn, wear sunscreen (SPF 15 or higher), protective clothing, a wide-brimmed hat, and sunglasses when you are hiking in sunny weather. If you do get sunburn, treat the area with aloe vera gel and protect the area from further sun exposure.

Blisters. Be prepared to take care of these hike spoilers by carrying moleskin (a lightly padded adhesive), gauze and tape, or Band-Aids. An effective way to apply moleskin is to cut out a circle of moleskin and cut the center out of it—like a doughnut—and place it over the blistered area. Cutting the center out of the moleskin will reduce the pressure applied to the sensitive skin. Other products that can help you combat blisters are Bodyglide and Second Skin. Bodyglide is applied to suspicious hot spots before a blister forms to help decrease friction to that area. Second Skin (made by Spenco) is applied to the blister after it has popped, and it acts as a "second skin" to help prevent further irritation.

Insect bites and stings. You can treat most insect bites and stings by applying hydrocortisone 1 percent cream topically and taking a pain medication such as ibuprofen or acetaminophen to reduce swelling. If you forgot to pack these items, a cold compress or a paste of mud and ashes can sometimes assuage the itching and discomfort. Remove any stingers by using tweezers or scraping the area with your fingernail or a knife blade. Don't pinch the area, as you'll only spread the venom. Some hikers are highly sensitive to bites and stings and may have a serious allergic reaction that can be life threatening. Symptoms of a serious allergic reaction can include wheezing, an asthmatic attack, and shock. The treatment for this severe type of reaction is epinephrine (Adrenaline). If you know that you are sensitive to bites and stings, carry a prepackaged kit of epinephrine (e.g., Anakit), which can be obtained by prescription only from your doctor.

Ticks. Ticks can carry diseases, such as Rocky Mountain Spotted Fever and Lyme disease. The best defense is, of course, prevention. If you know you're going to be hiking through an area littered with ticks, wear long pants and a long-sleeved shirt. You can apply a permethrin repellent to your clothing and a DEET repellent to exposed skin. At the end of your hike, do a spot check for ticks (and insects in general). If you do find a tick, coat the insect with Vaseline or tree sap to cut off its air supply. The tick should release its hold, but if it doesn't, grab the head of the tick firmly—with a pair of tweezers if you have them—and gently pull it away from the skin with a twisting motion. Sometimes the mouthparts linger, embedded in your skin. If this happens, try to remove them with a disinfected needle. Clean the affected area with an antibacterial cleanser and then apply triple antibiotic ointment. Monitor the area for a few days. If irritation persists or a white spot develops, see a doctor for possible infection.

Dehydration. Have you ever hiked in hot weather and had a roaring headache and felt fatigued after only a few miles? More than likely you were dehydrated. Symptoms of dehydration include fatigue, headache, and decreased coordination and judgment. When you are hiking, your body's rate of fluid loss depends on the outside temperature, humidity, altitude, and your activity level. On average a hiker walking in warm weather will lose four liters of fluid a day. That fluid loss is easily replaced by normal consumption of liquids and food. However, if a hiker is walking briskly in hot, dry weather and hauling a heavy pack, he can lose one to three liters of water an hour. It's important to always carry plenty of water and to stop often and drink fluids regularly, even if you aren't thirsty.

Heat exhaustion is the result of a loss of large amounts of electrolytes and often occurs if a hiker is dehydrated and has been under heavy exertion. Common symptoms of heat exhaustion include cramping, exhaustion, fatigue, lightheadedness, and nausea. You can treat heat exhaustion by getting out of the sun and drinking an electrolyte solution made of one teaspoon of salt and one tablespoon of sugar dissolved in a liter of water. Drink this solution slowly over a period of one hour. Drinking plenty of fluids (preferably an electrolyte solution such as Gatorade) can prevent heat exhaustion. Avoid hiking during the hottest parts of the day and wear breathable clothing, a wide-brimmed hat, and sunglasses.

Hypothermia can be a threat because of often unpredictable weather on the Oregon Coast. A combination of heavy rain and wind can leave you wet and shivering—the perfect recipe for hypothermia. More-advanced signs include decreased coordination, slurred speech, and blurred vision. When a victim's temperature falls below 92 degrees Fahrenheit, blood pressure and pulse plummet, possibly leading to coma and death. To avoid hypothermia, always bring a windproof/rainproof shell, a fleece jacket, noncotton tights (for example, Capilene), gloves, and a hat. Learn to adjust your clothing layers based on the temperature. If you are climbing uphill at a moderate pace, you will stay warm, but when you stop for a break, you'll become cold quickly unless you add more layers of clothing. If a hiker is showing advanced signs of hypothermia, dress her in dry clothes and make sure she is wearing a hat and gloves. Place her in a sleeping bag in a tent or shelter that will protect her from the wind and other elements. Give her warm fluids to drink and keep her awake.

Navigation

Whether you are going on a short hike in a familiar area or planning a weeklong backpack trip, you should always be equipped with the proper navigational equipment—at the very least a detailed map and a sturdy compass.

Maps. There are many different types of maps available to help you find your way on the trail. Easiest to find are Forest Service maps and Bureau of Land Management maps. These maps tend to cover large areas, so be sure they are detailed enough for your particular trip. You can also obtain National Park maps as well as high-quality maps from private companies and trail groups. These maps can be obtained from either outdoor stores or ranger stations. U.S. Geological Survey (USGS) topographic maps are particularly popular with hikers—especially serious backcountry hikers. These maps contain the standard map symbols such as roads, lakes, and rivers, as well as contour lines that show such details of the trail terrain as ridges, valleys, passes, and mountain peaks. The 7½-minute series (1 inch on the map equals approximately ⅖ of a mile on the ground) provides the closest inspection available. USGS maps are available by mail (U.S. Geological Survey, Map Distribution Branch, P.O. Box 25286, Denver, Colorado 80225), or you can visit them on-line at mapping.usgs.gov/esic/to_order.html.

If you want to check out the high-tech world of maps, you can purchase topographic maps on CD-ROM. These mapping programs let you select a route on your computer, print it out, and take it with you on the trail. Some mapping programs let you insert symbols and labels, download waypoints from a GPS unit, and export the maps to other software programs. One mapping software program that lets you do all of these things and more is Maptech's Terrain Navigator (888–839–5551; www.maptech.com).

The art of map reading is a skill that you can develop by first practicing in an area you are familiar with. To begin, orient the map so the map is lined up in the correct direction (i.e., north on the map is lined up with true north). Next, familiarize yourself with the map symbols and try to match them up with terrain features around you, such as a high ridge, mountain peak, river, or lake. If you are practicing with an USGS map, notice the contour lines. On gentler terrain these contour lines are spaced farther apart, and on steeper terrain they are closer together. Pick a short loop trail and stop frequently to check your position on the map. As you practice you will learn how to read the map so you will be able to anticipate a steep section on the trail or a good place to take a rest break, and so on.

Compass. First off, the sun is not a substitute for a compass. So, what kind of compass should you have? Some characteristics you should look for are a rectangular base with detailed scales, a liquid-filled housing, protective housing, a sighting line on the mirror, luminous alignment and back-bearing arrows, a luminous north-seeking arrow, and a well-defined bezel ring. You can learn compass basics by reading the detailed instructions included with your compass. If you want to fine-tune your compass skills, sign up for an orienteering class or purchase a book on compass reading.

Once you've learned the basic skills on using a compass, remember to practice the skills before you head into the backcountry.

Global Positioning Systems (GPS). If you are a klutz at using a compass, you may be interested in checking out the technical wizardry of the GPS device. GPS was developed by the Pentagon and works off of twenty-four NAVSTAR satellites, which were designed to guide missiles to their targets. A GPS device is a handheld unit that calculates your latitude and longitude with the easy press of a button. The Department of Defense used to scramble the satellite signals a bit to prevent civilians (and spies!) from getting an extremely accurate reading, but that practice was discontinued in May 2000, and GPS units now provide nearly pinpoint accuracy (within 30 to 60 feet).

There are many different types of GPS units available, and they range in price from $150 to $400. In general all GPS units have a display screen and keypad where you input information. In addition to acting as a compass, the unit allows you to plot your route, retrace your path, track your traveling speed, find the mileage between waypoints (straight-line distance), and calculate the total mileage of your route. Despite these advances in GPS technology, don't put all of your trust in your GPS. Per the USGS, "GPS units do not replace basic map and compass skills." Keep in mind that these devices don't pick up signals indoors, in heavily wooded areas, or in deep valleys. And most important to remember—they run on batteries.

Pedometers. A pedometer is a handy device that can track your mileage as you hike. This device is a small, clip-on unit with a digital display that calculates your hiking distance in miles or kilometers based on your walking stride. Some units also calculate the calories you burn and your total hiking time. Pedometers are available at most large outdoor and sporting-goods stores and range in price from $20 to $40.

Trip Planning

Planning your hiking adventure begins with letting a friend or relative know your trip itinerary so they can call for help if you don't return at your scheduled time. Your next task is to make sure you are outfitted to experience the risks and rewards of the trail. This section highlights gear and clothing you may want to take with you to get the most out of your hike.

Day Hikes

- daypack
- water and water bottles/water hydration system
- food and high-energy snacks
- first-aid kit
- headlamp/flashlight with extra batteries and bulbs
- maps and compass/GPS unit
- knife/multipurpose tool
- sunscreen and sunglasses
- matches in waterproof container and fire starter
- insulating top and bottom layers (fleece, wool, etc.)
- raingear
- winter hat and gloves
- wide-brimmed sun hat
- insect repellant
- backpacker's trowel, toilet paper, and resealable plastic bags
- camera/film
- guidebook
- watch
- water-treatment tablets
- wet wipes
- extra socks

Overnight Trip (in addition to what's listed for Day Hikes)

- backpack and waterproof rain cover
- bandanna
- biodegradable soap
- collapsible water container (two- to three-gallon capacity)
- clothing—extra wool socks, shirt, shorts, long pants
- cook set/utensils and pot scrubber
- duct tape
- stuff sacks to store gear
- extra plastic resealable bags
- garbage bags
- journal/pen
- nylon rope to hang food
- long underwear
- permit (if required)
- repair kit (tent, stove, pack, etc.)
- sandals or running shoes to wear around camp and to ford streams
- sleeping bag
- waterproof stuff sacks (one for hanging food)
- insulating ground pad
- hand towel
- stove and fuel
- tent and ground cloth
- toiletry items
- water filter
- wet wipes

Equipment

With the outdoor market currently flooded with products, many of which are pure gimmickry, it seems impossible to both differentiate and choose. The only defense against the maddening quantity of items is to think practically—and to do so before you go shopping. The worst buys are impulsive buys. Since most of your name brands will differ only slightly in quality, it's best to know what you're looking for in terms of function. Buy only what you need.

Clothes. Clothing is your armor against Mother Nature's little surprises. Buying clothing that can be worn in layers is a good strategy for dealing with the often wet and windy weather on the Oregon Coast. In the spring, fall, and winter months, the first layer you'll want to wear is a wicking layer of long underwear that keeps perspiration away from your skin. Wearing long underwear made from synthetic fibers such as Capilene, Coolmax, or Thermax is an excellent choice. These fabrics wick moisture away from the skin and draw it toward the next layer of clothing, where it then evaporates. Avoid wearing long underwear made of cotton, as it is slow to dry and keeps moisture next to your skin.

The second layer you'll wear is the insulating layer. Aside from keeping you warm, this layer needs to "breathe" so you stay dry while hiking. A fabric that provides insulation and dries quickly is fleece. It's interesting to note that this one-of-a-kind fabric is made out of recycled plastic. Purchasing a zip-up jacket made of this material is highly recommended.

The last line of layering defense is the shell layer. You'll need some type of waterproof, windproof, breathable jacket that'll fit over all of your other layers. It should have a large hood that fits over a hat. You'll also need a good pair of rain pants made from a similar waterproof, breathable fabric. A fabric that easily fits the bill is Gore-Tex. However, while a quality Gore-Tex jacket can range in price from $100 to $450, you should know that there are more affordable fabrics out there that work just as well.

Now that you've learned the basics of layering, you can't forget to protect your hands and face. In cold, windy, or rainy weather, you'll need a hat made of wool or fleece and insulated, waterproof gloves that will keep your hands warm and toasty. They'll allow you to remove your outer gloves for tedious work without exposing the skin.

Footwear. If you have any extra money to spend on your trip, put that money into boots or trail shoes. Poor shoes will bring a hike to a halt faster than anything else. To avoid this annoyance, buy shoes that provide support and are lightweight and flexible. A lightweight hiking boot is better than a heavy, leather mountaineering boot for most day hikes and backpacking. Trail running shoes provide a little extra cushion and are made in a high-top style that many people wear for hiking. These running shoes are lighter, more flexible, and more breathable than hiking boots. If you know you'll be hiking in wet weather often, purchase boots or shoes with a Gore-Tex liner, which will help keep your feet dry.

When buying your boots, be sure to wear the same type of socks you'll be wearing on the trail. If the boots you're buying are for cold-weather hiking, try the boots on while wearing two pairs of socks. Speaking of socks, a good cold-weather sock combination is to wear a thinner sock made of wool or polypropylene covered by a heavier outer sock made of wool. The inner sock protects the foot from the rubbing effects of the outer sock and prevents blisters. Avoid wearing cotton socks.

It's always a good idea to bring an extra pair of sandals or an old pair of tennis shoes along if you plan on hiking on the beach or fording creeks.

Once you've purchased your footwear, be sure to break them in before you hit the trail. New footwear is often stiff and needs to be stretched and molded to your foot.

Backpacks. No matter what type of hiking you do, you'll need a pack of some sort to carry the basic trail essentials. There are a variety of backpacks on the market, but let's first discuss what you intend to use it for. Day hikes or overnight trips?

If you plan on doing a day hike, a daypack should have some of the following characteristics: a padded hip belt that's at least 2 inches in diameter (avoid packs with only a small nylon piece of webbing for a hip belt); a chest strap (the chest strap helps stabilize the pack against your body); external pockets to carry water and other items that you want easy access to; an internal pocket to hold keys, a knife, a wallet, and other miscellaneous items; an external lashing system to hold a jacket; and a hydration pocket for carrying a hydration system (which consists of a water bladder with an attachable drinking hose).

For short hikes some hikers like to use a fanny pack to store just a camera, food, a compass, a map, and other trail essentials. Most fanny packs have pockets for two water bottles and a padded hip belt.

If you intend to do an extended overnight trip, there are multiple considerations. First off, you need to decide what kind of framed pack you want. There are two backpack types for backpacking: the internal frame and the external frame. An internal-frame pack rests closer to your body, making it more stable and easier to balance when hiking over rough terrain. An external-frame pack is just that, an aluminum frame attached to the exterior of the pack. An external-frame pack is better for long backpack trips because it distributes the pack weight better so you can carry heavier loads. It's easier to pack, and your gear is more accessible. It also offers better back ventilation in hot weather.

The most critical measurement for fitting a pack is torso length. The pack needs to rest evenly on your hips without sagging. A good pack will come in two or three sizes and have straps and hip belts that are adjustable according to your body size and characteristics.

When you purchase a backpack, go to an outdoor store with salespeople who are knowledgeable in how to properly fit a pack. Once the pack is fitted for you, load the pack with the amount of weight you plan on taking on the trail. The weight of the pack should be distributed evenly, and you should be able to swing your arms and walk briskly without feeling out of balance. Another good technique for evaluating a pack is to walk up and down stairs and make quick turns to the right and to the left to be sure the pack doesn't feel out of balance.

Other features that are nice to have on a backpack include a removable day pack or fanny pack, external pockets for extra water, and extra lash points to attach a jacket or other items.

Day hikers on the Saddle Mountain Trail in Saddle Mountain State Park

Sleeping bags and pads. Sleeping bags are rated by temperature. You can purchase a bag made of synthetic fiber such as Polarguard HV or DuPont Hollofil II, or you can buy a goose-down bag. Goose-down bags are more expensive, but they have a higher insulating capacity by weight and will keep their loft longer. However, keep in mind that if a goose-down bag gets wet it loses its insulating capacity. To help combat this problem, many goose-down bags are now sold with a Gore-Tex shell. You'll want to purchase a bag with a temperature rating that fits the time of year and conditions you are most likely to camp in. One caveat: The techno-standard for temperature ratings is far from perfect. Ratings vary from manufacturer to manufacturer, so to protect yourself you should purchase a bag rated ten to fifteen degrees below the temperature you expect to be camping in. Synthetic bags are more resistant to water than down bags, but many down bags are now made with a Gore-Tex shell that helps to repel water. Down bags are also more compressible than synthetic bags and take up less room in your pack, which is an important consideration if you are planning a multiday backpack trip. Features to look for in a sleeping bag include a mummy-style bag, a hood you can cinch down around your head in cold weather, and draft tubes along the zippers that help keep heat in and drafts out.

You'll also want a sleeping pad to provide insulation and padding from the cold ground. There are different types of sleeping pads available, from the more expensive self-inflating air mattresses to the less expensive closed-cell foam pads (e.g., Ridge Rest). Self-inflating air mattresses are usually heavier than closed-cell foam mattresses and are prone to punctures.

Tents. The tent is your home away from home while on the trail. It provides protection from wind, snow, rain, and insects. A three-season tent is a good choice for backpacking and can range in price from $100 to $500. These lightweight and versatile tents provide protection in all types of weather, except heavy snowstorms or high winds, and range in weight from four to eight pounds. Look for a tent that's easy to set up and will easily fit two people with gear. Dome-type tents usually offer more headroom and places to store gear. Other tent designs include a vestibule where you can store wet boots and backpacks. Some nice-to-have items in a tent include interior pockets to store small items and lashing points to hang a clothesline. Most three-season tents also come with stakes so you can secure the tent in high winds. Before you purchase a tent, set it up and take it down a few times to be sure it is easy to handle. Also sit inside the tent and make sure it has enough room for you and your gear.

Hiking with Children

Hiking with children isn't a matter of how many miles you can cover or how much elevation gain you make in a day; it's about seeing and experiencing nature through their eyes.

Kids like to explore and have fun. They like to stop and point out bugs and plants, look under rocks, jump in puddles, and throw sticks. If you're taking a toddler or young child on a hike, start with a trail that you're familiar with. Trails that have interesting things for kids, like piles of leaves to play in or a small stream to wade through during the summer, will make the hike much more enjoyable for them and will keep them from getting bored.

You can keep your child's attention if you have a strategy before starting on the trail. Using games is not only an effective way to keep a child's attention, but also a great way to teach him or her about nature. Play hide and seek, where your child is the mouse and you are the hawk. Quiz children on the names of plants and animals. If your children are old enough, let them carry their own daypack filled with snacks and water. So that you are sure to go at their pace and not yours, let them lead the way. Playing follow the leader works particularly well when you have a group of children. Have each child take a turn at being the leader.

With children, a lot of clothing is key. The weather on the Oregon Coast can be unpredictable, so you always want to bring extra clothing for your children no matter what the season. In the winter, spring, and fall months, have your children wear wool socks and warm layers such as long underwear, a polar fleece jacket and hat, wool mittens, and good rain gear. Good footwear is also important. A sturdy pair of high-top tennis shoes or lightweight hiking boots are the best bet for little ones. If you're hiking in the summer near a lake or stream, bring along a pair of old sneakers or sandals that your child can put on when he wants to go exploring in the water. Remember, when you're near any type of water, always watch your child at all times. Also when you are hiking on the beach, don't let your kids play on or around water-soaked logs—these logs can easily crush a child.

During the summer months, you'll want your kids to wear a wide-brimmed hat to keep their face, head, and ears protected from the hot sun. Also make sure your children wear sunscreen at all times. Choose a brand without PABA—children have sensitive skin and may have an allergic reaction to sunscreen that contains PABA. If you are hiking with a child younger than six months, don't use sunscreen or insect repellent. Instead, be sure that their head, face, neck, and ears are protected from the sun with a wide-brimmed hat, and that all other skin exposed to the sun is protected with the appropriate clothing.

Remember that food is fun. Kids like snacks, so bring a lot of munchies for the trail. Stopping often for snack breaks is a fun way to keep the trail interesting. Raisins, apples, granola bars, crackers and cheese, Cheerios, and trail mix all make great snacks. If your child is old enough to carry his/her own backpack, fill it with treats before you leave. If your kids don't like drinking water, you can bring boxes of fruit juice.

Avoid poorly designed child-carrying packs—you don't want to break your back carrying your child. Most child-carrying backpacks designed to hold a forty-pound child will contain a large carrying pocket to hold diapers and other items. Some have an optional rain/sun hood. Tough Traveler (800–GO TOUGH; www.toughtraveler.com) is a company that specializes in making backpacks for carrying children and other outdoor gear for children.

Taking a break on the summit of Neahkahnie Mountain

Hiking with Your Dog

Bringing your furry friend with you is always more fun than leaving him behind. Our canine pals make great trail buddies because they never complain and always make good company. Hiking with your dog can be a rewarding experience, especially if you plan ahead.

Getting your dog in shape. Before you plan outdoor adventures with your dog, make sure he's in shape for the trail. This takes the same discipline as getting yourself into shape, but luckily, your dog can get in shape with you. Take your dog with you on your daily runs or walks. If there is a park near your house, hit a tennis ball or play Frisbee with your dog.

Swimming is also an excellent way to get your dog into shape. If there is a lake or river near where you live and your dog likes the water, have him retrieve a tennis ball or stick. Gradually build your dog's stamina over a two- to three-month period. A good rule is to assume that your dog will travel twice as far as you will on the trail. If you plan on doing a 5-mile hike, be sure your dog is in shape for a 10-mile hike.

Training your dog for the trail. Before you go on your first hiking adventure with your dog, be sure he has a firm grasp of the basics of canine etiquette and behavior. Make sure he can sit, lie down, stay, and come. One of the most important commands you can teach your canine pal is to "come" under any situation. It's easy for your friend's nose to lead him astray or possibly get him lost. Another helpful command is the "get behind" command. When you're on a hiking trail that's narrow, you can have your dog follow behind you when other trail users approach.

Nothing is more bothersome than an enthusiastic dog that runs back and forth on the trail and disrupts the peace of the trail for others. When you see other trail users approaching, give them the right-of-way by quietly stepping off the trail and making your dog lie down and stay until they pass.

Equipment. The most critical pieces of equipment you can invest in for your dog are proper identification and a sturdy leash. Flexi-leads work well for hiking because they give your dog more freedom to explore but still leave you in control. Make sure your dog has identification that includes your name and address and a number for your veterinarian. Other forms of identification for your dog include a tattoo or a microchip. You should consult your veterinarian for more information on these last two options.

The next piece of equipment you'll want to consider is a pack for your dog. By no means should you hold all of your dog's essentials in your pack—let him carry his own gear! Dogs that are in good shape can carry up to 30 to 40 percent of their own weight. Companies that make good quality packs include Ruff Wear (888–783–3932; www.ruffwear.com) and Wolf Packs (541–482–7669; www.wolfpacks.com). Most packs are fitted by a dog's weight and girth measurement. Companies that make dog packs generally include guidelines to help you pick out the size that's right for your dog. Some characteristics to look for when purchasing a pack for your dog include a harness that contains two padded girth straps, a padded chest strap, leash attachments, removable saddle bags, internal water bladders, and external gear cords.

You can introduce your dog to the pack by first placing the empty pack on his back and letting him wear it around the yard. Keep an eye on him during this first introduction. He may decide to chew through the straps if you aren't watching him closely.

Once he learns to treat the pack as an object of fun and not a foreign enemy, fill the pack evenly on both sides with a few ounces of dog food in resealable plastic bags. Have your dog wear his pack on your daily walks for a period of two to three weeks. Each week add a little more weight to the pack until your dog will accept carrying the maximum amount of weight he can carry.

You can also purchase collapsible water and dog-food bowls for your dog. These bowls are lightweight and can easily be stashed into your pack or your dog's. If you are hiking on rocky terrain or in the snow, you can purchase footwear for your dog that will protect his feet from cuts and bruises. All of these products can be purchased from Ruff Wear (888–783–3932; www.ruffwear.com).

The following is a checklist of items to bring when you take your dog hiking: collapsible water bowls, a comb, a collar and a leash, dog food, a dog pack, flea/tick powder, paw protection, water, toys, and a first-aid kit that contains eye ointment, tweezers, scissors, stretchy foot wrap, gauze, antibacterial wash, sterile cotton-tip applicators, antibiotic ointment, and cotton wrap.

First aid for your dog. Your dog is just as prone—if not more prone—to getting in trouble on the trail as you are, so be prepared. Here's a rundown of the more likely misfortunes that might befall you canine hiking partner.

Bees and wasps. If a bee or wasp stings your dog, remove the stinger with a pair of tweezers and place a mudpack or a cloth dipped in cold water over the affected area.

Heat stroke. Avoid hiking with your dog in really hot weather. Dogs with heat stroke will pant excessively, lie down and refuse to get up, and become lethargic and disoriented. If your dog shows any of these signs on the trail, have him lie down in the shade. If you are near a stream, pour cool water over your dog's entire body to help bring his body temperature back to normal.

Heartworm. Dogs get heartworms from mosquitoes, which carry the disease in the prime mosquito months of July and August. Giving your dog a monthly pill prescribed by your veterinarian easily prevents this condition.

Plant pitfalls. One of the biggest plant hazards for dogs on the trail is foxtails. Foxtails are pointed grass seed heads that bury themselves in your friend's fur, between his toes, and even sometimes in his ear canal. If left unattended, these nasty seeds can work their way under the skin and cause abscesses and other problems. If you have a longhaired dog, consider trimming the hair between his toes and giving him a summer haircut to help prevent foxtails from attaching to his fur. After every hike always look over your dog for these seeds—especially between his toes and in his ears.

Other plant hazards include burrs, thorns, thistles, and poison oak. If you find any burrs or thistles on your dog, remove them as soon as possible before they become an unmanageable mat. Thorns can pierce a dog's foot and cause a great deal of pain. If you see that your dog is lame, stop and check his feet for thorns. Dogs are immune to poison oak, but they can pick up the sticky, oily substance from the plant and transfer it to you.

Protect those paws. Be sure to keep your dog's nails trimmed so he avoids getting soft tissue or joint injuries. If your dog slows and refuses to go on, check to see that his paws aren't torn or worn. You can protect your dog's paws from such trail hazards as sharp gravel, foxtails, lava scree, and thorns by purchasing dog boots.

Sunburn. If your dog has light skin, he is an easy target for sunburn on his nose and other exposed skin areas. You can apply a nontoxic sunscreen to exposed skin areas, which will help protect him from overexposure to the sun.

Ticks and fleas. Ticks can easily give your dog Lyme disease, as well as other diseases. Before you hit the trail, treat your dog with a flea and tick spray or powder. You can also ask your veterinarian about a once-a-month pour-on treatment that repels fleas and ticks.

When you are finally ready to hit the trail with your dog, keep in mind that some conservation and wilderness areas do not allow dogs on trails. Your best bet is to hike in national forests, Bureau of Land Management lands, and state parks. Always call ahead to see what the restrictions are.

Appendix

Hikes by Interest

Hikes for Beach Lovers

3: Fort Stevens State Park
4: Ecola State Park to Indian Beach
5: Cannon Beach
7: Oswald West State Park—Short Sand Beach
12: Cape Kiwanda State Natural Area
14: Kiwanda Beach to Porter Point
20: Yaquina Bay State Park and Lighthouse
23: South Beach State Park
24: Seal Rock State Recreation Area
25: Yachats 804 Trail
35: Coquille River Lighthouse
37: Cape Ferrelo to Whalehead Beach

Hikes for Children and Beginning Hikers

1: Fort Canby State Park
3: Fort Stevens State Park
4: Ecola State Park to Indian Beach
5: Cannon Beach
7: Oswald West State Park—Short Sand Beach
9: Cape Meares State Park
11: Munson Creek Falls
12: Cape Kiwanda State Natural Area
13: Pheasant Creek Falls and Niagara Falls
14: Kiwanda Beach to Porter Point
18: Devil's Punchbowl State Natural Area
19: Yaquina Head Outstanding Natural Area
20: Yaquina Bay State Park and Lighthouse
21: Hatfield Marine Science Center Estuary Trail
22: Mike Miller Educational Trail
23: South Beach State Park
24: Seal Rock State Recreation Area
25: Yachats 804 Trail
26: Alsea Falls and Green Peak Falls
27: Cape Perpetua Trails
28: Heceta Head Lighthouse

29: Sutton Creek Recreation Area
31: Siltcoos River Estuary Trails
32: Tahkenitch Creek
33: Lake Marie
35: Coquille River Lighthouse
36: Babyfoot Lake
40: Alfred A. Loeb State Park Nature Trails

Hikes for Lighthouse Lovers

1: Fort Canby State Park
9: Cape Meares State Park
19: Yaquina Head Outstanding Natural Area
20: Yaquina Bay State Park and Lighthouse
28: Heceta Head Lighthouse
33: Lake Marie
35: Coquille River Lighthouse

Hikes for Peak Baggers

6: Saddle Mountain
8: Neahkahnie Mountain

Hikes for Tide-Pool Lovers

5: Cannon Beach
12: Cape Kiwanda State Natural Area
18: Devil's Punchbowl State Natural Area
19: Yaquina Head Outstanding Natural Area
24: Seal Rock State Recreation Area
27: Cape Perpetua Trails

Hikes for Waterfall Lovers

11: Munson Creek Falls
13: Pheasant Creek Falls and Niagara Falls
17: Drift Creek Falls
26: Alsea Falls and Green Peak Falls

About the Author

Lizann Dunegan is a freelance writer and photographer and specializes in writing about outdoor activities and travel. Lizann has been hiking trails in the Northwest for more than ten years and is often accompanied by her partner, Ken Skeen, and her two border collies, Levi and Sage. Lizann is the author of multiple books about the Northwest, including *Canine Oregon*, *Hiking Oregon*, *Trail Running Oregon*, *Mountain Biking Northwest Oregon*, *Road Biking Oregon*, and *Insiders' Guide to the Oregon Coast*. Lizann also loves trail running, mountain biking, cross-country skiing, sea kayaking, and playing the violin and cello.